Teaching Economics

Joshua Hall • Kerianne Lawson
Editors

Teaching Economics

Perspectives on Innovative Economics Education

Springer

Editors
Joshua Hall
College of Business and Economics
West Virginia University
Morgantown
West Virginia, USA

Kerianne Lawson
College of Business and Economics
West Virginia University
Morgantown
West Virginia, USA

ISBN 978-3-030-20695-6 ISBN 978-3-030-20696-3 (eBook)
https://doi.org/10.1007/978-3-030-20696-3

This Springer imprint is published by the registered company Springer Nature Switzerland AG.
The registered company address is: Gewerbestrasse 11, 6330 Cham, Switzerland

Acknowledgements

We would like to thank the Center for Free Enterprise at West Virginia University for general research support.

Contents

Contributors

Nimish Adhia Manhattanville College, Purchase, NY, USA

Laura J. Ahlstrom Oklahoma State University, Stillwater, OK, USA

Abdullah Al-Bahrani Northern Kentucky University, Highland Heights, KY, USA

Carlos J. Asarta University of Delaware, Newark, DE, USA

Andrew Beckstrom Onalaska High School, Onalaska, WI, USA

Joab Corey University of California Riverside, Riverside, CA, USA

Hugo Eyzaguirre Northern Michigan University, Marquette, MI, USA

Tawni Hunt Ferrarini Lindenwood University, St. Charles, MO, USA

Judge Glock West Virginia University, Morgantown, WV, USA

Joshua Hall College of Business and Economics, West Virginia University, Morgantown, WV, USA

Adam Hoffer University of Wisconsin-La Crosse, La Crosse, WI, USA

Alice Louise Kassens Roanoke College, Salem, VA, USA

Ninos P. Malek De Anza College, Cupertino, CA, USA

M. Scott Niederjohn Lakeland University, Plymouth, WI, USA

Colin O'Reilly Creighton University, Omaha, NE, USA

Brian O'Roark Robert Morris University, Moon Township, PA, USA

Darshak Patel University of Kentucky, Lexington, KY, USA

Gordon Smith Anderson University, Anderson, SC, USA

Signè Thomas Florida State University, Tallahassee, FL, USA

Leith Thompson Burwood Girls High School, Croydon, NSW, Australia

Marcus M. Witcher University of Central Arkansas, Conway, AR, USA

David Youngberg Montgomery College, Rockville, MD, USA

Chapter 1
The Development of Interactive Classroom Activities to Teach Economic Freedom to Students of Various Learning Styles

Signè Thomas

Abstract I created eight lessons exploring economic freedom, designed with student-centered learning in mind. Seven of the eight lessons are interactive, and six of those seven involve students working together in collaborative groups. Multiple lessons involve physical activity, two of which (Lesson 2 and Lesson 6) involve students running around the classroom during the lesson. The interactive activities are perfectly suited for the flipped classroom or flipped learning. These lessons can also be implemented in a traditional style classroom, if an instructor wants to break up their lecture with an interactive activity. These lessons are designed for high school and undergraduate students, and provide an educator with ready-to-use activities to use within their classroom to teach their students about various aspects of economic freedom. Each lesson has a theme, description, learning outcomes, procedure, a final thought, and a glossary. The lessons also include any necessary handouts such as readings or signs, student directions, team answer sheets, answer keys, visuals, and any other resources needed for the activity. These thorough materials will significantly reduce the amount of time it takes an instructor to prepare and implement the lessons in their classroom. I have received positive verbal and written feedback from educators in the USA and Canada, as well as from my own Honors Principles of Macroeconomics and Honors Principles of Microeconomics students at Florida State University.

1.1 Literature Review

A flipped or inverted classroom, or flipped learning, is a pedagogical method where the learning process is said to be "flipped" from the traditional style of lecture or "chalk and talk." Rather than spending class time fully focused on a lecture, students

S. Thomas (✉)
Florida State University, Tallahassee, FL, USA
e-mail: sathomas3@fsu.edu

J. Hall, K. Lawson (eds.), *Teaching Economics*,
https://doi.org/10.1007/978-3-030-20696-3_1

do their reading assignments and watch lectures online outside of class time, so that class time can be utilized for engaging learning activities with the students (Roach 2014; Bishop and Verleger 2013). High school chemistry teachers Jonathan Bergmann and Aaron Sams are largely credited with the creation of this concept when they first started recording their chemistry lectures so students who missed class could view them online. The recordings spread, and they began utilizing class time for activities. The flipped classroom was born (Gasparic et al. 2017)! Its popularity grew in part due to the Khan Academy, an online system that has videos covering a large array of subjects that individuals can access at no monetary cost. The flipped classroom allows time spent in the classroom to be concentrated more toward active and collaborative learning (Roach 2014). Flipped classrooms tend to employ group interactive learning activities during class time to make the most out of time spent in the classroom.

As the concept of the flipped classroom evolved, so has the terminology for the concept. The concept first appeared in 2006 and was originally referred to as a flipped classroom, where video is used as a medium of teaching the subject matter and the teacher is at the center of instruction in the classroom. Later, the flipped mastery model emerged, which was similar to the aforementioned flipped classroom but it also adapted to the needs of individual learners. Now we have what is called flipped learning, which still makes use of videos to teach content but rather than the teacher being the center of instruction in the classroom, it is now the student at the center of the classroom (Gasparic et al. 2017). Flipped learning emphasizes rich learning experiences through methods that are student focused.

Research shows that the greater the incongruency between an economics instructor's teaching style and a student's learning style, the lower the student's performance in the economics course and the less the student is interested in the subject matter (Charkins et al. 1985). Others found supporting evidence when utilizing the Myers-Briggs Type Indicator to study student performance when taking into account a student's temperament type compared to their economics instructor's temperament type. Students whose temperament type matched that of their economics instructor performed better in the course than otherwise (Borg and Shapiro 1996). These findings suggest that economics instructors may want to incorporate numerous teaching styles in order to better reach students of various learning types. Research also supports the idea that when an economics instructor uses a variety of teaching styles, they are more likely to increase student performance, diversity of students, and student interest in economics (Bartlett 1996). Bartlett suggests that an instructor should encourage student interaction during class, and also recommends developing hands-on activities. By incorporating an array of teaching methods in one's economic class, an economics instructor can better reach students of various learning styles (Becker and Watts 1995, 1996). Becker and Watts suggest using hands-on demonstrations, classroom games, simulations, and the like as one of the ways to reach students, increase their learning, and increase student interest in the subject. They explain that while some students and teachers are natural-born listeners and lecturers, others prefer talking with their peers through discussions, and even others learn or teach best when using group activities that feature hands-on demonstrations of economic concepts and relationships (Becker and Watts 1995, 1996). The latter are now commonly referred to as interactive activities, or "econ games."

Some interactive activities involve physical activity. Physical activity has been shown to increase students' attention, concentration, focus, cognition, memory, and academic achievement (Donnelly and Lambourne 2011; Budde et al. 2008; Rasberry et al. 2011). In a systematic review of the literature, Rasberry et al. (2011) explored connections between physical activity and academic performance. Nine different studies were included in the category of classroom-based physical activity, which included short periods of physical activity of 5–20 min within the classroom, some of which were incorporated into learning activities. The nine studies examined how these brief physical activities in a classroom setting affected cognitive skills (aptitude, attention, and memory), attitudes (mood), academic behaviors (on-task behavior and concentration), and academic achievement (standardized test scores, reading literacy scores, and math fluency scores). Four studies reported all positive classroom associations between physical activity and that of classroom behaviors and academic achievement (DellaValle et al. 1986; Maeda and Randall 2003; Mahar et al. 2006; Norlander et al. 2005). Eight of the nine studies Rasberry et al. (2011) and her colleagues reviewed suggest these classroom-based physical activities may have favorable associations with indicators of cognitive functioning, academic behaviors, and/or academic achievement. The ninth study found no relationship. No negative relationships were found in the nine studies reviewed (Rasberry et al. 2011).

1.2 The Creation of Eight Lessons in Economic Freedom

Interactive activities can be utilized to accommodate a diverse range of learning styles. I incorporate different pedagogical approaches and learning styles to reach each student in the manner(s) in which they best learn. Ultimately, I strive to captivate students and peak their interest in the subject matter. Interactive activities—also known as "econ games"—are one of the many ways I like to bring economics to life for students.

When designing interactive "econ games," I account for different learning styles that are based on Howard Gardner's (1993) Theory of Multiple Intelligences. One lesson will focus on engaging visual learners, while another will be focused on aural learners and geared toward developing one's listening skills. Many of the activities involve more than one learning style at a time, merging different combinations of visual, aural, verbal, physical, social, and solitary learning styles. The purpose of these interactive activities is to engage different types of students to spark their curiosity in the subject matter and hopefully motivate them to learn more beyond the classroom.

In 2017, the Fraser Institute asked me to develop lessons that teach economic freedom to students in a fun, engaging manner (Thomas 2018). The Fraser Institute is the publisher of the *Economic Freedom of the World* (EFW) annual report by Gwartney et al. (2017). The *Lessons in Economic Freedom* I developed consists of eight lessons (interactive activities or "econ games"). Lesson 1, "What Does This Map Represent?" utilizes the visual (spatial) learning style, a bit of the physical (kinesthetic) learning style, and the social (interpersonal) learning style. This lesson uses photos and data of various countries, and later utilizes the 2016 EFW map to engage the students to explore country differences. Students work collaboratively in groups to discuss and try to determine which countries are depicted, and use critical thinking to hypothesize what the map on the wall represents. The titles (and the like) within the map are covered up until the end of the activity, when the instructor reveals that the map represents economic freedom.

Based on the literature suggesting physical activity within classroom activities can increase attention, cognition, and even academic achievement (Donnelly and Lambourne 2011; Budde et al. 2008; Rasberry et al. 2011), Lesson 2 is designed to put the students into motion. Lesson 2, "Map-Reading Relay Race," puts a physical (kinesthetic) learning style into action, combined with incorporating the visual (spatial) learning style and the social learning style. Students are grouped together into teams of three to five students, and they participate as a team in the map-reading relay race. Not only do they gain practice in honing their world map reading abilities, but they also learn to read and identify key information presented in the map itself as well as in the bar graphs along the bottom of the map.

In an effort to differ which learning styles are at the forefront of the various lessons, Lesson 3, "Economic Freedom Trivia," utilizes the aural (auditory) and verbal (linguistic) learning styles, along with the social learning style. First, students read a handout that explains how economic freedom is measured. Then, the students work in a team as they carefully listen to statements being read aloud by the instructor, and determine if each is true or false.

Lesson 4, "The Rapid Response Quiz Show: Why is Economic Freedom So Vitally Important?" incorporates visual and aural/verbal learning styles, a bit of the physical learning style, and the social learning style. Before starting the game, students first read a handout that explains the difference between political freedom and economic freedom (how political institutions differ from economic institutions). The reading handout also demonstrates how a greater amount of economic freedom is associated with better outcomes when it comes to many measures of an individual's well-being, standard of living, and life satisfaction, including higher income per capita, larger economic growth rates, higher income for the poorest of the poor in their country, lower poverty rates, a higher life expectancy, more political rights and civil liberties, greater gender equality (less gender inequality), and happier lives. After the students have read the handout, they split into teams, listen to each statement read aloud by the instructor, and try to correctly fill in the blank within each statement based on the information they read in the handout. Speed also comes into play in this game, as the first team to write down the correct answer to each fill-in-the-blank will receive double the points for that round.

Lesson 5, "The Rules of the Game: How Policies Influence Incentives," utilizes visual and physical learning styles, along with the social learning style. Each team of students is given an envelope of "policy cards," and they must determine the secondary effects of each policy. They are given glue sticks and sheets of paper (or poster board) that say "Expand Business Activity" and "Reduce Business Activity," and they work together to determine what secondary effects would likely result from each policy.

Since even 5 min of physical activity has been shown to have positive learning outcomes for students (Maeda and Randall 2003), Lesson 6 (in addition to Lesson 2) has the students up and running. Lesson 6, "Economic Freedom Runners," combines physical, social, and aural/verbal learning styles. Students split into teams and when it is their turn to run, they listen to the instructor state a policy or factor of the economy, and a student from each team will run to the other side of the room to grab the appropriate sign—either "Consistent" or "Inconsistent"—depending on whether the statement is consistent or inconsistent with economic freedom. Students have a chance to work both independently in this exercise and with their team if needed. Speed is a factor in Lesson 6 as well, as the first team member to make it back to their team with the correct answer earns double the points for that round. The teams also have a chance for a few bonus points if they can correctly identify which of the five main areas of the EFW index that the given concept falls within. (It would be a good idea for the students to have already played the Lesson 3 game before participating in Lesson 6, so they each have already read the handout explaining how economic freedom is measured, and what each of the five main areas of the EFW Index measures.)

While the other lessons incorporate a social (interpersonal) learning style, Lesson 7 is the one lesson that is designed to utilize the solitary (intrapersonal) learning style. Lesson 7, "Learning The Ropes of Research: EFW on the Web," utilizes a visual learning style to teach students how to utilize the functions of the Fraser Institute's Economic Freedom of the World website. Following the directions in the worksheet, students learn how to quickly and easily identify data points relating to Economic Freedom of the World. Students also learn how to access the entire EFW dataset so they can use it in the future research if this topic sparks their interest.

Lesson 8, "Economic Freedom Line," utilizes visual, aural/verbal, social, and physical learning styles. Students are each assigned a country without knowing the real-world name of the country. They only know a couple of data points about their country, and must use the general relationships they have learned thus far about how economic freedom relates to those variables, to try to place themselves in a line from most-economically free to least-economically free. This lesson is meant to be a humbling experience for the students, as some might be thinking they know all there is to know about economic freedom at this point. But there are a few "surprise" countries placed in the deck of country cards, and hopefully such surprises will induce curiosity for the student to learn more about why/how it is that certain countries rank where they do in terms of economic freedom.

1.3 Conclusion

When designing the lessons to teach about various concepts, relationships, and facts surrounding economic freedom, I was careful to incorporate features that will be beneficial for students of different learning styles. I have found that students (and educators!) are not only more engaged during these games and activities, but that they also absorb, understand, and retain the information better. Many students have told me that it is much easier to remember a concept when one is not simply memorizing from a textbook. I have witnessed my Honors Principles of Microeconomics and Honors Principles of Macroeconomics students at Florida State University discover and apply concepts for themselves while participating in these econ activities. In fact, my students enjoy these activities so much that outside of class time, they come to the economic education center where I work in order to participate in more activities, and some students have even brought friends who are not enrolled in my course. Many of my FSU students have told me in person, via email, in their course evaluations, and even written on the back of their final exams that they really enjoyed the interactive activities, and that the economic freedom lessons helped them learn and truly grasp the economics concepts.

While sharing my interactive educational activities with Canadian educators in a workshop setting, I discovered that even those already familiar with the concepts still enjoy this method of learning by doing. It is a delight to see these instructors and other educators in the USA excited and eager to implement these tools in their own classrooms. These activities can be incorporated in classrooms at both the high school and college/university setting. While economics courses are the obvious choice for implementing these activities, teachers and professors in other areas of study such as history, civics, political science, social studies, and geography could also benefit from incorporating these Lessons in Economic Freedom into their classrooms when exploring differences across countries.

References

Bartlett R (1996) Discovering diversity in introductory economics. J Econ Perspect 10(2):141–153

Becker WE, Watts M (1995) Teaching tools: teaching methods in undergraduate economics. Econ Inq 33(4):692–700

Becker WE, Watts M (1996) Chalk and talk: A national survey on teaching undergraduate economics. Am Econ Rev 86(2):448–453

Bishop JL, Verleger MA (2013) The flipped classroom: a survey of the research. In: ASEE national conference proceedings, Atlanta, GA

Borg M, Shapiro S (1996) Personality type and student performance in principles of economics. J Econ Educ 27(1):3–25

Budde H, Voelcker-Rehage C, Pietraßyk-Kendziorra S, Ribeiro P, Tidow G (2008) Acute coordinative exercise improves attentional performance in adolescents. Neurosci Lett 441:219–223

Charkins R, O'Toole DM, Wetzel JN (1985) Linking teacher and student learning styles with student achievement and attitudes. J Econ Educ 16(2):111–120

DellaValle J, Dunn K, Dunn R, Geisert G, Sinatra R, Zenhausern R (1986) The effects of matching and mismatching students' mobility preferences on recognition and memory tasks. J Edu Res 79(5):267–272
Donnelly JE, Lambourne K (2011) Classroom-based physical activity, cognition, and academic achievement. Prev Med 52:S36–S42
Gardner H (1993) Frames of mind: the theory of multiple intelligences. Basic Books, New York
Gasparic RP, Bergmann J, Sams A (2017) Flipped learning: gateway to student engagement, international society for technology in education: Eugene, Oregon and Washington, DC, 2014. Center Educ Pol Stud J 7(3):173–176
Gwartney JD, Lawson R, Hall JC (2017) Economic freedom of the World: 2017 annual report. Fraser Institute, Vancouver
Maeda JK, Randall LM (2003) Can academic success come from five minutes of physical activity? Brock Educ J 13(1):14–22
Mahar MT, Murphy SK, Rowe DA, Golden J, Shields AT, Raedeke TD (2006) Effects of a classroom-based program on physical activity and on-task behavior. Med Sci Sports Exer 38(12):2086–2094
Norlander T, Moâs L, Archer T (2005) Noise and stress in primary and secondary school children: noise reduction and increased concentration ability through a short but regular exercise and relaxation program. Sch Eff Sch Improv 16:91–99
Rasberry CN, Lee SM, Robin L, Laris B, Russell LA, Coyle KK, Nihiser AJ (2011) The association between school-based physical activity, including physical education, and academic performance: a systematic review of the literature. Prev Med 52:S10–S20
Roach T (2014) Student perceptions toward flipped learning: new methods to increase interaction and active learning in economics. Int Rev Econ Edu 17:74–84
Thomas S (2018) Lessons in economic freedom. Fraser Institute, Vancouver

Chapter 2
Video Games in Teaching Economics

David Youngberg

Abstract While economic education considers a large body of valuable classroom activities which demonstrate the efficacy of economic ideas, these activities mainly serve as illustrations and are constrained to the classroom. But video games hold even more pedagogical promise and to illustrate their potential, I present a working video game designed to reinforce students' understanding of comparative statics. The game plays as if it was built solely to entertain but rewards players who have a solid grasp of how to shift supply and demand curves. It thus incentivizes command of the subject matter without the pressure of grades. And because the game is not obviously homework, students who have trouble would be encouraged to stay engaged as they practice shifting curves. Though the game lacked many features a final version would include, student test results suggested that the video game improved student learning.

2.1 Introduction

The popular stereotype of economics is that of a dry, heartless, and highly mathematical discipline. Economists are "bean counters," concerned only with efficiency in the worst sense of the word. Nothing could be further from the truth. Economic insights have diverse applications to not just understanding human behavior but also to get the most out of life. Part of the job of the economic educator is to correct this misperception and games are a powerful tool at the educator's disposal. By playing a role in some scenario, the learner puts herself in the shoes of a stranger and understands why that person acts as they do. Students do not merely see how theory works in practice, but discover they act in a way the theory predicts. The concept transforms from a chalkboard abstraction to a real thing that practically impacts

D. Youngberg (✉)
Montgomery College, Rockville, MD, USA
e-mail: david.youngberg@montgomerycollege.edu

J. Hall, K. Lawson (eds.), *Teaching Economics*,
https://doi.org/10.1007/978-3-030-20696-3_2

lives and predicts behavior. At their very best, games help the student recognize economics as lively, humane, and relevant to their daily life.

As valuable as in-class games are, they have their limitations. Students and professors face computational limits concerning how different parties interact. Even elementary math performed in class takes time and can lead to simple errors which sabotage the instructive goals of the game. Such games are usually used to demonstrate ideas rather than practicing the concepts, a task typically left to conventional homework and studying.

Augmenting instructional techniques with electronic supplements in the form of video games addresses this disconnect. While they no means should replace conventional assignments, video games don't make mathematical errors and students find them much more engaging. By sparking interest in novices—where interest is scarcest—these games can transform apathy into curiosity which in turn can lead to greater enthusiasm for conventional instruction.

To illustrate the potential of game-based learning, I present a video game called *Merchant of the Seas*, I created with computer programmer Kyle Pittleman, and I implemented in my introductory economics class. The game attempts to draw a clear parallel to its main teaching goal—comparative statics—to its game play. The video game is described in detail along with how it was used in class. Preliminary results suggest the potential of this kind of instruction is well-justified.

2.2 Game Typology

Video games, broadly defined, fall into one of two categories. Commercial-off-the-shelf (COTS) games are what we typically think of as video games. They are the first-person shooter, strategy, role-playing, sports, puzzles, and fighting games which are sold for their entertainment value. Serious games (SG) form the other category. Also called game-based learning (GBL) games, they are designed to teach students and professionals particular skills (Aleksić and Ivanović 2017).

There is a fair amount of blurring between these types. Serious games, when properly executed, can be enjoyable enough to be played solely for their entertainment value. And COTS games could be used in an educational setting to teach certain skills. For example, students who played the popular puzzle game Tetris showed an improved spatial reasoning, though this improvement was limited to rotating shapes only found in Tetris (Sims and Mayer 2002).

While the Tetris finding puts the general pedagogical value of COTS games in doubt, these games increasingly include "toolkits" called modding software that allows users to create their own add-ons to the base game. This "middleware" drastically reduces technical barriers to creating custom games because much of the programming is handled by the computer (Castronova 2005). Lawson and Lawson (2010) used it to alter the popular role-playing game *Neverwinter Nights*, creating *Journey to Akerlof*, a game designed to teach concepts such as diminishing marginal utility and the profit-maximizing level of output. They also recruited three students with no knowledge of programming to create a new learning module for the game. Though the students found the task difficult, they were able to complete the project in 7 weeks.

Regardless of the type of game used, using video games to teach economics would follow a pattern similar to in-class games educators often use to illustrate or reinforce various concepts. There are three types of simulations used in economic education: optimization, exploratory, and market simulations. Optimization refers to users attempting to maximize a given goal (profit, utility) under some constraint; exploratory refers to identifying the component parts of a simulated economy; and a market simulation involves participants interacting in a market context, resulting in a price (Porter et al. 2004).

Economists are well aware games encourage student engagement. Classroom games cover a wide range of topics including the connection between quality and cost, entry and exit, and profit-maximizing price, to name a few (Bernard and Schulze 2000; Cheung 2005; Eckalbar 2002). Games that use computers are similarly prolific. Kirche et al. (2011) support use of Applet programs for single-user simulations while noting several barriers to their use exist, such as time to the development and a necessary skill set. Many other attempts created numerical Excel-based simulations (Brown 2000; Saitone and Sexton 2009; Gilbert and Olad 2007, 2011). However, these simulations offer no inherently engaging context but rather a list of adaptive-learning questions (such as Myeconlab, Aplia, and Connect) or a series of inputs into a program that outputs some economic idea (e.g., a shift in a demand curve). Repeating fill-in-the-blank questions may improve understanding but it doesn't help the sizable portion of students who give up out of frustration before learning can take hold (Katz 1999). While there is value in practicing concepts outside of class, there is a role for practice which resembles a game more than it resembles conventional homework. There is a role for fun.

2.3 Game-Based Learning Potential

Activities and simulations are a vastly different method of instruction compared to lectures. Participants are actively engaged in lesson rather than passively learning. Depending on the activity, there may be more or less text to read, graphs to interpret, and words to listen to. Computer games allow for any number of activities to be digitized with audible, textual, and/or visual stimulations be enhanced or subdued. Moreover, computing technology is available for any faculty and students often possess not one but several computers, enabling them to explore the games outside of classroom time. Citing increasing student expectations for more technological integration in instruction, Goffe and Sosin (2005) argued for the value of integrating technology with instruction, specifically mentioning computer games.

But the most salient motivation for game-based instruction lies in the recognition of how diverse learners can be. Students vary in their past experiences, ability to handle stress, work and family commitments, language capacity, willingness to ask questions, and numerous other factors. Video games cannot address all of the considerations but they can help students with learning styles and intelligence types that do not work well with conventional instruction.

A learning style describes how a person best understands new information (Sharda 2007). The number of ways to categorize learning styles is seemingly endless with one literature review estimating 71 distinct models, categorized into 13 major groups (Coffield et al. 2004). For example, Fleming's (2006) VARK model categorizes learning styles into one of four types: visual, auditory, read and write, and kinesthetic. Visual learners best understand new concepts using pictures and graphs. Auditory learners prefer hearing information in the form of discussion or lecture. Learners with the read and write style learn best when the information is presented as literacy: reading the relevant information and writing down what they understand. Kinesthetic learners favor "learning by doing," using their hands, feet, or whole body in some learning-based game or activity.[1]

Complicating differences in learning styles is differences of intelligence. Psychologists have long pulled away from the popular notion that there is one single kind of "intelligence" and instead think of intelligence as multi-faceted. Horn and Cattell (1966) made a distinction between crystallized intelligence—mastering ideas and deducing from a set of facts—and fluid intelligence—understanding how to absorb new information and adapt to unfamiliar circumstances. Crystallized intelligence is what we normally think of as general intelligence and specializes in abstract modeling and memorizing definitions. In contrast, people with a high fluid intelligence have excellent inductive reasoning skills. They can aptly extrapolate from previous experiences and information to draw accurate conclusions about the broader world (Lohman 2001). Gardner (1993) goes further than dual intelligences, arguing that there as many as eight different kinds of intelligence, though this interpretation is controversial among psychologists (Lohman 2001).

Lectures dominate typical college-level classes. Educators focus on delivering key concepts and theories to students who've spent most of their life learning in this traditional format. It's a format that favors crystallized intelligence and auditory learning. Because such intelligence matters and such learners exist, it would be a mistake to completely abandon this style of learning.

But it would behoove educators to incorporate other learning styles into their pedagogy and offer an opportunity for students with greater fluid intelligence to flourish. This is not a matter of hand-holding students but recognizing that the nature of working and learning is changing. The proliferation of information in various media—including videos (Mateer and Stephenson 2011), podcasts (Hall 2012), traditional text (Chamlee-Wright 2011), and games—enables future workers and citizens to learn how they feel most comfortable. And the rapidly changing nature of what constitutes best practices, from software to customer service, mean workers who can learn and adapt on the job will have an advantage. Indeed, "trainability" is a skill employers increasingly seek (Beaton 2017).

[1]Learning style theory has fallen out of favor among psychologists in recent years. The theory, however, remains popular with the general public and preferences for content delivery are genuinely diverse.

Gee (2003) outlined 36 principles of good instructional-based game design. There is no need to go through all principles here but the following should convey the underlying idea (pp. 208–211):

> **#7 Committed Learning Principle.** Learners participate in an extended engagement (lots of effort and practice) as extensions of their real-world identities in relation to a virtual identity to which they feel some commitment and a virtual world that they find compelling.
> **#12 Practice Principle.** Learners get lots and lots of practice in a context where the practice is not boring (i.e., in a virtual world that is compelling to learners on their own terms and where the learners experience ongoing success). They spend lots of time on task.
> **#14 "Regime of Competence" Principle.** The learner gets ample opportunity to operate within, but at the outer edges, of his or her resources, so that at those points things are felt as challenging but not "undoable."
> **#16 Multiple Routes Principle.** There are multiple ways to make progress or move ahead. This allows learners to make choices, rely on their own strengths and styles of learning and problem solving, while also exploring alternative styles.
> **#27 Explicit Information On-Demand and Just-in-Time Principle.** The learner is given explicit information both on-demand and just-in-time, when the learner needs it or just at the point where the information can best be understood and used in practice.
> **#28 Discovery Principle.** Overt telling is kept to a well-thought-out minimum, allowing ample opportunity for the learner to experiment and make discoveries.

Seasoned educators will notice many points of overlap between Gee's principles and their own experience in pedagogy. Good lecturers are entertaining and hold students' attention. Questions are best addressed by not simply telling the student the answer but by asking a series of probing questions so they discover and grasp the answer on their own. Only if they are truly stuck is the answer given but even then, it's done to highlight key ideas from the aforementioned questions. With this in mind, an appropriate video game is when: a participant pursues a particular goal using one or several strategies; that in the pursuit of that goal it is possible to lose in some way; and that the mere pursuit of the goal can reasonably be described as an enjoyable process.

2.4 Evidence

The evidence of video games on learning outcome is slim. While a meta-analysis of 115 studies by Gosen and Washburn (2004) suggests wide-spread effectiveness in learning, none of the studies had potential design or measurement flaws. Other analyses come to similar conclusions: the evidence is, at best, mixed (Wideman et al. 2007; Sitzmann 2011).

But there are tantalizing indications that game-based learning has potential, especially when considering the role of different kinds of intelligence. A review of the empirical evidence by Aleksić and Ivanović (2017) suggests certain types of students learn particularly well playing video games: students with higher levels of intelligence in logical/mathematical, visual/spatial, and bodily/kinesthetic and students with the visual and kinesthetic learning styles. However, they also note that sample bias may be an issue and it's difficult to untangle the effect of the treatment from noise.

Dobrescu et al. (2014) put special attention towards creating a well-designed experimental study and their work is worth exploring in depth. They developed a multi-stage game designed to teach students the production possibilities curve, comparative advantage, and gains from specialization and trade. After an initial instructional video, players would make bundles of two goods by selecting various points on a two dimensional grid. The player would learn some combinations are impossible while others are wasteful, discovering their unique production possibilities curve in the process. The game would then introduce a computer-controlled player that the human player could trade with. Players who identified their comparative advantage and traded smartly with the computer player attained a level of consumption beyond their personal production possibilities curve. Players also had access to a media library with definitions and videos explaining the underlying concepts, some of which was required in an initial instructional video.

Eighty-one randomly selected students were assigned at random to either the video game group or a control group. Both groups included introductory microeconomics students and noneconomics students, with the experiment conducted before the material would be covered in the introductory microeconomics class. Each group had 1 h to learn the material, with the control group reading a textbook chapter and the other group playing the game (this includes the time it took to complete the game's tutorial). Afterwards, students were given identical tests composed of multiple choice and essay questions. Isolation of participants—from each other and from the Internet—was carefully maintained. Game behavior was monitored and recorded.

Despite the video game group never formally reading about these underlying economics concepts—arguably the most counter-intuitive in introductory economics—they performed no worse than the students who formally learned the material by reading the textbook chapter. This might sound like a failure of video games but it should also be noted that many students enjoyed learning the material through the game much more than reading. On that note alone, this is a promising find: video games offer a more enjoyable learning experience with no educational loss. The experiment also contained a time constraint as students were not allowed to practice more than an hour before they were tested. In the real world, students would practice the material more if it's more enjoyable to practice. Video games are a more efficient way to understand material.

The experiment also found evidence that game play and more conventional instruction (as captured by the videos the media library provided) are pedagogical complements. Controlling for media library use, the more the learner played through the game, the better she did at both the multiple choice and essay questions. The more students watched videos, holding the number of playthroughs constant, the better she did at essay questions (though not multiple choice questions). In other words, game play and video learning each had a positive effect on learning and the nature of that effect changed based on the type of assessment used, suggesting players with certain learning styles disproportionately benefited from game-based learning.

2.5 Applications in Class

As exciting as their pedagogical potential is, instructional video games cannot stand alone. Despite the promising work of Dobrescu et al. (2014), it would be mistake to claim that video games could replace all conventional instruction. The evidence that such a transformation would be beneficial does not exist and it would run into conflict what psychologists know about intelligence and learning styles. Some people really do learn better from conventional instruction. What is more promising is to leverage its entertainment and convenience advantages of video games to diversify instruction delivery.

Instructional games are best when granular. Each game should focus on a single idea or inter-related ideas, much how in-class activities are used to illustrate a specific topic. Such modular design allows other educators to pick games that best suit their style and syllabus, lowers the chance the lesson of the game is not lost in unrelated ideas, and makes it easy for students to practice a single concept they are having trouble with.

Video games, no matter how instructional, should not be played in class. Video games are solitary activities which can be done at virtually any time, especially if they can be done on a smartphone. They require a tutorial and, if well designed, are enjoyable enough to not need the structure of class to incentivize engagement. There are much better ways to use class time, from conventional instruction to activities which can take advantage of the availability of multiple participants.

Video games could be assigned for either before or after the relevant class. In the after class approach, the game serves the same function as homework. After completing the tutorial, students practice the relevant concept. When students complete the game, the game could automatically send a message of completion to the professor (or, if the game lacks this capacity, the student could email the professor a screenshot of a completion message), thus allowing the student to "turn in" the assigned game. But unlike homework, the game could reinforce key ideas through explicit messages, acting as a sort of tutor instead of simply as low-stakes assessment.

Instructors might prefer to assign video games before the relevant class. This may be jarring for students as they may require some explicit background before understanding how the game connects to the relevant concepts. The tutorial and accompanying video game would act as the student's first exposure to the material. The game's tutorial could give a crash course in not just the game but the ideas the game is meant to illustrate. The game would thus serve as a platform for class discussion, much like an assigned reading. Students come to class with questions about the material, having a shared experience to discuss. They could bond over common difficulties and confusions. And because the game should be fun, they are far more likely to complete it compared to a conventional reading assignment. The biggest advantage to this approach lies in the ability to immediately address any deviations of the game from the material the game represents. The game acts as "baby steps" to a more sophisticated understanding covered in class. In either approach, the game is available for students to return to if they wish to practice for an upcoming exam or project.

2.6 Trade-Offs

Instructional video games must strike a delicate balance between subject accuracy, player enjoyment, and technical sophistication. A game that perfectly reflects what a player may experience on an exam will feel very much like an exam and will unlikely be enjoyable. A game that is incredibly fun will likely lack any transferability of skills. And while players may enjoy accurate market simulations, such simulations require an artificial intelligence to act as competitors. For any given skill level in computer programming, there's a trade-off between enjoyment and accuracy. It is not a one-for-one trade-off: each factor has diminishing returns. A very enjoyable game can be made slightly less enjoyable but add a great deal of instructional value. Similarly, a very dull game can take a few minor liberties the material and but vastly increase its appeal.

While technical limitations can be addressed with modding software, mods have limitations. Manufacturers encourage the use of modding software because mods require the original game to run and manufactures find that additional mods increase the appeal of their game. Game "modders" create add-ons that encourage new players, including modders' friends, to buy the game (Castronova 2005). But an educational game created with a mod requires students to purchase the base game, an expense that can easily amount to $50 or $60. While this may be small compared to a textbook, the game, in pursuit of modularity, may only cover a few different concepts. One could imagine many different mods for the same base game, with each mod covering a single concept. But mods are constrained by the base game. It's doubtful that any single base game could be a workable platform for all the necessary mods one would have to create. As more colleges encourage faculty away from textbooks and towards (free) open educational resources, requiring students to purchase a video game seems impractical.

With these issues in mind, *Merchant of the Seas* focuses on a single idea that students often struggle with—supply and demand shifts—though other lessons concerning arbitrage and the cost of obtaining information inevitably seep through as well.

2.7 Game Description

Comparative statics is one of the trickier concepts for economics students. The ability to master it through simple memorization is limited and students with excellent memories but poor reasoning skills could easily be befuddled by shocks outside the standard examples. Doing it regularly and well is a skill that requires practice. Because supply and demand manipulation leads to many insights about how markets work and adapt and is one of the most practical lessons covered in introductory economics, it is the focus of *Merchant of the Seas*.

The player takes on the role of a sea-based merchant at the height of the Roman Empire (approximately 100 C.E.), trading six different goods—cloth, fish, incense, pottery, timber, and wine—between six different cities—Alexandria, Byzantium, Leptis Magna, New Carthage, Rome, and Salamis. They begin the game in a random location with 100 gold. Throughout the game market shocks will disrupt prices and create new opportunities by shifting the supply or demand curves. The player's goal is to navigate these shocks, buying and selling goods until her treasury reaches or exceeds 1000 gold pieces. Players who correctly anticipate which curve shifts and how will find reaching the goal much easier. Players who are very poor at interpreting these shocks will struggle or lose the game.

The game consists of land and sea hexes organized to resemble the Mediterranean Sea. The ship, representing the player, can move up to three hexes a turn. If the player is adjacent to a city, a city window on the right-handed side of the screen displays options to buy and sell. When the turn is complete, the player clicks on the "End Turn" bottom, gold is subtracted from the player's treasury, and the ship's movement is reset.

Each city supplies two different goods and demands two different goods. Prices follow linear supply and demand equations. For example, Byzantium supplies fish using the equation: $P = 35+Q$. The first unit the player buys will cost 36 gold, then 37 gold, then 38 gold, etc. Alexandria demands fish at $P = 50-Q$; the first unit will sell for 49 gold, the second unit for 48 gold, then 47 gold, etc. Thus, the game begins with many obvious profit opportunities to exploit. Players can easily buy commodities cheaply in some locations and sell them at higher prices elsewhere, pocketing the profit made. The player generates a cushion of gold that allows her to make mistakes as she learns. A consequence of this approach is that the merchant is effectively a perfect price discriminator, collecting all the consumer surplus as well as producer surplus as profit. While this is immediately strange to those well-versed in economic theory, novices are unlikely to notice. It is more likely that they will notice each additional unit is more and more costly to buy and each additional unit generates smaller and smaller revenue. In other words, this strange approach encourages students to think in terms of increasing marginal cost and decreasing marginal benefit. Having players follow along the curves also eliminates the possibility that there will be a persistent profit opportunity players could utilize without having to apply the lesson.

There are not enough profit opportunities for players to win the game by mindlessly buying low and selling high. They have to take advantage of supply and demand shifts. The game captures a shift in supply or demand by increasing or decreasing the curve's intercept. These shifts are reflected in the market shocks which appear in the top-center of the screen every three turns. Some shocks are straightforward, such as "The citizens of Alexandria develop a new way of cooking fish, resulting in a better tasting meal." This clearly affects the market for fish (and Alexandria's other goods—supplying cloth, supplying incense, and demanding timber—would clearly not be affected by a new fish recipe) and since Alexandria demands, and does not supply, fish, it must affect the demand curve (and indeed it does; it would add five to the intercept so now Alexandria's equation for buying fish is $P = 55-Q$). This creates a new arbitrage opportunity that savvy players can exploit.

Since students often have trouble determining which curve to shift, roughly two-thirds of shocks are not so obvious. Most of these affect two cities, one which supplies the good and one which demands it.[2] One such example is: "A sage in New Carthage develops a better potter's wheel; the invention quickly spreads to Rome." This most closely resembles the kind of question a student might see on an exam "In the market for pottery, what happens after the invention of a better potter's wheel?" and the player must decide: do the citizens of New Carthage willing to pay more for pottery (demand shifts up/right) or is pottery from Rome now cheaper (supply shifts down/left)? Since each good has two cities buying and two cities selling, it is not obvious what the player should do unless she knows what should shift. And since it is expensive to travel, there is an incentive to knowing what should happen without having to check it by visiting each city. Appendix 1 offers sample instructions for students explaining how to play the game, how it connects to supply and demand shocks, and how interpreting these shocks help players win the game.

Merchant of the Seas has other lessons integrated into it. The many profit opportunities players can exploit in the game's opening ends up teaching arbitrage; learners will discover how easy it is to earn money under these conditions so it would not surprise them that, in competitive markets, these opportunities are hard to find and quickly exhausted once they become common knowledge. When the arbitrage opportunities are exhausted, another lesson concerning the cost of obtaining information emerges. The learner must spend gold to travel, bringing him further away from winning. While this turn-by-turn cost intended to discourage learners from simply traveling to cities at random to learn where the best prices were, it also had the effect of making information gathering costly. The game thus illustrates search costs. Knowing where to go without exploring directly saves the player time and tedium, it also means they spend less gold, avoiding these search costs. Moreover, a shock that creates a profit opportunity is less likely to be undone by a different shock if it can be exploited more quickly. In multiple ways, the learner experiences how costly it is to acquire information.

2.8 In Practice

In 2015, I integrated a prototype of the video game into my introductory economics class. Over the course of a spring and fall semester, students were required to win the game and submit a screenshot of the victory screen to document their completion.

[2]Other shocks that are not as obvious as the price of clay rising involve changing a city's population or income.

In the spring semester, students were only required to complete the game. In the fall semester, students were required to complete the game in 100 turns or fewer. The assignment preceded an in-class explanation of supply and demand shifts similar to a standard lecture. They also had an in-class overview of the game which took roughly 15 min. The overview looked much like a game tutorial, explaining how the controls work, the goal of the video game, the basic process of completing the game, and how the game's content connected to the material we had just covered. It also included instructions on how to download and activate the game. It later became clear that directing students to a YouTube video might have been just as effective and would not have taken up valuable class time. Such a video would have followed a script similar to what's found in Appendix 1. A handout as presented in Appendix 1 could have also worked.

Students typically enjoyed the game and understood the connection between the game and the course material. It took an average of about 45 min to win the game and roughly twice as long to play it long enough to win. That students had to spend 50–55 min practicing the game before they were able to even start a winning session suggests it has potential as a pedagogical tool. This was not an easy game: students had to practice to complete it. It also highlights the value of a tutorial. Though the game was explained in detail in class, students might have spent a fair amount of time familiarizing themselves with the controls. This practice time might have acted as a clumsy tutorial. The lack of a structured tutorial also might help explain why students didn't use the game to help them study for the exam (Table 2.1).

Students tended to be better when they played *Merchant of the Seas*. Comparing students who played the game in the fall of 2015 with the students who did not one year previous, the game playing students did better by approximately one point on a four-part question covering comparative statics. Students in the spring semester of 2015 had an even stronger improvement but the typical student in the fall is likely different compared to the typical student in the spring (Table 2.2).

Technical difficulties prevented some students from playing the game and were thus required to complete an alternative assignment. The alternative assignment involved 24 multiple choice questions on comparative statics using the same shocks found in the game. Since technical difficulties are more or less random, this provided a natural experiment opportunity. In 2015, the spring semester had twenty such

Table 2.1 Student reaction

Statement	Average (6 = Strongly Agree)	N
"I enjoyed playing *Merchant of the Seas*"	4.93	121
"I felt that playing *Merchant of the Seas* helped me learn supply and demand shifts"	4.12	121
"I played *Merchant of the Seas* again to help me study for this exam"	2.08	121
"I see the connection between *Merchant of the Seas* and supply and demand shifts"	4.68	120

Table 2.2 Time to complete

Questions (2015 Fall semester only)	Average (hours)	N
For the *Merchant of the Seas* screenshot you submitted as your assignment, about how long did it take you to complete that particular play-through?	0.76	60
While attempting to complete the assignment, about how long, in total, did you spend playing *Merchant of the Seas*?	1.66	59

Table 2.3 Performance

Semester	Average (out of 16)	Variance	*p*-value (compared to Fall 2014 average)	N
Fall 2014	12.4	5.78	N/A	95
Fall 2015	13.5	7.54	0.0294	43
Spring 2015	13.9	3.83	0.0000	62

students and the fall semester had ten. In both cases, students who completed the alternative assignment did the same as students who completed the game. Similar to the findings of Dobrescu et al. (2014), the game doesn't improve scores over conventional practice but it doesn't make them any worse (Table 2.3).

The tested game was a prototype and lacked many features likely to improve student comprehension. When the player arrives at a city that had experienced a supply or demand shift, there is no graphical indication to confirm that's why the price changed. The game lacks a tutorial and in-game reference that would enhance understanding of the interface, the material, and the game's connection to the concepts. The game presents a few of the shocks in a confusing or arbitrary manner and only the most recent shock is viewable. But despite these shortcomings, students found the game enjoyable and the evidence suggests they learned from it.

2.9 Complications of *Merchant of the Seas*

Video games are stepping stones for student engagement. They should focus on deepening student understanding for one key lesson without robbing the player of a pleasurable game experience. Designing instructional video games requires striking a balance between content accuracy, enjoyment, and technical expertise. This may mean that the video game may not perfectly represent related concepts. Such instances should be treated as valuable opportunities for the instructor to launch a discussion.

For example, *Merchant of the Seas* focuses on cementing comprehension of supply and demand shifts. It does this by allowing a single middle-man—the player—to buy and sell goods. But as the only merchant, the player has a huge amount of market power and that is in stark contrast to how competitive markets work. In competitive models, no one person should be able to influence the price but that is exactly the situation in *Merchant of the Seas*. Each additional unit bought increases the price and each additional unit sold decreases the price. The game should arguably have prices that don't change with each transaction.

While technically more accurate, this creates dangers. As designed, any profit opportunities the player discovers are short-lived. You cannot win the game based on correctly interpreting a single shock. But if prices are mostly static after a shock, arbitrage opportunities could persist far longer than. The game will not be challenging and the player will be poorly incentivized to understand the material. If it's easy, it won't be fun. Attempting to make the game more accurate risks failing to reinforce anything altogether.

It's possible to instead add other middle-men to better reflect competitive markets. With this would enhance accuracy and may even make the game more enjoyable, even a basic artificial intelligence is difficult to program. Video game programming is a major endeavor and avoiding unnecessary complications is advised.

Because of the structure of the game, some effects might seem confusing to players. A demand shock which occurred in both a supplying city and a demanding city would arguably affect both supply and demand. If the citizens in both New Carthage and Rome started entertaining themselves with a jug-throwing contest, wouldn't the price of pottery in Rome (a pottery supplier) increase as locals start buying locally made pottery to break? Technically, this is true since the model of the game assumes the people of the city of Rome only make pottery and never buy it. It should therefore be highlighted to inquiring players that the game is a simplification and the separation of the market between cities is an artificial construct for purposes of instruction.

Alternatively, one could argue that the game assumes such local demand (or local supply) are simply too small to be reflected in the price that way. The reason why New Carthage is listed as demanding pottery is because it demands pottery on a scale that far outstrips all other cities (save Leptis Magna).[3]

2.10 Should Learning Be Fun?

Despite the promise video games have for student learning, making learning more enjoyable may have a negative impact on students. More education is correlated with more income. One possible reason for this connection is skills (human capital): workers with more education are more productive and thus can command a higher wage. Engineers and accountants learn skills that employers find valuable and pay a premium for labor apt in those abilities. But employers' skill needs are too

[3]It should be noted that neither myself nor Kyle Pittleman is a trained historian. Goods were assigned to cities based on if the relevant distances would result in an enjoyable and instructional game.

varied and vague to be covered by all disciplines. They also value general attributes like intelligence, grit, and diligence. This is reason number two: more education demonstrates to potential employers that candidates have these desired traits. Smart, hard-working, and careful people find passing college classes to be easy. Stupid, lazy, and careless people have a difficult time getting a college, or even a high school, degree. This "signaling theory" doesn't claim a perfect connection between the signal and the trait but since such attributes are hard to observe directly, it's the best available.

Unlike human capital, signals are relative. If everyone can send the signal, the signal means nothing. When a small portion of the US population had a college degree, having one was a big deal. You stood out. Now such degrees are much more common. Having one is a weaker signal and employers are no longer impressed, forcing students to run clubs, take on internships, and maintain perfect grades to signal greatness. It amounts to an arms race, ultimately resulting in students having to get graduate degrees when a bachelor's would have sufficed.

So far we've assumed that students are better off if learning is more enjoyable. And while the incentive gains to learn in a more compelling environment seem obvious, there are certain areas that it should be avoided. In economics' most practical areas—supply-and-demand shifts, comparative advantage, sunk costs—it makes sense that learning should be fun. A better grasp of these ideas leads to better workers and a smarter voting population. But if we make concepts which have little practical value to most students easier to learn, we will only push the arms race farther.

Consider a video game that teaches people how to have a great job interview. It's an incredibly advanced program, able to simulate many possible questions and reactions from interviewers. Players upload their resumes and the game uses it to formulate custom interview questions. It understands not only nuances in how the player chose to word her answers, but also picks up on subtle pauses, changes in volume, and tones of confidence. It hooks up to the computer's camera and will pick up on the player's body language and facial reactions. It blows the Turning test out of the water.

It's also very fun to play. Players get useful feedback and enjoy "interviewing" for hours on end. They might even forget they're practicing their interview skills. They learn to "game" the game, faking it in all the right ways. It's so much fun, everyone plays it and everyone can give a great interview, even mediocre workers. But interviews are signals: they are used to demonstrate favorable personality traits and attitudes. If it becomes easy to learn how to act this way, including faking that you have certain traits, the signal loses significance. It's no longer notable if you had a great interview. It would be like dressing up for the interview; it's only notable if you don't send the signal. In this world, great interviews become minimum standards of success and genuinely great candidates have to work even harder to find new ways to stand out.

Enjoyable learning ends up being wasteful if what's being learned is signaling. If a game made impractical, but difficult, concepts easy to learn, we risk robbing that concept of its signaling benefit. This would not make students better off but only push the arms race forward, akin to making it easier to build nuclear weapons during the Cold War. As educators particularly interested in avoiding wastes of time and money, we should resist applying educational games to concepts that are more about showing off than improving productivity.

2.11 Conclusion

Pedagogical techniques should include video games that are not obviously instructional. There is tremendous value in students developing economic concepts in nontraditional formats. At minimum, different media helps maintain a student's attention. But an instructional video game a student finds fun could also encourage outside studying, encouragement, or a deeper appreciation of discipline as its practical implications become more evident.

The video game presented here suggests such a game is possible. The shocks players encounter emulate test questions and real-world phenomena. Because the turn-by-turn decreasing gold is paired with increasingly hard-to-find profit options, the game incentivizes players to learn the material in a way reminiscent of conventional video games. It's fun to try to stay "alive," especially if you can try again once you fail. Its focus on a single economic idea is deliberate. The authors suspect other enjoyable games could be designed to teach a wide variety of topics, and encourage others.

Appendix 1: Sample Instructions

Obtaining information is costly. Because relevant knowledge is spread out in different places and that knowledge is constantly changing, there is a need for people who focus on gathering information and using it in beneficial ways. The better you are information gathering, the more value you add.

Merchant of the Seas is a game about how costly it is to get information and how to anticipate informational changes. You know this as supply and demand curve shifts, or comparative statics. This game offers a chance to practice one of introductory economics' most practical skills in an enjoyable setting.

In *Merchant of the Seas*, you are a merchant at the height of the Roman Empire, approximately 100 C.E. There are six cities to trade in and in each city, there are two goods to buy and two goods to sell. You start on a random point on the map with 100 gold to buy any goods you wish. But be careful how you spend it! Your ship moves only three spaces a turn. Click the ship and the game highlights the hexes you can travel to. Click a hex to go there. Whenever you proceed to the next turn (by clicking the End Turn button in the upper-right hand corner), you pay the sailors that help you run your ship two gold. You win when you reach 1000 gold.

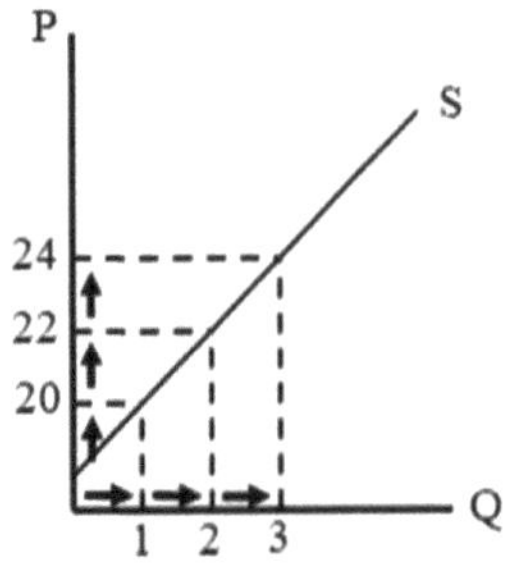

Fig. 2.1 Supply curve

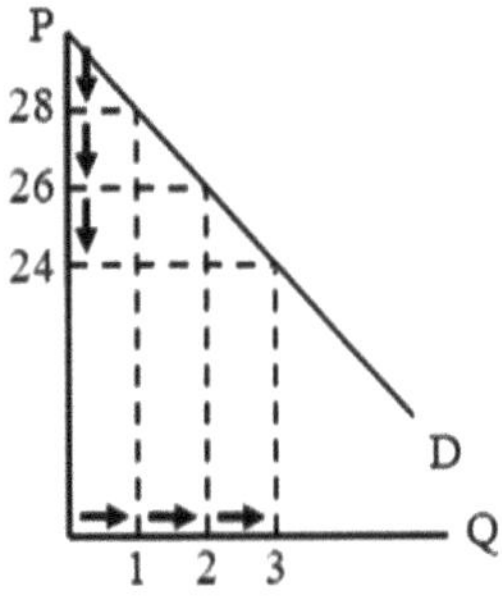

Fig. 2.2 Demand curve

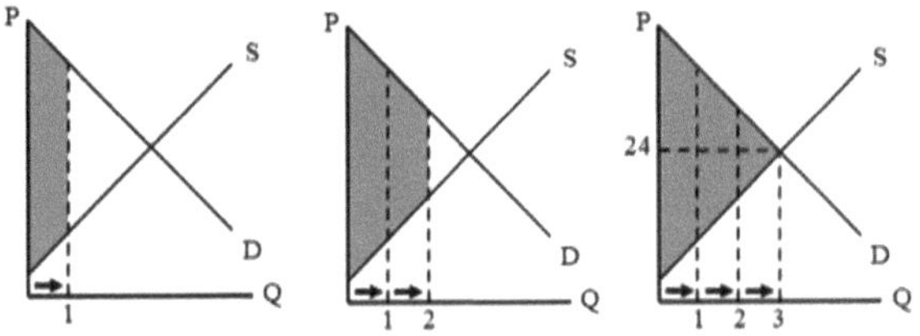

Fig. 2.3 Demand and supply

When you move next to a city, you can see prices for the goods the city is buying and selling. Every unit you buy increases the price of the next unit you buy. Since you're buying the good, the city is a producer and you can think of yourself as moving up the good's supply curve (Fig. 2.1) with each unit bought.

No city sells and buys the same good, so you'll have to travel to a different place to sell your wares. When you sell, each unit you sell results in a lower and lower price. Since you're selling the good, the people in the city in question is now the consumer and you can think of yourself as traveling down the demand curve (Fig. 2.2) with each unit sold.

The profit you make equals the difference between the two curves: the shaded area in Fig. 2.3. In the beginning of the game, there will be many profit opportunities from buying low and selling high, what economists call *arbitrage*. But the game remembers how many times you've bought and sold every good; these arbitrage opportunities will soon be exhausted. On their own, it won't be enough to get to 1000 gold. That's when you have to be clever!

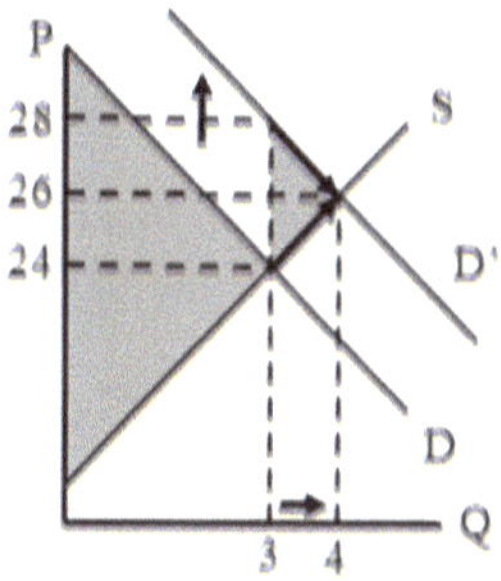

Fig. 2.4 Shifting demand curve

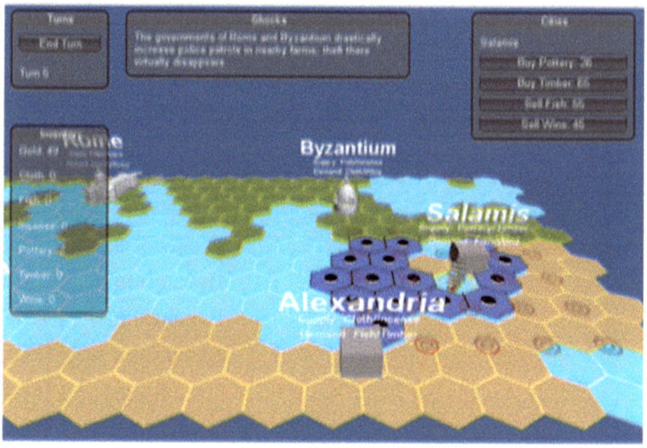

Fig. 2.5 Screenshot of *Merchant of the Seas*

Every three turns, you get news about something that happened in the Empire. These news events, called shocks, shift a demand or supply curve for one or more of the goods. This creates new profit opportunities for you to exploit! Figure 2.4 illustrates how an upward shift in demand makes trading a fourth unit profitable, when before it wasn't.

You can find out which prices have changed by traveling to each city but traveling is expensive. It's far better if you can determine which goods have become cheaper to buy (from downward shifts in supply) and which goods have become more expensive to sell (from upward shifts in demand) by interpreting these shocks as they appear. But be aware: demand can also shift down and supply can also shift up. Understanding these shocks not only tell you which cities to visit if you're trading a particular good but also which ones to avoid.

Figure 2.5 is a sample screenshot which includes the user interface. It depicts your ship docked at Salamis with the window on the upper right displaying current prices. The window at the top center displays the latest shock. The inventory on the left displays current money and current inventory; this player has 49 gold and two units of pottery in the ship's cargo hold. The window in the upper left displays the current turn and includes the button players click to proceed to the next turn. The purple hexes represent the ship's range this turn. The red circles are an artifact of the game's engine and have no in-game consequence.

You can view the entire map by zooming out (pressing CTRL while using the mouse wheel) and you can scroll by pressing the arrow keys. Each city displays what you can buy in that city (the good's supply curve in that city) followed by what you can sell in that city (the good's demand curve in that city). In Byzantium, you can buy Fish and Incense and you can sell Cloth and Wine.

Appendix 2: Goods Equations

See Table 2.4.

Table 2.4 All goods' supply and demand equations

City	Good	Supply/Demand	Equation
Alexandria	Fish	Demand	50−Q
Alexandria	Timber	Demand	90−2Q
Alexandria	Cloth	Supply	40+2Q
Alexandria	Incense	Supply	45+2Q
Byzantium	Cloth	Demand	70−4Q
Byzantium	Wine	Demand	50−2Q
Byzantium	Fish	Supply	35+Q
Byzantium	Incense	Supply	35+4Q
Leptis Magna	Incense	Demand	75−4Q
Leptis Magna	Pottery	Demand	45−Q
Leptis Magna	Cloth	Supply	35+5Q
Leptis Magna	Fish	Supply	30+2Q
New Carthage	Cloth	Demand	70−2Q
New Carthage	Pottery	Demand	55−2Q
New Carthage	Timber	Supply	60+4Q
New Carthage	Wine	Supply	20+Q
Rome	Incense	Demand	70−2Q
Rome	Timber	Demand	85−Q
Rome	Pottery	Supply	35+Q
Rome	Wine	Supply	20+2Q
Salamis	Fish	Demand	55−2Q
Salamis	Wine	Demand	45−Q
Salamis	Pottery	Supply	20+3Q
Salamis	Timber	Supply	65+6Q

Appendix 3: Game Shocks

See Table 2.5.

Table 2.5 All shocks in the game and their effects

Shock	Effect(s)			
	City	Good	D/S	Impact
A cold snap strikes the Empire	Byzantium	Cloth	D	+10
	New Carthage	Cloth	D	+10
A wealthy merchant in New Carthage dies and leaves his vast collection of clothes to the poor	New Carthage	Cloth	D	−5
A wealthy merchant in Byzantium dies and leaves his vast collection of clothes to the poor	Byzantium	Cloth	D	−5
In New Carthage and Leptis Magna, the price of dye dramatically falls	New Carthage	Cloth	D	+10
In Byzantium and Alexandria, the latest fashion requires a completely new set of clothes	Byzantium	Cloth	D	+5
An artisan in Alexandria develops a way to store cloth using less space without harming the product	Alexandria	Cloth	S	−5
An artisan in Leptis Magna develops a way to store cloth using less space without harming the product	Leptis Magna	Cloth	S	−5
Corruption spreads through the police in Leptis Magna after major cuts in their pay; theft from warehouses increases	Leptis Magna	Cloth	S	+10
	Leptis Magna	Fish	S	+10
A fire in Alexandria destroys several looms	Alexandria	Cloth	S	+5
In Alexandria and New Carthage, improvements in animal husbandry increase the birth rate of sheep	Alexandria	Cloth	S	−10
The price of looms fall in Byzantium and Leptis Magna	Leptis Magna	Cloth	S	−5
A sickness hits Alexandria which the sages say comes from eating too much fish	Alexandria	Fish	D	−10
The price of beef rises in Alexandria and Leptis Magna	Alexandria	Fish	D	+5
In Byzantium and Salamis, the price of olive oil falls	Salamis	Fish	D	+5
The citizens of Salamis develop a new way of cooking fish, resulting in a better-tasting meal	Salamis	Fish	D	+5
	Salamis	Wine	D	+5
The citizens of Alexandria develop a new way of cooking fish, resulting in a better-tasting meal	Alexandria	Fish	D	+5

(continued)

Table 2.5 (continued)

Shock	Effect(s)			
	City	Good	D/S	Impact
Calm weather in Leptis Magna and Alexandria make fishing safer	Leptis Magna	Fish	S	−10
The local governments in Leptis Magna and Salamis improve their respective harbors, allowing for greater fishing boat traffic	Leptis Magna	Fish	S	−5
A fire in Byzantium destroys most of the fishing nets	Byzantium	Fish	S	+10
In Byzantium and Salamis, slaves talented at repairing nets become available for sale	Byzantium	Fish	S	−5
In Alexandria and Byzantium, tinkers improve fishing boat design	Byzantium	Fish	S	−10
Priests in Alexandria and Leptis Magna introduce a new ritual using incense that proves popular with the local citizenry	Leptis Magna	Incense	D	+5
The cities of Byzantium and Leptis Magna each build a new temple (incense is used in religious ceremonies)	Leptis Magna	Incense	D	+5
The city of Rome cuts taxes; incomes rise	Rome	Incense	D	+10
	Rome	Timber	D	+10
In the cities of Alexandria and Rome, a series of bad omens drive citizens to the temples (incense is used in religious ceremonies)	Rome	Incense	D	+10
The Emperor's sponsoring an elaborate series of games; attendance prevents citizens from going to religious ceremonies	Rome	Incense	D	−15
The Alexandrian government improves their roads leading to Arabia Felix, where incense is grown	Alexandria	Incense	S	−5
In Alexandria and Leptis Magna, the price of camel feed increases (camels are used to transport incense)	Alexandria	Incense	S	−10
A new law in Alexandria increases the pay of porters (those who transport goods within a city)	Alexandria	Incense	S	+5
	Alexandria	Cloth	S	+5
In Byzantium and Rome, the price of gems (which, like incense, is imported from distant lands) falls	Byzantium	Incense	S	−10
The Byzantium government improves their roads leading to Arabia Felix, where most incense is grown	Byzantium	Incense	S	−5
Wall paintings become unfashionable in Leptis Magna but the love of painted art remains	Leptis Magna	Pottery	D	+5
Angry mobs in Rome and New Carthage threaten to lynch any citizen how keeps decorated pottery in his home	New Carthage	Pottery	D	−10

(continued)

Table 2.5 (continued)

Shock	Effect(s)			
	City	Good	D/S	Impact
Wall paintings become unfashionable in New Carthage but the love of painted art remains	New Carthage	Pottery	D	+5
New Carthage moderately grows as more people immigrant to the Empire	New Carthage	Pottery	D	+5
	New Carthage	Cloth	D	+5
The sages in Leptis Magna and Salamis claim eating food stored in clay pots is bad for your health	Leptis Magna	Pottery	D	−5
In the cities of Leptis Magna and Rome, citizens increasingly entertain themselves with jug throwing contests	Leptis Magna	Pottery	D	+5
Salamis prevents fire outbreaks in warehouses with regular patrols	Salamis	Pottery	S	−5
	Salamis	Timber	S	−5
In Rome, the price of clay rises	Rome	Pottery	S	+10
A sage in New Carthage develops a better potter's wheel; the invention quickly spreads to Rome	Rome	Pottery	S	−10
The price of bricks in Rome and Leptis Magna fall (clay is used to make bricks as well as pottery)	Rome	Pottery	S	−10
The cities of New Carthage and Salamis receive slaves who are very good at safely transporting large numbers of clay pots	Salamis	Pottery	S	−5
A massive fire burns a large residential area of Rome!	Rome	Timber	D	+15
The sages convince the people of Alexandria that stone chairs are good for your health	Alexandria	Timber	D	−5
A massive fire burns a large residential area of Alexandria!	Alexandria	Timber	D	+15
The citizens of Alexandria and New Carthage become interested in making custom wooden toys for their children	Alexandria	Timber	D	+5
Rome and Salamis have a warm winter; fireplaces are rarely used	Rome	Timber	D	−5
Hoards of hostile barbarians are found in the forests near Salamis	Salamis	Timber	S	+10
A more efficient saw appears throughout the Empire	New Carthage	Timber	S	−10
	Salamis	Timber	S	−10
Barbarians retreat from the vicinity of Alexandria and Salamis; the local forests become a much safer place	Salamis	Timber	S	−10

(continued)

Table 2.5 (continued)

Shock	Effect(s)			
	City	Good	D/S	Impact
The price of hiring talented forest guides in New Carthage and Rome falls	New Carthage	Timber	S	−5
The price of wheat (sometimes grown on deforested land) in Alexandria and New Carthage notably increases	New Carthage	Timber	S	+10
The governors of Rome and Byzantium declare a celebration of the gods; drunken revelry soon to follow	Byzantium	Wine	D	+10
The Salamis city government agrees to cut taxes; incomes rise	Salamis	Wine	D	+5
	Salamis	Fish	D	+5
The sages in Rome and Salamis claim that water, rather than wine, is best for your health	Salamis	Wine	D	−5
A very dry and salty cracker becomes a popular snack in New Carthage and Salamis	Salamis	Wine	D	+5
The Byzantium government agrees to cut taxes; incomes rise	Byzantium	Wine	D	+5
	Byzantium	Cloth	D	+5
The wells of Byzantium and New Carthage become polluted; the city water smells terrible!	Byzantium	Wine	D	+10
The price of raisins in Byzantium and Rome rises	Rome	Wine	S	+10
Favorable weather in New Carthage leads to a bumper crop of grapes	New Carthage	Wine	S	−5
In New Carthage and Salamis, improvements in irrigation are adopted in nearby farms	New Carthage	Wine	S	−5
The governments of Rome and Byzantium drastically increase police patrols in nearby farms; theft there virtually disappears	Rome	Wine	S	−15
Favorable weather in Rome leads to a bumper crop of grapes	Rome	Wine	S	−5

References

Aleksić V, Ivanović M (2017) A literature review of empirical research on the effects of digital games on learning styles and multiple intelligences. Croat J Edu 19(2):511–562

Beaton C (2017) Top employers say millennials need these 4 skills in 2017. Forbes, New York, NY, January 6, 2017. Available at: https://www.forbes.com/sites/carolinebeaton/2017/01/06/top-employers-say-millennials-need-these-4-skills-in-2017/#62d9cc517fe4. Accessed 25 Oct 2017

Bernard JC, Schulze W (2000) Teaching marginal cost, supply, and efficiency with an English-auction experiment. J Econ Educ 31(1):52–59

Brown B (2000) Interactive learning: Vignettes from America's most wired campuses. Anker, Bolton, MA

Castronova E (2005) Synthetic Worlds: the business and culture of online games. University of Chicago Press, Chicago

Chamlee-Wright E (2011) Cultivating the economic imagination. J Econ Financ Edu 10(2):41

Cheung S (2005) A classroom entry and exit game of supply with price-taking firms. J Econ Educ 36(4):358–368

Coffield F, Moseley D, Hall E, Ecclestone K (2004) Learning styles and pedagogy in post-16 learning: a systematic and critical review. Learning and Skills Research Centre, London

Dobrescu LI, Greiner B, Motta A (2014) Learning economic concepts through game-play: an experiment. Int J Edu Res 69(1):23–37

Eckalbar JC (2002) An extended duopoly game. J Econ Educ 33(1):41–52

Fleming ND (2006) Teaching and learning styles: VARK strategies. ND Fleming, Christchurch

Gardner HE (1993) Multiple intelligences: the theory in practice. Basic Books, New York

Gee JP (2003) What video games have to teach us about learning and literacy. Palgrave MacMillan, New York

Gilbert J, Olad R (2007) Excel models for international trade theory and policy: an online resource. J Econ Educ 42(1):95

Gilbert J, Olad R (2011) Simulating tariffs vs. quotas with domestic monopoly. J Ind Organ Edu 2(1):1–11

Goffe W, Sosin K (2005) Teaching with technology: May you live in interesting times. J Econ Educ 36(3):278–291

Gosen J, Washburn J (2004) A review of scholarship on assessing experiential learning effectiveness. Simul Gaming 35(2):270–293

Hall JC (2012) Incorporating econtalk podcasts into the principles classroom. J Priv Enterprise 28(1):113

Horn JL, Cattell RB (1966) Refinement and test of the theory of fluid and crystallized intelligence. J Edu Psychol 57(5):253–270

Katz A (1999) A computer-aided exercise for checking novices' understanding of market equilibrium changes. J Econ Educ 30(2):148–162

Kirche E, Tharp T, Zalewski J (2011) Embedding web applications into a learning process for courses in quantitative methods and economics. Int J Edu Res 6(2):135–146

Lawson CL, Lawson LL (2010) Adventures in learning: creating role playing video games to teach and learn economics. Int Rev Econ Edu 9(1):93–110

Lohman DF (2001) Talent development IV: Proceedings from the 1998 Henry B. and Jocelyn Wallace national research symposium on talent development. Great Potential Press, Scottsdale AZ

Mateer GD, Stephenson EF (2011) Using film clips to teach public choice economics. J Econ Finance Edu 10(1):28–36

Porter TS, Riley TM, Ruffer RL (2004) A review of the use of simulations in teaching economics. Soc Sci Comput Rev 22(4):426–443

Saitone TL, Sexton R (2009) A flexible oligopoly-oligopsony model for classroom simulations and policy analyses. J Ind Organ Edu 4(1):1–16

Sharda NK (2007) Creating innovative new media programs: need, challenges, and development framework. In: Proceedings of the international workshop on educational multimedia and multimedia education, pp 77–86. Available at: https://doi.org/10.1145/1290144.1290157. Accessed 10 Oct 2017

Sims V, Mayer R (2002) Domain specificity of spatial expertise: the case of video game players. Appl Cogn Psychol 16(1):97–115

Sitzmann T (2011) A meta-analystic examination of the instructional effectiveness of computer-based simulation games. Pers Psychol 64(2):489–528

Wideman HH, Owston RD, Brown C, Kushniruk FH, Pitts KC (2007) Unpacking the potential of educational gaming: a new tool for gaming research. Simul Gaming 38(1):10–30

Chapter 3
One-Shot Game: A Free-Market Approach to the Principles of Microeconomics Class

Ninos P. Malek

Abstract This paper addresses what topics should be ignored in a principles of microeconomics class, what the goal of the principles class should be, a preferred philosophical paradigm for the introductory class, the effectiveness of online classes compared to traditional classes, and the topics that should be covered in a principles class. Professors who teach a principles class should approach the class with the philosophy that students will only take one economics class in their academic career and that fundamental economic principles and economic thinking should be emphasized, not mathematical calculations and advanced graphs better left to an intermediate-level class. Professors should use examples relevant and familiar to the typical college student in order to help students learn and appreciate the economic way of thinking. Most students have encountered pro-government intervention teachers in high school and most of their professors will come from the same perspective with respect to various economic policy issues. The role of the economics professor should be to balance out the education of the students by assigning normative, pro-free market articles to read and by showing video clips demonstrating the unintended consequences of government intervention. The principles professor should want to primarily teach and should be able to communicate in a clear, engaging manner.

3.1 Introduction

Economics education has been a topic of research interest to many economists (Bach and Saunders 1965; Paden and Moyer 1969; Mandelstamm 1971; Horton 1972; Hansen 1975; Charkins et al. 1985; Watts 1987; Case 2002; Watts and Lynch 1989; Salemi and Siegfried 1999; Becker 2000; Becker and Watts 2001; Walstad 2001; Colander 2004; Becker 2004; Becker et al. 2006; Harter et al. 2015; Hall et al. 2015;

N. P. Malek (✉)
De Anza College, Cupertino, CA, USA
e-mail: malekninos@deanza.edu

J. Hall, K. Lawson (eds.), *Teaching Economics*,
https://doi.org/10.1007/978-3-030-20696-3_3

Allgood et al. 2015). Books have been published that share best teaching practices and alternative teaching methods to "chalk and talk" (Walstad and Saunders 1998; Becker and Watts 1998; Becker et al. 2006; Salemi and Walstad 2010; Hoyt and McGoldrick 2012). In addition, the philosophical and moral/ethical content of economics and its role in economics education has been an issue of discussion (Boulding 1969; Hall et al. 2016). Economists have also shared their experiences as to what makes an effective teacher (Elzinga 2001).

The reality that economists must understand is that the public knows very little about economics (Hansen et al. 2002) and high school and college-level economics does not help very much (Walstad and Rebeck 2002). The question that must be asked is "How can economics be taught so that students by the end of the course can understand the kinds of economic problems they will be reading about and involved in throughout their adult lives?" (Hansen 1975).

Is economics education a topic worthy of further research or is the opportunity cost of that research to the economist too high? Is it inefficient for the economist to view himself or herself as a teacher first and a researcher second? In other words, if a young academic economist is told, "You are the best teacher in the university and your students learn a tremendous amount because of you," is he or she (1) Hurting his or her career in terms of getting tenure and in terms of losing respect among mainstream economists? and (2) Is he or she allocating his or her mental and physical resources in a suboptimal manner?

The next question that must be asked is "What is the role of morality or normative economics in economics education?" There are those who believe that it is unethical for professors to advocate normative positions in class. Others believe that it is beneficial to the student if he hears the different political (normative) viewpoints on various economic policies. Finally, the last question that must be considered is "Who should teach the principles course and what topics should be covered?"

Economics can illuminate and better explain *all* other subjects because ultimately economics is the study of human actors making choices. Because of this, the principles of economics course is arguably the most important subject that a college student will take.

Approaching the topic of economics education with my diverse teaching background (I have taught at the high school level, community college level, and university level), I have seen how economics has impacted the lives of many students and I have seen how teaching philosophy and the topics that are covered make a difference in student interest, participation, and ability to "think like an economist."

This paper is divided into six sections. Section 3.1 covers what topics should be ignored in a principles of microeconomics course. Section 3.2 discusses what the goal of the class should be. Section 3.3 deals with the philosophy of teaching. Section 3.4 addresses the rise and use of online courses as substitutes for the regular classroom setting. Section 3.5 lists what topics should be covered in a principles course. Section 3.6 offers opinions as to what the necessary tools are for successful teaching. Section 3.7 concludes the paper.

3.2 What Needs to be Ignored in a Principles Class and Why

An economics professor must first accept the reality that most students have a negative perception of economics because of (1) the poor quality of teaching at the high school level or (2) a bad experience in another college economics class. Twenty-two states as of 2018 required students to take an economics course before graduating from high school. Twenty-five states require that an economics course be offered and all fifty states and the District of Columbia require economics be part of their education standards. The main problem is that most teachers at the secondary level who teach economics did not major in economics and many have not ever taken an economics course at all.

As to the second issue, most students who had a previous experience with economics did not really take an economics course. Courses that pass for economics tend to be a personal finance class or, at the university level, just another math and art (technical drawing) class applied to economic theory.

The philosophy of economics education at most institutions seems to be that a principles course is the stepping stone to more advanced courses. In essence, economics departments arrogantly assume that students who take a principles of economics course will major in economics and even go on to graduate school. With this perspective, it is not surprising that economics professors feel the pressure to use mathematics in their lectures and feel the need to cover more advanced material like elasticity calculations, indifference curve analysis, cost curves, and product curves. It is true that many modern-day textbooks leave these topics to an appendix, but, nevertheless, the need (or desire) that professors feel to teach more technical economics is evident.

However, this philosophy has tremendous costs. Economics departments must realize that most students in the principles class are not economics majors. In addition, the economics instructor must come to the semester (or quarter) with this view: "I am going to teach this class as if it will be the only economics class these students will ever take." With this philosophy comes the freedom to teach the really important lessons of our discipline and it is these lessons that will be most useful to the students throughout their lives. And if students do move on to advanced courses, a foundation of solid economic reasoning and practical applications of economics will prove to be most useful. Moreover, it is this teaching approach that will get students to appreciate and, dare I say, love the power of economics in their everyday lives. Ironically, this philosophical approach to teaching economics will lead students to take another economics course and, perhaps, minor or major in economics. I will call this approach the Intuitive/Everyday Life Approach (IEL).

The concept of elasticity should be taught at the principles level, but class time should not be lost on teaching calculations. The concept of diminishing marginal utility should be taught, but not marginal utility calculations. Indifference curves, cost curves, product curves, and optimization problems requiring calculus are also an impediment to the teaching of principles of economics. The technical and theory-only lessons are ineffective at piquing student interest and they are not effective tools for teaching the principles of economics. As Frank (2002) argues, "At some point, of course, it becomes more productive to spend time talking about tangencies than to work through yet another example of the opportunity cost concept. In my view, however, that point arrives well after the Principles course."

Some people might balk at the reference to student interest. They might say "Who cares what students find interesting? We are not here to entertain them. We know what they need." But this attitude does not accept reality. A good teacher knows what motivates students and he or she manipulates their interests and passion into a love, or at least an appreciation, for economics. Is this unethical? No. It is the ethical, vigorous competition for the minds of the students taking the class.

3.3 What Is the Fundamental Goal of the Principles Class?

The principle of economics class is an opportunity to change not only a student's perspective about the real world, but also the course of public discourse. Our teaching should be viewed as a stone thrown out on a pond, not knowing how far the ripples will go, but knowing that ripples will be created by our teaching. As Hansen et al. (2002) state, "The Principles of Economics course, as taught at most colleges and universities, is a missed opportunity to improve economic literacy." It is this lack of economic literacy which results in the electorate either supporting public policy legislation without understanding the unintended consequences of those policies or supporting candidates who favor interventionist policies that reduce our freedom.

The most important goal of the principles class should be to teach the "economic way of thinking." As Becker (2000) points out quoting Siegfried et al. (1991), "The primary goal of undergraduate courses in economics is to enable students to think like economists." Gregory Mankiw in his well-written and popular principles textbook begins with his "Ten Principles." Gwartney et al. (2015) have their "Eight Guideposts" and the Council for Economic Education has their "Handy Dandy Guide." If students can understand and apply a list such as one of these, economics instructors should consider the semester a success.

It is also critical to tell students what they can do with an economics degree. Even though the teaching paradigm should be to approach the principles class as if it were the only economics class the students will ever take, it should be a goal to persuade students to take more economics classes and even major in economics. It is perfectly ethical to recruit students, and the IEL method works better because it "hooks" the students first it allows them to see the power and beauty of economic reasoning in their daily lives and this whets their appetites for more economics learning.

Many students have an interest in economics because they are politically minded and want concrete analysis and, yes, answers to their political and public policy questions. Too many economists are afraid or uncomfortable with providing answers or they feel less like "scientists" when they offer policy recommendations or normative analysis. So, students get short-changed and are left to professors in other departments for answers to policy issues. As Fels (1955) stated:

> Clearly, a course in elementary economics cannot also be a course in philosophy, religion, and ethics; but clearly economic goals are too specific to be left entirely to other parts of the curriculum. The elementary course ought to encourage students to think through what goals they want policy to pursue. Ideas can be more effectively taught if the ideas and their applications go hand-in-hand. This means a course designed to teach principles should really be oriented around policy problems. We economists are interested in economics for its own sake; our beginning students are not. For them, policy problems are intrinsically more interesting and can be a vehicle for arousing their interest in ideas.

The most important "sub-goal" of the principles course is to teach the unintended consequences of actions. In other words, to teach students to not look at just the short term, but the long term; to look not just at one group that is being affected, but all groups Hazlitt (1946). Too many journalists and politicians support ideas or pass legislation without considering the long-term effects of those policies (or they know them but also know that most voters do not either because they are uneducated or rationally ignorant).

To increase student interest in economics, economics instructors should do two things: first, use various public policy examples that students are either directly familiar with (like minimum wage or smoking laws) or at least have heard of and explain the unintended consequences of various public policy measures and legislation, and second, use "fun" and everyday life examples of economics. Yes, economics can be fun even if most economists are not.

If an instructor can verbalize, for example, Thomas Sowell's Basic Economics, he will have achieved so much more than teaching mathematical techniques and technical drawing (e.g., learning how to draw indifference curves and cost curves) (Sowell 2004). What I mean by "fun" economics is using examples or puzzles based on books like The Armchair Economist (Landsburg 1993), Freakonomics (Levitt and Dubner 2005), The Undercover Economist (Harford 2006), The Joy of Freedom (Henderson 2002), or The Economics of Everyday Life (Becker) or at least incorporating examples from these books or websites that have succinct, yet entertaining economics articles. In addition to good, intuitive-type textbooks that use real-life examples and pop culture like The Economic Way of Thinking (Heyne et al. 2014), Microeconomics: Private and Public Choice (Gwartney et al. 2015), or Principles of Microeconomics (Mateer and Coppock 2014), books such as Economics in One Lesson (Hazlitt 1946) and The Economics of Public Issues (Benjamin, Miller, and North) are excellent sources that students find easy to grasp, and yet, are effective at teaching solid economic reasoning. The Foundation for Teaching Economics, The Federal Reserve Banks (especially the Dallas Fed), and Council for Economic Education also have resources that are topical and intuitive which engage students effectively and pique their interest.

A slightly more controversial suggestion is to talk about blunt, "adult" issues like sex, drugs, prostitution, and excessive alcohol consumption. The reality is that most college students have direct experience with these issues. Many professors will take the moral position that they do not want their students' lives damaged by certain lifestyle choices. Well, what better course (perhaps other than a religion class) to teach students to count the cost of their actions and to think about not just the short-term, but the long-term, than economics? But, more to the point, educationally this method works because students can relate to the subjects. It is then easier to explain economics principles from this framework.

Lastly, it is important to make students better consumers of politics. They need to know the ramifications of trade policy, price controls, drug prohibition, the illegality of selling of organs, labor laws, and other public policies on their lives and on the economy as a whole. If students do not analyze and discuss these issues in their economics course, then where will they learn how to think about these issues in a clear, logical manner?

3.4 The Role of Philosophy and Normative Economics in Teaching

There is nothing wrong with discussing and advocating normative economic positions. Of course, the positive aspects of a policy issue (notice I am assuming policy issues are being discussed) should be taught first. For example, before teaching about rent control, it is necessary to teach the fundamentals of supply and demand, then introduce price controls (ceilings in this case) and their effects, and then get to the specifics of rent control. After discussing the positive analysis that rent controls reduce the cost of discrimination by the landlord, that they encourage overuse of space, that they reduce the incentive to the landlord of up keeping the apartments, and that in the long-run, there will be a shortage of rental units, it is not only necessary, but in the interest of a well-rounded education, to discuss the normative aspects of having rent control laws.

My contention that discussing normative economics is vital for a well-rounded education rests on my experience as a teacher and from student-feedback. First, let's be clear most university faculty members tend to be Democrats (Klein et al. 2005). The platform of the Democratic Party can hardly be characterized as pro-free market on economic issues. That is well and fine. However, what this means to the average college student is that he or she is inundated either directly or indirectly with normative views on political, public policy, and economic issues by most of their professors. Therefore, the role of the free-market economist should be to balance out the education of the students he or she encounters by giving them normative, pro-free market articles and lectures and showing videos or video clips that come a free-market perspective (such as Stossel in the Classroom , Free to Choose, and www.learnliberty.org) on these policy topics. Is this biased? Yes. Is it unbalanced on the whole? No. Not even close. Remember, for most students, the principles class is the only economics class they will ever take, so it is critical to at least expose them to free market philosophy not just more technical jargon, graphs, and equations that they will soon forget.

3.5 Why Online Courses Are Not a Good Substitute for Face-to-Face Teaching

There have been papers that have researched the effectiveness of web-based courses (Brown and Liedholm 2002; Coates et al. 2004; Pyne 2007). My main criticism is unique because my view of what should be taught in an economics course is not typical of most economics instructors. Again, my view is that first we should focus on teaching certain core principles and "drilling" those principles into the minds of our students with various examples that are relevant and interesting, and second, that we should use the economics course as a platform for shedding light on not only the efficiency but also the morality of the free-market. A web course might be able to achieve the first goal but the second goal is, if not impossible, very difficult. The importance of a powerful and persuasive communicator, class discussions, and videos where the entire class is watching it together (I believe there are positive externalities watching movies or videos as a group) are simply not able to be duplicated by a web-based course.

3.6 What Topics the Semester Should Cover

In a Principles of Microeconomics class, there are seven main topics that should be covered. They are:

1. Fundamental concepts (scarcity and opportunity cost)
2. Voluntary trade as a positive-sum game
3. The importance of institutions, private property, and what real free-enterprise (capitalism, market economy, free-market) means
4. Supply and demand and its applications to various policy issues
5. Public choice analysis
6. Public goods theory, externalities, and government failure
7. Competition as a dynamic process not a static state of affairs.

It is important to teach some economics jargon. After all, economists have their own language and students must learn it. However, we must be able to teach this jargon using examples and stories. I emphasize the intuitive over the mechanical and I point out the moral aspects of the economics. Leaving out the mathematics and technical aspects of the unit allows time for thorough teaching and discussion. For example, with trade, after the usual teaching of absolute and comparative advantage and the logical conclusion that voluntary trade benefits both parties, I then discuss outsourcing, sweatshops, and free trade from a free-market perspective. Again, I begin the lecture with the positive analysis and, conveniently, the benefits of free trade from this positive analysis, but then I get to the normative dimension such as why sweatshops are obviously (from the revealed preference of the workers) good and I ask the students, "What's wrong if Nike wants to pay as little as possible for their workers? Are you evil when you want to get paid as much as possible for your work?"

With supply and demand after the usual diagrams and concepts, the moral dimension becomes stimulating. I focus on the terms "price gouging" and "rip offs" in this section. Again, I inject the moral questions to get the students thinking. For example, the public generally considers many things as "too expensive" or "highway robbery" but people are hypocritical, as I like to point out to the students, and there is an inherent anti-business mentality that pervades our society. It is the responsibility of the free-market economist to make students uncomfortable by asking them, "Are you evil when you want to pay as little as possible for that Starbucks Mocha even if you could pay more?" or "Is it your right to get that gallon of gasoline from Exxon?" or "Is it your right to rent an apartment or work for somebody else?" I then give them a good dose of Walter Williams, Thomas Sowell, David Henderson, Milton Friedman, and other free-market economists and philosophers to round out the particular unit.

Many readers of this paper will claim that I am proselytizing. Yes, I am. The free-market economics education community needs to understand its "Great Commission" because the interventionist professors (some of whom are inside the Economics Department) understand theirs!

I emphasize the public choice analysis which sheds light on why we have so much government intervention in our economy and it explains to students why we have policies that have unintended consequences. And when I teach on market structures, I give them the definitions and the characteristics of the various structures but I eliminate the cost curves and mathematics and then get to the heart of the issue: What is real competition? Do we have a right to get the products companies make? If there is one big company, don't they deserve to be the "King of the Hill?" From here I get into the topic of antitrust legislation and what free-market economists believe on this topic.

Lastly, I emphasize the real meaning of capitalism (free-enterprise). We must make sure that students know that we do not live in a free-market. So, when they hear that corporations are receiving welfare or subsidies, they will realize that this is evidence of a non-capitalist system, not capitalism gone awry.

3.7 Necessary Tools

I think it is necessary for the Economics Department of the college or university to be committed to excellence in teaching. Unfortunately, it is the "technical wizard" who has numerous mainstream journal publications who is highly recruited rather than the person who can communicate clearly and engage students. It is also necessary that the person teaching the principles course respects the discipline as something vital to his students and to society at large. If one has the philosophy that having to teach a class of students is not the optimal use of his time, he should not call himself a "professor" and continue to damage this beautiful subject of economics. If one would rather research than explain the power of economic analysis to students, he should leave the classroom.

Unfortunately, when economics departments recruit, they want the top-ten school graduate who has demonstrated excellent mathematical and econometric skills, but they overlook the person (who might not come from the "right" school) who can actually communicate economics and can relate to the typical student. Actually, research does not seem to improve teaching (Friedrich and Michalak Jr 1983). The reason that economics department go after the top-ten program graduates, in my opinion, is that the principles class is viewed as either a stepping stone to advanced economics (which I already addressed as a mistake) or it is not taken seriously. Therefore, it is more valuable to hire the technician who can focus on research and advanced courses (even though at the advanced level good teaching ability is more important than the professor's intellectual power or educational background).

Economics departments should invest resources into developing better principles teachers. By better I mean, not getting faculty to publish more journal articles, but better teaching ability and skills. There is something to be said for economics professors who invest in their own human capital by learning better methods of teaching and by attending conferences specifically related to economics education.

3.8 Conclusion

The Principles of Microeconomics class is arguably the most important subject college students can take. After all, economics studies the choices we humans must make and whether it is in our religion, the time we spend studying, exercising, our diet, dating, or spending time with our family, it is the human action of having to make choices that binds all these facets of our lives together. In addition to adding clarity to the lives of students, economics can help them become better consumers of the media and the rhetoric of politicians. Our goal in the principles class should be to teach basic concepts using stories and everyday examples.

Students in our society today get bored easily. Economics has a bad reputation outside the Ivory Tower. However, economics is a subject that is interesting and relevant. The subject is unfortunately becoming more and more abstract and technical in order to prove its claim as a science. Moreover, the economist who can clearly relate to "the Everyman" (Klein 1999) is brushed aside as not being rigorous enough. The economist who spends his time writing for the public at large is not taken as seriously by the profession (unless he has proved himself mathematically already by getting published in top journals). Unfortunately, economics departments in their hiring seem to reflect the same attitude, but that is a topic for another paper.

The principles class is something very precious to the Economics Department and to society. As Case (2002) stated, "It is the Principles course that connects the discipline to the world and establishes it relevance." We should have the motto, "Teach this class as if it were the only economics class my students will take." I also believe that it is our responsibility as advocates of free-markets to discuss the morality of the market, private property, voluntary exchange, and the importance of freedom. We should not be ashamed or feel unethical when we blend good positive economics with good normative economics. This I hope will radically change not only the teaching of economics, but society as well. Ironically, teaching with the IEL method tends to motivate students to enroll in additional economics courses, even deciding to pursue a minor or major in economics. If they do that, then for better or worse, they can get their fill of indifference curves, Edgeworth boxes, optimization problems, and "scientific" economics.

References

Allgood S, Walstad W, Siegfried J (2015) Research on teaching economics to undergraduates. J Econ Lit 53(2):285–325

Bach GL, Saunders P (1965) Economic education: aspirations and achievements. Am Econ Rev 55(3):329–356

Becker WE (2000) Teaching economics in the 21st century. J Econ Perspect 14(2):109–119

Becker WE (2004) Economics for a higher education. Int Rev Econ Educ 3(1):52–62

Becker WE, Watts M (1998) Teaching economics to undergraduates: more alternatives to chalk and talk. Edward Elgar Publishing, Cheltenham

Becker WE, Watts M (2001) Teaching economics at the start of the 21st century: still chalk-and-talk. Am Econ Rev 91(2):446–451

Becker WE, Watts M, Becker S (2006) Teaching economics: more alternatives to chalk and talk. Edward Elgar Publishing, Northampton

Boulding KE (1969) Economics as a moral science. Am Econ Rev 59(1):1–12

Brown B, Liedholm CE (2002) Can web courses replace the classroom in principles of microeconomics. Am Econ Rev 92(2):444–448

Case KE (2002) Reconsidering crucial concepts in micro principles. Am Econ Rev 92(2):454–458

Charkins RJ, O'Toole DM, Wetzel J (1985) Linking teacher and student learning styles with student achievement and attitudes. J Econ Educ 16(2):111–120

Colander D (2004) The art of teaching economics. Int Rev Econ Educ 3(1):63–76

Coates D, Humphreys BR., Kane J, Vachris MA (2004) No significant distance between face-to-face and online instruction: evidence from principles of economics. Econ Educ Rev 23(5):533–546

Elzinga KG (2001) Fifteen theses on classroom teaching. South Econ J 68(2):249–257

Fels R (1955) The teaching of elementary economics. Am Econ Rev 45(5):919–932

Frank RH (2002) The economic naturalist: teaching introductory students how to speak economics. Am Econ Rev 92(2):459–462

Friedrich RJ, Michalak Jr SJ (1983) Why doesn't research improve teaching? Some answers from a small liberal arts college. J High Educ 54(2):145–163

Gwartney JD, Stroup RL, Sobel RS, Macpherson D (2015) Economics: private and public choice, 15th edn. South-Western Cengage Learning, Mason

Hall JC, Hodges CD, Malek NP (2015) A review and analysis of the effectiveness of alternative teaching methods on student learning in economics. Perspect Econ Educ Res 9(1):75–85

Hall JC, Hodges CD, Malek NP (2016) The relationship between economics and ethics and the effectiveness of normative economics on student attitudes and learning. J Econ Econ Educ Res 17(1):16–24

Hansen WL (1975) New approaches to teaching the principles course. Am Econ Rev 65(2):434–437

Hansen WL, Salemi MK, Siegfried JJ (2002) Use it or lost it: teaching literacy in the economics principles course. Am Econ Rev 92(2):463–472
Harford T (2006) The undercover economist. Oxford University Press, New York
Harter CL, Schaur G, Watts M (2015) School, department, and instructor determinants of teaching methods in undergraduate economics courses. South Econ J 81(4):1169–1188
Hazlitt H (1946) Economics in one lesson. Harper & Brothers, New York
Henderson DR (2002) The joy of freedom: an economist's odyssey. Prentice Hall, New York
Heyne P, Boettke P, Prychitko D (2014) The economic way of thinking, 13th edn. Pearson Education, Upper Saddle River
Horton RV (1972) Values and the economics principles courses. J Econ Educ 3(2):118–123
Hoyt GM, McGoldrick K (2012) International handbook on teaching and learning economics. Edward Elgar, Northampton
Klein DB (1999) What do economists contribute? New York University Press, New York
Klein DB, Stern C, Western A (2005) Political diversity in six disciplines. Acad Quest 18(1):40–52
Landsburg SE (1993) The armchair economist: economics and everyday life. The Free Press, New York
Levitt SD, Dubner S (2005) Freakonomics. HarperCollins Publishers, New York
Mandelstamm AB (1971) The principles course revisited. J Econ Educ 3(1):41–48
Mateer D, Coppock L (2014) Principles of microeconomics, 1st edn. WW Norton and Company, Inc., New York
Paden DW, Moyer ME (1969) The relative effectiveness of three methods of teaching principles of economics. J Econ Educ 1(1):33–45
Pyne D (2007) Does the choice of introductory microeconomics textbook matter? J Econ Educ 38(3):279–296
Salemi MK, Siegfried JJ (1999) The state of economic education. Am Econ Rev 89(2):355–361
Salemi MK, Walstad WB (2010) Teaching innovations in economics: strategies and applications for interactive instruction. Edward Elgar, Northampton
Sowell T (2004) Basic economics: a citizen's guide to the economy. Basic Books, New York
Walstad WB (2001) Economic education in US high schools. J Econ Perspect 15(3):195–210
Walstad WB, Rebeck K (2002) Assessing the economic knowledge and economic opinions of adults. Q Rev Econ Finance 42(5):921–935
Walstad WB, Saunders P (1998) Teaching undergraduate economics: a handbook for instructors. Irwin-McGraw Hill, New York
Watts M (1987) Ideology, textbooks, and the teaching of economics. Theory Pract 26(3):190–197
Watts M, Lynch GJ (1989) The principles courses revisited. Am Econ Rev Pap Proc 79(2):236–241

Chapter 4
A Highly Simplified Pollution Abatement Game

Nimish Adhia

Abstract The version of the pollution abatement game presented here, compared to other versions, is simpler for an instructor with a tight timeline looking for an easy and fun way to demonstrate the cost-effectiveness of pollution permits. The absence of equations, tables, or worksheets and the presence of tangible objects makes this version less effort-intensive, more intuitive, and more fun than other versions. The idea behind the creation of this version has been to make the game more like playing monopoly and less like doing taxes. The players in this version hold their wealth in the form of tangible objects, pay taxes using poker chips, and calculate the social cost of abatement by adding up fridge magnet numerals on a collection plate.

4.1 Introduction

Pollution abatement games are an excellent way to help students grasp the strengths and weaknesses of various pollution abatement policies such as command and control, tradable pollution permits, and pollution tax. The games presented by Walbert and Bierna (1998) and Hazlett (1995) are classics. Ando and Harrington (2006) present a simplified version that makes fewer assumptions about the economics background of the players. Corrigan (2011) presents a variation which allows the instructor to demonstrate and compare the cost-effectiveness of the permits and tax policies under realistic conditions such as abatement costs uncertainty and information asymmetry.

These games, however, are quite complex, and require more time, exposure to the economics, and willingness to perform more math than is necessary to grasp the one big lesson—that market-oriented policies such as pollution taxes and tradable permits are relatively cost-effective compared to a command and control policy. Ando and Harrington (2006) present a game which, albeit simpler, requires players

N. Adhia (✉)
Manhattanville College, Purchase, NY, USA
e-mail: nimish.adhia@mville.edu

J. Hall, K. Lawson (eds.), *Teaching Economics*,
https://doi.org/10.1007/978-3-030-20696-3_4

to solve equations and fill out worksheets in order to figure out their abatement costs. Corrigan (2011) encourages firms to think strategically and overstate their abatement costs, and asks the regulator to anticipate, estimate, and compensate for such overstatement.

A likely consequence of such complexity is that time-pressed instructors facing students with limited exposure to the economic way of thinking (such as in a "Global Economy" course that I teach for students majoring in International Studies) will give such games a pass. This would be a shame, since much of the complexity is not required for a game to be useful for students in, say, an international relation course to understand the cost-effectiveness of a global cap-and-trade regime. Even if such an instructor were to valiantly attempt the game, some students might get too bogged down in calculating their marginal costs to be able to get the "big picture." A weary student might end up concluding that the classroom game was nothing but a problem set with some role-play thrown in.

This paper presents a highly simplified version of the pollution abatement game I have devised for my courses. Players are not required to perform long calculations. Their costs are as conspicuous to them as bright colored fridge magnets can be. Their wealth is represented by tangible items held in their hands, and so their gain and loss are immediately obvious. The decision making required of them here is therefore quicker and more intuitive, and decisions of their neighbors more transparent. Their attention is consequently free to wander towards other aspects of the game such as what the other players are doing and how their choices interact. They are thus more likely to grasp the underlying logic of a policy regime. Finally, being handed poker chips and fridge magnets, rather than worksheets and calculators, calls forth within them a touch of playfulness and strengthens students' mental association of positive feelings with learning.

The trade-off of such simplification is, of course, that the robustness of the main lesson (market-oriented policies reduce pollution at the least cost) cannot be demonstrated under more realistic and complex situations. I find the gains in student engagement, enjoyment, and insight to be worth the trade-off.

4.2 The Setup

Time required: 50 min, including discussions.
Needed items:

- 400 poker chips
- 2 sets of fridge magnets in the shape of numerals 0 to 9
- 10 pieces of paper that say "pollute one," or anything that can serve as pollution permits
- a collection plate labeled "the total social cost of reducing pollution"
- recommended: a hat (or anything else that could serve as a visible sign that the instructor is speaking in the role of the pollution regulator).

4.3 Conducting the Game

I start out by grouping students into 10 teams and handing out to each team:

- 40 poker chips (while announcing that each is worth $1)
- 2 randomly chosen fridge magnets
- the following instruction sheet for all teams (while giving them time to read it and seek clarifications)

Information Sheet for All Teams

The Game

The game ask you to observe and discuss the strengths and weaknesses of three pollution abatement policies: (i) command and control, (ii) tax, (iii) and tradable permits. Each round will implement one policy.

Your Team's Role

- Your team is a firm generating two units of pollution every year when there is no regulation.
- Your team's wealth ($) = number of poker chips + sum of your two fridge magnets.
- The value of each fridge magnet numeral represents the abatement cost ($) for a unit of pollution you produce.
- Your team's goal in each round is to maximize its wealth while complying with the regulator's pollution control policy. In this context, that would mean preserving as much of wealth as possible.

Your Instructor's Role

- Your instructor is a pollution regulator, whose goal is to limit the society-wide total number of pollution units.
- There will be three rounds, and in each round the regulator will experiment with a different policy.

How to Play the Game

- The regulator will begin each round by announcing a policy and the actions that firms should undertake to comply.
- Then a collection plate labeled "total social cost of reducing pollution" will be passed around.
- Each team must give up a certain number of poker chips, or one (or both) of your fridge magnet(s), in accordance with the regulator's policy.
- If you give up a fridge magnet, it means that you have abated your pollution emission by one unit, and bore the cost equal to the value of the fridge magnet.

I create on the blackboard Table 4.1 to be filled in at the end of each round.

Table 4.1 Blackboard table

	Total social cost of abatement ($)
Round 1 command and control	
Round 2 pollution tax	
Round 3 tradable permits	

Before the rounds begin, I announce, "my target as a regulator is to allow pollution emission of no more than 10 units." In interest of simplicity, I have set the target equal to the number of teams, which also works out to be the half the number of pollution units emitted in the absence of regulation. I point out to players that each player has different pollution abatement costs, and ask them to think of reasons why that might be the case (such as different technologies).

4.4 Round One

I begin by announcing "In this round I am going to control our pollution levels by commanding that each firm abate its pollution by one unit." I pass out the collection plate, and to comply each team must give up a fridge magnet.

If I see a team about to give up its higher-value magnet, I remind them about their wealth maximization goal. This is usually sufficient to ensure that all teams abate their unit with the least cost. I retrieve the fridge magnets from the collections plate and note their sum of on the *Total Social Cost of Abatement* table on the blackboard.

4.4.1 Discussion Questions

(i) *Was this policy able to limit pollution in a way that was minimized the total social cost? Why or why not?*

To illustrate the fact that the total cost of the policy was not minimized, I point to one of the magnets (e.g., a "4") still held by a team and compare it to one of the magnets (e.g., a "6") on my collection plate. It shows that a pollution unit with lower abatement cost ($4) continues to be emitted while another unit with a higher abatement cost ($6) does not.

(ii) *Is this policy equitable? Why or why not?*

It could be argued that the policy is equitable in the sense that each firm is required to reduce pollution by the same amount. But since firms have different costs of abatement, some people might consider the burden of abatement to have been distributed inequitably.

(iii) *Suppose that to minimize the total social cost of abatement, a real-world regulator were to require only the firms with low costs of abatement to curb pollution. What problems might arise?*

It would seem patently inequitable to have only some firms bear the entire social cost of abatement. Also, the regulator has less knowledge about each firm's abatement costs than the firms themselves do, and so the firms would have an incentive to overstate their costs in order to avoid being required to abate.

At the end of each round, I return to each team the fridge magnet numerals placed on the collection plate.

4.5 Round Two

I announce that "the policy of this round is a pollution tax. For each unit of pollution that you emit, you must pay a $4.99 tax using your poker chips, or else abate." When I pass out the collection plate, each team must either give up (i) both fridge magnets, or (ii) one fridge magnet and $4.99 worth of poker chips, or (iii) $9.98 worth of poker chips. Since each team has poker chips of $1 denomination only, they will need to put $5 of poker chips on the plate. If they ask for a penny back, I announce "No change is given. I can give you credit worth a penny though."

To preserve its wealth, each team should be giving up its fridge magnet numerals of value less than 4.99, but pay the tax to keep the numerals of value greater than 4.99. There would exactly 10 such magnets. I have chosen the tax amount to be $4.99 rather than $5, so that those with the magnets "5" will not abate. It is necessary, given the setup of the game, to ensure no more than 10 units are abated. If I see a team about to give up a numeral that is a "5" or higher, I ask them to explain openly how they arrived at their decision. Doing this one team is usually sufficient to get all teams on the right track.

I retrieve the fridge magnets from the collections plate and note their sum on the appropriate line in the *Total Social Cost of Abatement* table in the blackboard. The sum is inevitable lower than under command and control.

4.5.1 Discussion Questions

(iv) *Why was the policy able to limit pollution at lower total social cost than command and control?*

To illustrate the reason, I point to the fact that all the magnets on the collection palate are lower than "5." Only units with an abatement cost lower than $5 were abated.

(v) *What are some of the problems that a regulator might face in setting the tax rate?*

One possible answer: the regulator might not know the distribution of the abatement costs among the units emitted, as such information is known privately by the firm, and they might not be willing to report it accurately. Without such knowledge, the regulator might not be able to predict accurately the number of pollution units that will be emitted at any given tax rate, making it hard to hit a target. I ask students to consider, for example, how many more units of pollution would have been emitted if I had set the tax rate at $3.

4.6 Round Three

I start by handing out a permit to each team and making the following announcement:

> You cannot pollute in this round without a permit. Each permit you possess will allow you to emit one unit of pollution. Everyone has been granted one permit for free to start.
>
> There will be a 4-minutes trading period for pollution permits. You can either buy or sell a permit using poker chips at the market price, determined by a Walrasian auction.
>
> I will call out a price. I will ask the teams willing to buy a permit at that price to raise their hands. Next, I will ask the teams willing to sell their permit at that price to raise their hands. I will repeat the process for several prices. Only raise your hand if you would increase your wealth at that price. We will set the market price as one for which the quantity of permits demanded is equal to the quantity supplied, or failing that, the one with the smallest gap between the quantity demanded and quantity supplied.
>
> After we set the market price, I will announce the start of a 4-minute trading period, during which you can trade permits with other teams at the market price.
>
> When I come around with my collection plate at the end of the trading period, for each one of your two pollution units you will have to either show me a permit or abate it.
>
> Before I begin the Walrasian auction, I am giving you three minutes to discuss the price range at which your team would be willing to buy or sell a permit. Start by asking yourself: at $1, would it make sense for you to buy a permit, or sell one? At $2? And so on.

Given the wealth maximization goal, it does not make sense for any team to buy a permit for a price higher than its lowest valued magnet, or sell at a price lower than its highest valued magnet. For example, if I have magnets "4" and "6," then for permit prices less than $6 it would make sense for me to keep my permit to use on the "6" while giving up my "4." But it would increase my wealth if I were able to sell my permit for a price higher than $6. Similarly, it would increase my wealth to be able to buy a permit for a price less than $4 so that I can avoid giving up my "4."

To ensure each team has figured out their ranges accurately, I start by asking a team to share them. If their buy and sell ranges are not accurate given their abatement costs, I keep prodding them with questions ("how about at $3? Would you buy at $3? How about $4?") until they arrive at the accurate ranges. It is usually sufficient to do this with one team for others to get the idea.

Once they have determined their buy and sell ranges, I announce the start of a Walrasian auction. The idea for the auction has been adopted from Ando and Harrington (2006). Such auction eliminates the need to discover the market price through a series of potentially chaotic and time-consuming series of bilateral exchanges. It also makes it very likely that the market clears. I, as the auctioneer, carry out the steps explained in the earlier instructions, keeping track of the number of buyers and sellers at each price on a table on the blackboard. Once I have determined the price, I begin the 4-min trading round.

After the trading period ends, I walk around with my collection plate, demanding their fridge magnets unless they can show me permits. I add up the values of the fridge magnets on the plates and announce the total cost of pollution abatement in round three, and note these costs on the table on the blackboard. These costs are bound to be lower than in round one.

4.6.1 Discussion Questions

(vi) *Why was the policy able to limit pollution at lower total social cost than command and control?*

To illustrate why the costs were lowered, I point to a permit trade that took place, and how it allowed a firm with high cost of abatement (e.g., $7) to transfer its abatement obligation to a firm with a low cost of abatement (e.g., $4).

(vii) *Compared to the command and control policy, are the teams buying permits better off? How about the teams selling permits?*

Correct Answer: Yes, all the teams are better off. The teams buying a permit pay a price that is lower than what it would cost that team to abate, and the firms selling a permit gets a price that is higher than what it would have saved by using the permit.

(viii) *Compared to the command and control policy, is this policy more equitable?*

One possible answer: Under the command and control policy, the firms unlucky to have high costs of abatement bore a higher burden of compliance. Now such firms get to buy their way out of abatement at a price that is lower than the cost of abatement, so their financial burden is lower.

(ix) *What about the cost spent on buying permits? Should that be included in the social cost of pollution abatement.*

Correct answer: That money represents transfers between firms, and therefore are not part of the social costs of pollution. One firm lost the money, the other firm gained it, and no real resources were expended (except a small amount to administer the permits market).

References

Ando A, Harrington D (2006) Tradable discharge permits: a student-friendly game. J Econ Educ 37(2):187–201

Corrigan J (2011) The pollution game: a classroom game demonstrating the relative effectiveness of emissions taxes and tradeable permits. J Econ Educ 42(1):70–78

Hazlett D (1995) An EPA-style auction of pollution permits. Classr Expernomics 4(1):3–7

Walbert MS, Bierna TJ (1998) The permits game: conveying the logic of marketable pollution permits. J Econ Educ 29(4):383–389

Chapter 5
Assignments to Engage Students in Economics Study Abroad Programs

Darshak Patel

Abstract Economic educators are continually searching for new ways for students to apply economics. In this paper, the author presents a writing assignment where students are to replicate the *Humans of New York* photojournalism project with an emphasis on concepts learned in class. The author shares guidelines and resources for instructors to implement into their economics study abroad curriculum.

5.1 Introduction

As faculty members, we know that content learning happens in and out of the classroom. While we can manage what happens in the classroom, our efforts to engage students outside of the classroom can drastically increase student learning. We challenge students to communicate using economics outside the classroom with the hopes that they will gain a deeper understanding of the content. Traditionally, assessment of student learning outside of the classroom has been in the form of homework, paper assignments, group projects, or online discussion forums. Frank (2006) provides a writing assignment that tests students on the mastery of basic economic principles applied to an event or application they have observed. Using this idea, I present this paper to provide a more interdisciplinary assignment for students by incorporating visual media, writing, and communication to extend the learning experience outside of the classroom, specifically in a study abroad setting.

The goal of this assignment is to help students critically identify concepts discussed in class to a story of a human or building in a certain place. The idea of interviewing (or researching in the case of a building) and sharing their story comes from the creator of *Humans of New York* (HONY) photojournalism project that

D. Patel (✉)
University of Kentucky, Lexington, KY, USA
e-mail: darshak.patel@uky.edu

J. Hall, K. Lawson (eds.), *Teaching Economics*,
https://doi.org/10.1007/978-3-030-20696-3_5

focuses on sharing images and stories of New Yorkers.[1] From an instructors point of view, Acchiardo et al. (2017) do an excellent job in connecting and illustrating economic concepts in each of these HONY stories, making class content relevant and bonding the audience with the power of the story. The idea shared in this manuscript is briefly mentioned in their paper as one way for instructors to take advantage of HONYEcon, extending their discussion by providing all the tools and resources for instructors to easily adopt in their class.

Humans/Buildings of "Place" is an engaging exercise for students to enhance their understanding of economics. These types of non-traditional assignments help make economics relevant to students across various diversity spectrums: major, age, gender, etc. (Al-Bahrani et al. 2016). There is increased discussion and debate in the economics literature on the idea that economics class lectures are too dependent on traditional teaching styles (Becker and Watts 1996). Instructors have adjusted and adopted active learning styles, like flipping the classroom, to connect better with students and enhance their overall experience. Activities include but are not limited to using literature, music videos, popular media, and art to teach economics.

Such diversity has also spread into assignments to push students to become producers of material that convey a strong understanding of their economic knowledge: artistic projects (Al-Bahrani et al. 2017),[2] student-generated podcasts (Moryl 2016), testing theories using FRED applications (Patel and Saunoris 2016), and EconJourney (Niman et al. 2018).[3] Other assignments, such as Econ Beats, take advantage of interdisciplinary learning by incorporating economics with media and communication and engaging the community through a semester-long group-project that also acts as a motivation to the Humans/Building assignment (Al-Bahrani et al. 2016). On a follow-up paper, Al-Bahrani and Thompson (2019) find that their interdisciplinary assignment helps students learn more.

Educators using this assignment encourage the following student learning objectives: (1) correctly identify economic concepts outside the classroom (real-world application), (2) gain practice writing and successfully conveying the economics message in "simple" terms using 500–750 words and, (3) promote interdisciplinary learning. The objective of this paper is to provide instructors with a fun project to adopt in their study abroad program as well as their classrooms.

[1]A detailed explanation of HONY and HONYEcon is available in Acchiardo et al. (2017).

[2]These include and not limited to: Rockonomix, ECON Behind the Music Media Analysis, Infographonomics, Video Scrapbooking, St. Patrick's Day/Valentine's Day Card Poems, Halloween Costumes, Pumpkin Carving, Easter Eggs, Dismal Art Project, Know-It-All Project, Everyday ECON, ECON Selfies and ECON Memes, ECON Ads and ECON Today, and Live-Tweet an Event.

[3]Students are asked to apply economic concepts of a made-up character over the course of the semester. More details can be found on their website www.econjourney.com.

5.2 The Assignment

The author uses this assignment for his study abroad trips every summer. The assignment is an extension of the idea mentioned in Acchiardo et al. (2017) on ways to incorporate HONY in classrooms.[4] For the study abroad setting, students extend their storytelling to buildings in addition to interviewing a human. I found the assignment is a way to push students to be practitioners and apply economics in real-world scenarios. Similar to a regular classroom, study abroad students can be equally diverse in both their academic and social skills. This assignment provided motivation for students to move outside their comfort zones and learn about different cultures.

As a required portion of their travel, the assignment is broken down into two parts: Human and Building of "Place". Below are "Instructions for Assignment" that provides generalized verbiage for instructors looking to adopt the assignment. For the first part, the goal is for students to interact with as many locals as possible and relate economics to their stories. Students are asked to interview a "human" native of that country/city and write a 500-word summary of what they learned about their "human" and relate it to Economic concepts from class. The "human" has to be born in that country, and students are usually surprised at how many humans one has to interview until they find one born in that country. Students also gain a first-hand experience on the impact of globalization, also surprised by how many naturalized citizens live in a country. After students find a "human" native to the country, they then complete the assignment as presented below.

Instructions for Assignment

Humans & Buildings of "Place"

Due: Share your due date and forms of submission. No late essays will be accepted.

Grades: Share points earned.

Goal: Travel/Study abroad provides an opportunity to learn about a different culture. I want you to take what you love the most about "Economics" and connect/relate it and explain it through the different culture. That way, you get to learn about the cultures and also think about Economics.

The "Humans and Businesses of Place" project gives you the opportunity to creatively demonstrate your understanding of an economic principle(s) discussed during this course. As you prepare for this project, listen to people you encounter during your day, and think about how what they're saying applies to economics. For example, while I was walking to school today (May 12th, 2016) at the garage, the girl next to me was on her phone saying, "Yeah, I pay a lot for my parking, but I don't care, because I make a lot of money." Wow! That was a perfect example of income as a determinant of price elasticity of demand. If we had more time, I would have liked to ask her if she had always felt that way about paying for parking and what circumstances had brought her to that decision.

1. For Humans of "Place", you have to interview a human (someone you don't know). If you are not comfortable striking up a conversation with a complete stranger, talk to

[4] Professor Charity-Joy Acchiardo uses a version of this assignment in her classes at the University of Arizona "Humans of Arizona." Professor Acchiardo has provided approval to use some of the language in the assignment and use of the grading rubric in Table 5.1.

Table 5.1 Grading rubric: Three primary components are considered the story you have based your project on, the essay that connects the relevant economic principle(s), and the paragraph

Grade/Points	Grading summary	Comments
A	Among the best in the class	The entire project is of the highest quality, well written, and original. The story is highly engaging. The writer clearly and skillfully uses their story to illustrate an economic principle(s). The essay is free or nearly free of errors in grammar, punctuation, and mechanics. The photograph shows care in composition, engages the viewer, and connects them to the person in the essay
B	Better than average	The project is competent, satisfactorily composed, and mildly original. The story is interesting. The essay is good and at times impressive. The essay manifests minor, occasional errors in grammar, punctuation, or mechanics. The photograph is clear and of good quality
C	Average	The project is adequate and meets the requirements outlined in the assignment. The story may somewhat interesting. The essay suffers from poor organization and unclear application of the economic principles in question and has frequent errors in grammar, punctuation, or mechanics. The photograph is of average quality or uninteresting
D	Barely adequate	The discussion is trivial and unoriginal. The essay demonstrates serious deficiencies or severe flaws in command of course material
E	Inadequate	The project is unsuccessful and indicates a student's neglect and lack of effort in the course

people you know (not an option for study abroad). Ask them to tell you a little about themselves or share an interesting story from their life, and see if you can identify the economics in their story. You may need to interview a few people before you hear a story you want to use for your project. Once you find the person and story you want to focus on, take a photograph of the person (quality and creativity counts!), record their story and a key quote, and explain the connection to the economic principle(s) you want to highlight.

2. Do the same for the Buildings in "Place". First, share with the reader what the building is (more like a story of the building). Second, share with the reader the economic significance of that building to the city or the country. Take a good quality picture with you in front of it.

Submission rules: The essay portion for each should be no more than 500 words. Quick tips: avoid complex terminology, write for someone who has never taken a course in economics and avoid the use of algebra and graphs.

The inspiration for this project comes from the Humans of New York photojournalism project begun by Brandon Stanton in 2010. Stanton shared his photographs and short stories of everyday New Yorkers (and extended this to different countries) on social media and now has over 22 million combined followers on Facebook, Instagram, and Twitter! You can read his blog at http://www.humansofnewyork.com/.

To further enhance the students' overall experience and interests, they are asked to replicate the "human" assignment for any building of that country. Buildings can constitute any of the following but are not limited to: businesses (large, medium, small), museums, historic buildings, cafes, etc. In some cases, students choose their building to be one of the site visits in the agenda. Students do not realize the importance of many of the buildings to that city, and this gives them a chance to research a particular structure and talk about its economic implications. Buildings and structures can communicate a lot about economic history and landscape of the country. Encouraging students to examine this can open their eyes to the role of economics within the economy. For example, a couple of students took the opportunity to write a story on the Berlin wall and the role economics played in its construction. Guidelines of Human and Building of "Place" assignment are shown below. Instructors are welcome to tweak this for their use.

5.3 Pitfalls and Concerns

One major concern of this assignment is that, in a few circumstances, shy students will be very hesitant to approach a stranger. The instructor may have to be flexible with the guidelines. In one scenario in Germany, a student had high level of anxiety and was not able to approach anyone for most of the trip. However, I was able to introduce her to a friend born in the city who was more than happy to engage with the student. In a more recent scenario in Australia, I managed to talk to a few individuals on a train ride and was able to notify students that they would be great humans to interview. One shy student took advantage of the situation. Overall, the essence of the assignment still existed where the student engaged with the stranger, took a picture, and wrote economic content. No such issues arise with the building portion of the assignment.

Another issue for an instructor to consider is a concern for the safety of the students. I extend two simple rules for students to follow for this assignment and their safety: (1) do not interview someone alone—always have a friend close, and (2) find a "human" preferably during the day (avoid nights).[5]

[5]Students are often creative in ways in which they find their humans and building.

5.4 Assessment

Instructors are welcome to use several possible grading criteria. One option is the peer-reviewed system. There are quite a few positives for using this system. One, in particular, is that students come across economics applications several times enhancing their learning experience. For grading purposes, students can use the textbook or other resources to familiarize themselves again with the concepts and see if their peer correctly identifies the concepts in their "human" story. It also reduces the grading requirement, especially if one has a large class. Frank (2006) shares important tips on how to reduce an instructor's workload with the help of peer reviews and teaching assistants.

For instructors thinking of grading on their own, Table 5.1 provides a sample rubric, and points can be assigned at the instructor's discretion. This is my preferred method of grading, as it does not take long since study abroad classes are typically small. Furthermore, student submissions are fun to read and provide an opportunity to reminiscence about the study abroad. The assignment, rubric, and past examples are shared with students in their syllabus and Learning Management System.

5.5 Student Examples

The assignment can be best appreciated through student submissions. In this section I present three student examples with permission. The first one is a human example, the second a building example from a study abroad trip to Berlin in 2016, and then a human example from a student in Professor Acchiardo's class at the University of Arizona.

5.5.1 Student Example: Humans of Berlin, Germany (Fig. 5.1)

So different structures or different types of organizations bring other benefits but also downsides. So you gotta know those benefits and know if that's what you're looking for. For example if you're working for a global player its always a solid job and you earn a lot of money and they give you a good image but on the other hand you have not so much of a say in change. Like if you want to change processes or structure or improve them it is mostly a lot of work, very difficult. So if you are more hands on and want to move and change the structure and the business then I would rather prefer to start in a startup because they are more like evolving very fast and there's more you can do there. But it's also very chaotic. In a startup you are starting a project and after 3 days it seems like it's a completely different project because so many things change like what your client wants or what the product should look like or who you're working for. I prefer working for startups because on the one hand you have a say in things, a big influence, this is good on the other hand (this is even more important for me) the people working for startups are more like me, the culture is more like me. They dress like me- jeans, t-shirt- this is the environment I like to work in. But on the other hand, if you work for a global player its more often that you come

Fig. 5.1 Humans of Berlin, Germany

in suits. A good example is that I worked for Coca-Cola, they have a fresh young image. When I worked for them in the headquarters in Germany, I had an office in the 7th floor and it was really nice but the people there wear the image, they wear suits, they're distanced they aren't as nice.—Sandro (Direct quote, some sentences edited out for brevity.)

Sandro talked to me for around 30 min about his long career in the Human Resources field. He had worked for many different industries and companies in all stages of development, varying from big players such as Phillip Morris and Coca-Cola to fresh start-up IT firms. Like the typical rational consumer that economics is based on, he weighs the costs and benefits of different jobs to figure out which offers to accept. Sandro prefers working for start-ups. He sees many benefits to working for start-ups such as the casual environment that allows him to wear jeans and a t-shirt, the ability to have more control over the processes in the business, and the opportunity to make more of a difference in the company. There are also costs associated with working for a young company like the chaos there can be in an environment where everything is new and changing. There are also trade-offs he gives up by choosing a start-up over an established global firm. He gives up possibly a better salary and a more steady, solid job and perks like a nice office. Weighing all of these costs and benefits, Sandro has decided that start-ups are the place for him.

5.5.2 *Student Example: Building of Germany (Fig. 5.2)*

Less than a block away from Hotel 38 stands the Tacheles, a massive, run down building boasting a distinct, six story mural that reads "how long is now?" The question provokes thought, with no real answer or clear meaning. Although it may be easy for some to overlook, within its walls lies one of the richest histories of any building in Berlin. The Tacheles is a standing relic of the turbulent phases of Berlin's recent history, having played a pivotal role in each one.

Fig. 5.2 Building of Germany

Built in 1909, the building began its life as a large shopping mall that linked Oranienburgerstrae with Friedrichstrae. Later, an electric company purchased the building, where it held the world's first live broadcast of a sporting event. Soon after, Nazis seized the building and converted it into an SS headquarters. At that time, bombs badly damaged the building. During the Cold War, Russian soldiers and the GDR government occupied the building.

Communist struggle and oppression over years gave birth to an artistic counterculture in Berlin, with art becoming a communication medium for anti-authority thinking. In the 1990s, immediately after the Berlin Wall fell, the Tacheles blossomed into headquarters for this counterculture. Artists collaborated, painting the building's walls, showcasing sculptures in its courtyard. The Tacheles boasted a nightclub, a bar, and a biergarten, all of which centered around the arts. Squatters occupied the building until 2012, when the forces of capitalism began to take hold. Efficient use of the land and building overtook a locally beloved, but not economically productive, artistic phase. Still, the mural remained.

A German bank now owns the Tacheles and plans to completely remodel the building, converting it into apartment spaces. According to dw.com, the housing market in Berlin has become extremely competitive. Following in the footsteps of places like New York and London, apartment viewings commonly draw crowds of eighty or more people. Demand for housing nearly doubles its supply. Berliners seek approximately 18,000 new apartments a year in the midst of a 10,000 supply. The bank capitalized on the principle that in the face of high demand, scarcity will lead to high value. If permitted to do so, banks and investors will likely continue to renovate historical buildings like the Tacheles, at least until the supply meets demand.

The Tacheles conversion raises the question: should Berlin more heavily regulate its historic real estate market? Although the buildings lining Berlin's streets appear old, many are recreations after World War II's mass destruction. Should buildings still standing from the pre-war era be preserved in their former glory, or should they be swept up by rapid growth to achieve economic efficiency? Berliners will no doubt choose up sides, much like we do in our United States' urban cores. For now, the Tacheles' mural continues to beg the existential question—how long is now? Given Berlin's turbulent history and the building's many faces, perhaps the artist questioned whether the mural itself could withstand capitalism's creative and destructive forces.

5.5.3 Student Example: Human of University of Arizona (Fig. 5.3)

> I love music but not as a money maker but it does make me happy that people would want to listen. I'm more about a secure job for my future. My guitar is more like my friendly and supportive companion.
>
> My guitar and I have been winging it from the moment I made the decision to come study at the U of A. I came here so unprepared without knowing where I was going to live or how I was going to sustain myself. All I knew was that I had to get out of my town and begin a career, like, now, or else I would never get out of there; even if it means being away from my family and my church.

This University of Arizona freshman student speaks about the choices she's made. To her, earning a reliable degree that will land her a secure job is of high importance, for she realizes that an education adds her value as human capital to potential employers. For this reason, coming here to study is a priority above all the tradeoffs. From her story, one could tell that her opportunity cost would have been to enroll in a community college so that she could save some money while working to help her family with expenses. She also spoke about the difficulties from having to give up being close to her family and involved in her church's quire band, aspects also included in her opportunity cost of leaving her home town. However, she is well aware that there are not many career opportunities in her town, plus the experiences she has access to here at the U of A are what added the most wealth to her. Another thing this student considers as wealth is dedicating time and energy into her hobby of playing the guitar regardless of an earning potential. Her subjective value of playing the guitar and the occasional people who enjoy her music is greater than monetary value.

Fig. 5.3 Human of University of Arizona

5.6 Student Feedback

> I personally greatly enjoyed the Humans and Buildings of Ireland assignment, largely because of being given the freedom to pick what 'human' or 'building' we wanted to do the assignment on. In my case I chose to do it on the Guinness Storehouse as a way to do an assignment on two of my favorite subjects, alcohol and economics.

> I think the buildings and humans assignment is a fascinating project that allows for students to get acclimated to a new culture through meeting new people and appreciating different architecture. I would have never asked some of the questions to strangers if it was not for the project, but the conversations and things I learned as a result of doing so was stimulating. Furthermore, I normally do not take the time to appreciate buildings/architecture, and I never ask questions about or try to learn more about the respective place. Thus, it forced me to pay more attention to detail and appreciate beauty that I otherwise would not have noticed.

> I really liked the humans and buildings assignments. At first I was nervous about striking up a conversation with locals, but I'm so glad I did because everyone I talked to was so kind.

5.7 Conclusion

This manuscript provides economics educators with a detailed explanation of an interdisciplinary and global assignment to motivate and engage their students. Humans and Buildings of a "Place" take advantage of storytelling to relate economics to a real-world application. By making students the producers of the economic content, students are able to apply the "Economics is Everywhere" principle in practice to an environment unfamiliar to them.

References

Acchiardo CJ, Al-Bahrani A, Holder K, Mateer D (2017) Through the lens of life: teaching principles of economics with Humans of New York. J Econ Financ Educ 16(2):19–28

Al-Bahrani A, Thompson L (2019) Making economics stick with econ beats. In: Hall JC, Lawson K (eds) Perspectives on economic education and teaching

Al-Bahrani A, Holder K, Patel D, Wooten J (2016) Art of econ: incorporating the arts through active learning assignments in principles courses. J Econ Financ Educ 15(2):1–17

Al-Bahrani A, Libis B, Drabik S, Gibson J (2017) Econ beats: a semester long, interdisciplinary, project-based learning assignment. J Econ Financ Educ 16(3):1–11

Becker WE, Watts M (1996) Chalk and talk: a national survey on teaching undergraduate economics. Am Econ Rev 86(2):448–453

Frank R (2006) The economic naturalist writing assignment. J Econ Educ 37(1):58–67

Moryl R (2016) Pod learning: student groups create podcasts to achieve economics learning goals. J Econ Educ 47(1):64–70

Niman N, Furnagiev S, Lemos S, Tischer R (2018) Developing the journey process: a novel approach to teaching undergraduate economics. J Econ Financ Educ, Forthcoming

Patel D, Saunoris J (2016) Using the FRED excel-based application to improve learning outcomes in economic courses: from student to practitioner. J Econ Financ Educ 15(2):37–49

Chapter 6
The Economic Principles of My Cancer Treatment: How to Use Medical Experiences to Teach Economics

Joab Corey

Abstract This paper uses specific examples from my cancer treatment to illuminate multiple concepts that are typically covered in principles of economics classes. Economics is a method of thinking that reveals itself in all aspects of life and a good economics instructor should be able to see and adapt these economic concepts in even his or her most severe life experiences. The real events of my treatment serve to illustrate and further clarify basic economic concepts such as inelasticity, cost-benefit analysis, product bundling, how people respond to incentives, and marginal decision making. The more advanced concepts of a second-best world and the logic of the rational voter model are also explained using situations that arose during the treatment. These real-life incidences further clarify these ideas and provide effective examples that can be used in the classroom to bolster students' confidence in the economic way of thinking.

6.1 Teaching Economics

Economics is a discipline that can very easily be applied to everyday occurrences and situations. However, students tend to have trouble understanding economic concepts because they get caught up in the abstract theory and what they often perceive to be unrealistic over-simplified models that permeate many economic textbooks. It is the case that some students who are otherwise able to grasp the economic concepts taught in principles classes are skeptical of the viability of these concepts due to the assumptions that economists tend to make in order to simplify the lesson. Upon teaching concepts such as cost-benefit analysis, marginal decision making, and other basic economic principles I am often asked by students if people really think this way. Ironically, the reason behind the existence of these various concepts is that people do indeed think this way, even without realizing it.

J. Corey (✉)
University of California Riverside, Riverside, CA, USA
e-mail: joab.corey@ucr.edu

J. Hall, K. Lawson (eds.), *Teaching Economics*,
https://doi.org/10.1007/978-3-030-20696-3_6

It is also true that many believe economics to be primarily concerned with the study of money and business, making those who are unconcerned with such issues quickly lose interest. It is important to show students that economics is the art and science of decision making in all aspects of life and using real examples from a life event that is seemingly unrelated to the study of economics will help students appreciate how they can adopt the economic way of thinking in their own lives. After all, the simple act of being alive requires one to engage in economic decision making, the only thing that separates the economist from the non-economist are the terms and definitions used to describe this way of thinking.

Entertaining and informative economic examples can be found everywhere. There has been significant use of the media to motivate and supplement economic lectures. For example, Leet and Houser have developed an entire course that centers on the economic concepts found within classic movies (Leet and Houser 2003). Sexton (2006) uses clips from popular movies and television shows to discuss various economic concepts. Mateer (2005) also uses music and movies clips to provide more entertaining ways to teach the dismal science. In his article (and book) "Homer Economicus: Using The Simpsons to Teach Economics," Hall (Spring 2005, 2014) discusses ways to use examples from the popular animated television series to relate economics to his students. This demonstrates how economics is frequently found within pop culture and offers amusing examples that help students internalize the material. Such educational tools are important for the common student to remember his or her economic lessons even after leaving the classroom, which is the true mark of an effective and helpful class.

In addition to classic movies and popular media, there exists a great deal of economic examples in peoples' everyday experiences, whether they be as mundane as shopping at a convenience store or as dramatic as being locked in a World War II POW camp (Radford 1945). Every term I give out an anonymous midterm teacher evaluation asking students what their favorite and least favorite parts of class are to hopefully improve their economics education experience and, invariably, in terms of frequency of responses, the number one favorite part of class listed by my students are the instructor's personal stories and examples. They often accompany their response with statements like "they just really help me remember the material" and "they allow me to tie economics into everyday life." The students have spoken, and clearly, personal stories and experiences are among the best ways to deliver the material!

Personal health care experiences and decisions are no exception to this effective medium of economics education. Many professors, as they age, will likely run into various medical ailments and problems. Those who are not shy about such issues can use these situations to generate examples of existing economic concepts. This can extend well beyond the typical hypothetical posturing of how much medical insurance one should carry and how this is based on an individual's level of risk aversion, as it only requires that one with an understanding of basic economics be observant in how to relate their situations to a good classroom discussion. I incorporate this method of teaching by using personal examples from my cancer treatment to illustrate economic concepts that many students tend to find difficult. The nature and severity of some of these examples make the lessons even more compelling.

6.2 The Nature of My Cancer Diagnoses and Treatment

In January of 2007, at the age of 24 years old and in my second year of an economics Ph.D. program, I was diagnosed with testicular cancer, which is the cancer made famous by seven-time Tour-de-France winner Lance Armstrong and his autobiography "Its Not about the Bike" (Armstrong and Jenkins 2001). This cancer is often referred to as a young man's cancer because it is most common in males aged 18–35 and it is relatively rare. Testicular cancer only makes up about one percent of all incidences of cancer among males, or roughly 8000 cases annually. The nature of the cancer is that it originates in the testicles where it can then travel to the lymph nodes, lungs, and eventually the brain if given enough time (Moss 2007). While potentially lethal, it is one of the most curable of all cancers as it can be removed with surgery if localized in the testicle or can be cured through a combination of surgery and chemotherapy if it has spread. The day of my surgery, which occurred two days after my diagnosis, I found out that the CT scan I had taken revealed that the cancer had spread to my lymph nodes and that I required chemotherapy.

The type and amount of chemotherapy one afflicted with cancer receives depends on how far the cancer has spread and the size of the tumors. Having reached what is known as stage 2B, I required a chemotherapy schedule that required two drugs, cisplatin and etoposide, taken through an IV every day for five straight days followed by two weeks with no chemotherapy for a total of four cycles. During this treatment I encountered many situations that serve as good examples of the following economic concepts. Using these examples should help the students comprehend the information and increase their confidence in the veracity of the lesson.

6.3 Example 1: Inelasticity

Perfectly inelastic demand is represented by a vertical demand curve and occurs with goods where the buyer will purchase the same quantity regardless of the price. Most students have trouble grasping the concept of purchasing a good regardless of the price and often ask if such a good really exists. It is then revealed by the instructor that this vertical demand curve is more theoretical than practical (that is it exists in the minds and textbooks of economists more than it does in the real world). However, there are a few goods that come incredibly close to having this perfectly inelastic relationship between price and quantity demanded, and when pressed by students for examples of such a good, the most common response by economists is life-saving medications. While in reality, there will always be some price high enough to induce people to create or search for available substitutes, or just have to forgo the treatment altogether, the idea that life-saving medication is very inelastic, and perhaps the good most likely to be perfectly inelastic, remains. My cancer treatment was filled with very expensive, but very necessary medications (including the chemotherapy itself) that I would have purchased regardless of the price. However, the most vivid example of this (and the story I often tell my students) is when I went to purchase some necessary medications before my first chemotherapy treatment. One of the prescriptions was for the pill Emend which consists of three pills, one taken each day the first three days of a chemotherapy cycle. The purpose of this pill is to help prevent nausea and is so necessary that the hospital will provide it for you (and charge you for it) before they start your chemotherapy cycle if you don't purchase it on your own. One Emend pack, which consists of three pills, costs about $330 as of this writing. While waiting for my prescriptions to be filled the pharmacist and I engaged in the following dialogue:

Pharmacist: This prescription for Emend costs $330. Do you still want it?[1]
Myself: Do I still need it?
Pharmacist: Well, yes.
Myself: Then I guess I still want it.

The basic point of this dialogue is that she could have said that the pills cost $1000, or even $5000, and I still would have wanted them. This story drives home the point of inelasticity as whether the price for the Emend prescription was $1 or $5000, I still would have purchased the same amount.[2] The same is true for the chemotherapy itself. Even a considerable change in the price of chemotherapy would not have changed my demand for the treatment. If the price rose substantially, then I would have still wanted the prescribed number of cycles and if the price dropped substantially (even as low as one cent per cycle), then I would have not wanted any more chemotherapy above the prescribed dosage for reasons obvious to anyone who has received chemotherapy treatments before.[3] Chemotherapy is truly a good where price has little to no effect on quantity demanded in either direction. This idea can be applied to any number of medications used for a variety of medical afflictions. Even a professor who suffers from severe migraines can use inelasticity when discussing how much he or she would pay to be free of their headaches. An economics professor in the hospital or in a pharmacy is the perfect storm for memorable classroom inelasticity examples.

---

[1]In retrospect, I think the pharmacist was trying to find a polite way of asking if I could still pay for the expensive medication rather than if I really wanted it. However, this thought did not enter my head at the time.

[2]Despite the necessity of the Emend pills, I still never got over the thought that, at the margin, I was swallowing over $100 with every one of those pills.

[3]The side effects of chemotherapy are very unpleasant. They often include but are not limited to nausea, hair loss, fatigue, dizziness, ringing of the ears, headaches, mouth sores, blood clots, and low blood cell count levels that result in a higher risk of other disease and infections. It also includes other long-term negative effects such as increased risk of other cancers and sterility.

6.4 Example 2: Second-Best World

In economics, a second-best world is one in which a problem already exists as opposed to an ideal (first-best) world that has no economic problems. For example, in a first-best world, subsidies are often considered to be economically inefficient as they create an uneven playing field and bolster inefficient producers. However, in a second-best world where a monopoly exists, a subsidy may be efficient as it will cause the monopoly to increase output towards the socially optimal quantity. Throughout my cancer treatment there were many examples of this concept.

An example of this presented itself during my second round of chemotherapy. One of the side effects of chemotherapy is clotting of the blood (usually as the result of the cancer dying). After my first round of chemotherapy, multiple blood clots formed in both of my arms so that I had to receive chemotherapy through a central line put into my chest. A central line is a medical procedure where a needle and tube are put into your chest (or sometimes neck) so that it taps into the vein that sits on top of your lung. A drawback of this procedure is that there is a small (one to two percent) chance that the needle could miss the vein and puncture your lung. During the procedure when the doctor was inserting the needle into my chest she claimed to be struggling because of the dense musculature of my chest.[4] She then had to increase her efforts at pushing the needle in my chest which increased my fear of her puncturing my lung. Again, in a first-best world with no cancer, having dense musculature in your chest may be efficient. However, in a world with cancer, having dense musculature is problematic.

Another simple, and probably more relatable, example of this concept refers to the changes in one's diet that often must be made when being diagnosed with some medical ailment. I had to change my, otherwise healthy, diet during my cancer treatment. Before my diagnoses, I would take a multivitamin every day and eat a large quantity of vegetables, particularly broccoli, for its health enhancing benefits. However, after being afflicted with the multiple blood clots in my arms, I had to take both blood thinner pills and blood thinner injections every day and also reduce my consumption of vitamin K, a known blood coagulant. This included the immediate halt to my multivitamin which contained vitamin K and the further elimination of leafy green vegetables such as kale and broccoli. So, while my diet was considered healthy before my diagnosis, it became inefficient when the blood clots formed. Conditions that elicit necessary changes to ones' diet are widely experienced and this serves as a great example for explaining to an economics class what an economist means when distinguishing between a first-best and second-best world, and how the most economically efficient choices are based on the circumstances and constraints in which those decisions are made. For example, in a first-best world, it may be efficient for an individual to choose steak over grilled chicken salad if he or she prefers steak and the two cost the same. However, in a second-best world,

[4]Upon hearing this I cursed all the mornings that I got up and went to the gym to perform bench presses in what I thought at the time was a sacrifice that would help me live a healthy life.

where an individual has high cholesterol and blood pressure or a family history of heart disease, then it may change the person's preferences to where it is more efficient to choose the grilled chicken salad.

6.5 Example 3: Cost-Benefit Analysis and Economic Efficiency

One of the primary tools economics students can equip themselves with is cost-benefit analysis. This technique demonstrates how economics is the study of decision making by teaching students how to break down the costs and benefits of a situation, how to think at the margin, and how to make an efficient decision (one in which the marginal benefits outweigh the marginal costs). I used this technique in an effort to get the hospital to treat me at a lower cost as an out-patient.

The blood clots I received in my arm as a reaction to the chemotherapy forced me to stay in the hospital overnight while receiving periodic treatments of blood thinner and antibiotic through an IV. While being admitted to the hospital I learned that the bed and room alone would cost me (or, subsequently, my insurance company) roughly $1200 a night, and this did not include any medication, medical procedures, or visits from doctors.[5]

Upon hearing this I talked to the hospital staff about the possibility of receiving treatment sitting in a chair outside of the room so I would not have to pay the exorbitant room and bed fee. The hospital personnel told me that because I would have to receive periodic treatment throughout the night that it was necessary for me to be an in-patient (which means I had to stay in the room) because they did not treat out-patients at such hours as 3:00 in the morning. I insisted that I could sit in a chair (ten feet away) outside of the room and receive the treatment throughout the night.

I dipped into my economic toolbox and pulled out a simple cost-benefit analysis in my explanation to the hospital staff as to why this was a good idea for everyone involved. I started by explaining the idea that the benefit of the treatment outweighed the cost of the treatment to me, but that the benefit of the bed and room did not outweigh the cost of the bed and room to me. At the time all of the rooms on the floor were filled and there were patients who were waiting for a room to open up. I used this fact to explain to the hospital that, by allowing me to receive treatment outside of the room, another patient could use the room and receive the treatment that he or she needs. This way the hospital would be able to admit another patient and make money from that patient's treatment and room expense along with my treatment (option A) as opposed to just my treatment and room fee (option B).

[5]My medical coverage at the time had a $100,000 per year cap on it, so even when the insurance company would be billed, I was still very much concerned with the costs of the treatment.

For the profit maximizing hospital: option A–(room revenue + revenue from my treatment + other patient's treatment) > option B–(room revenue + revenue from my treatment). So, by removing me from the room, the hospital, the patient waiting for a room, and myself would have all been made better off (I explain to my students that such a situation is called a Pareto superior move, an adjustment that makes at least one person better off without making anybody worse off). After explaining this to the hospital staff, my extensive scientific analysis was shot down with "it makes sense, but it's against hospital policy," and so I remained in my $1200 a night accommodation. This situation, which provides an example of cost-benefit analysis and Pareto optimality, also demonstrates how economic efficiency is frequently destroyed by poor centrally planned policy. While this example is unique to my particular situation, it is the case that many individuals who suffer from medical afflictions must engage in internal cost-benefit analysis and make decisions about their treatment. This can serve as a great way to explicitly break down costs and benefits so that students can understand and later incorporate this tool into their own lives. An economics professor can easily use his or her own medical history to drudge up examples of cost-benefit analysis, and in doing so, encourage his or her students to do the same. Students frequently cite this as one of their favorite examples that I use in my classroom.[6]

6.6 Example 4: Bundling

Bundling occurs when two or more goods or services are sold together. Product tying is a type of bundling that occurs when two goods are tied together so that the purchase or use of one necessitates the purchase or use of the other. This is often used to describe the market solution to the problem of providing public goods. Tying a private good (advertising) to a public good (radio broadcasts) can assure that the socially optimal quantity is provided. Tying can also refer to connecting two private goods so that the purchase of one good is dependent on the purchase of another. While product bundling can increase the number of choices to the consumer, the situation where the sale of one product is contingent on the sale of another will limit the choices of the consumer and make that consumer worse off. In the previous example, the hospital did a good job of tying together a very elastic good (the bed and room) with a very inelastic good (the treatment). Therefore, in buying the treatment, I was forced to pay the high price of the room as well. I often use this example of product tying in my classes when talking about price discrimination to illuminate how effective this strategy can be for a producer and how problematic this can be for the consumer.

[6]The doctors and hospital staff also thought it to be particularly amusing, especially as I drew out the cost-benefit chart above with the chemotherapy IV still in my arm.

6.7 Example 5: Principal–Agent Problem

The basic idea behind the principal–agent problem is that the purchaser (the principal) of a service lacks the necessary information to appropriately monitor the provider of the service (the agent), and thus, the agent may be working towards objectives that are not in the principal's best interest. A common example used to teach this topic is the idea of taking your car to a mechanic. Customers rarely have enough knowledge of automobiles to make sure that the mechanic correctly fixes their car at the lowest possible cost. Therefore, a mechanic can do a poor job that only temporarily fixes the automobile's problem and charge a high price for doing so. This problem is very evident in medical care where the patient (the principal) does not have the knowledge to fully monitor the hospital (the agent) and determine whether or not their care is adequate or over-priced.

I never had any doubts that the doctors and hospitals were doing their very best to cure me, but I was equally certain they were not trying to do so at the lowest cost.[7] There were many examples of this, but one in particular stands out. Typically, before you receive chemotherapy, you need to have your chest X-rayed to check for potential complications. One also needs his or her chest X-rayed after a central line is placed in order to determine that the line was placed correctly. I had to have a central line placed in any case to receive a blood thinner (Heparin) through an IV. Before undergoing the placement of the central line, the hospital asked me to have my chest X-rayed to determine if I could receive chemotherapy. Since I had to have a central line placed anyway I concluded that it would be better to wait until after the central line was placed to have my chest X-rayed so that a single X-ray could determine that the both the central line was placed correctly and that I could undergo chemotherapy. This way I would only have to pay for one X-ray as opposed to two. The hospital concluded that this was a good idea and even complimented me for thinking of it. I was only able to make this suggestion because I was far enough along in my treatment to be familiar with these procedures. Without knowing any better I would have paid for the X-ray twice. The absence of knowledge about various medical procedures makes it easy for health care practitioners to treat illnesses at costs that are higher than necessary, a clear example of the principal's agent problem, and likely the result of having a system where a 3rd party pays the majority of the bill.

6.8 Example 6: Health Care Systems Debate

How healthcare should be provided, whether it be through private insurance or a universal single-payer system, is a constant source of debate that has only become more contested since my cancer experience. Many are in favor of a universal single-

[7]The fact that I am sitting here writing this shows that they were successful in their efforts to cure me.

payer system where the government pays for all healthcare expenditures, citing the financial hardships that medical catastrophes can place on people. Others cite the problems of universal single-payer systems, such as long waiting lines for treatment and less medical innovation, when arguing for a privatized system handled by voluntary interactions between patients, doctors, and insurance companies. As a relatively poor graduate students living on a meager teaching assistantship stipend and with only the school's health insurance policy, I can appreciate both sides of the debate, and relay my first-hand experience to students so that they can further appreciate both sides of the debate as well.

It is true that, even with health insurance, I had to pay several thousand dollars out of pocket for my various treatments and hospitalizations. I was also constantly embroiled in payment disputes between the hospital and the insurance company. The hospital would often double-bill certain procedures (whether accidentally or intentionally, I never knew), causing the health insurance company to refuse to pay, and I spent a lot of time on the phone with both entities to get things straightened out. Even with my graduate level economics education, I had trouble figuring out the logistics of this inefficient billing procedure. Spending hours on the phone serving as an intermediary between the hospital and the insurance company while undergoing my cancer treatments was certainly not ideal, and there were certain times where I wished I lived in a universal healthcare system so I wouldn't have to deal with all of the payment procedures. Those who advocate such a system will appreciate such a story.

At the same time, I believe my success in overcoming the disease is a large result of the speed in which I was treated, as it was determined that my cancer was growing at an accelerated rate. Within weeks of seeing my primary care physician, I had an appointment with a specialist, where I was diagnosed on a Tuesday, received a CT scan, X-Ray, and EKG the next day, and then had surgery the following day on Thursday. My chemotherapy treatments were also promptly scheduled to start two weeks later. Had I been in a system where it would have taken me longer to receive these procedures, or these advancements had never been invented, someone else would likely be teaching my economics students today.

6.9 Example 7: Rational Risk

The Downs (1957) rational voter model discusses the costs and benefits of voting and concludes that people are rational in their choice not to vote. The Downs model lists the benefit of voting as the difference in how much you like the candidates multiplied by the probability that your vote will be the deciding vote in the election. The cost of voting is the time it takes to inform yourself about the candidates and the cost in terms of time and effort to actually vote. The probability that a person casts a decisive vote in a nation-wide election is so small that the cost of voting typically outweighs the benefit, so people rationally choose not to vote. One argument to why so many people do vote is the idea that they are playing a minimax strategy that involves avoiding the worst-case scenario, which in this case is that the preferred candidate lost because you did not vote.[8] However, there is reason to believe that people do not live their life by trying to avoid the worst-case scenarios. If this were true, nobody would cross the street for fear of being run over by a bus.

This was also evident by how I made decisions during my cancer treatment. Before putting the central line into my chest or neck I had to receive doses of plasma in order to prevent excessive bleeding since I was on blood thinners to treat my blood clots. As is the case with any blood or plasma transfusion, I had to sign a release form where I acknowledged that there was a potential risk of acquiring HIV or hepatitis, no matter how thoroughly the plasma was screened. I was told by the doctor that the chance of this occurring was about 1 in every 300,000. I could have avoided the transfusion, but doing so would result in being in the hospital an extra three days while my blood coagulation levels stabilized themselves. Obviously, the minimax strategy would be to avoid the plasma transfusion and the chance of getting HIV, but because the probability of acquiring these diseases is so low I rationally chose to get the transfusion rather than spend an extra three days in the hospital. This real-life example is evidence that the minimax strategy is usually not realistically employed, but that people will engage in what could be termed risky activity (such as the avoidance of voting in an election you care about) if the probability of creating the undesirable outcome is low enough. This example is very applicable as many people often have to sign medical waivers before undergoing operations, transplants, or various other treatments. Presenting this example to the class is a powerful way to illustrate this economic concept.

6.10 Conclusion

These examples are best used after fully explaining the lesson to which the specific example pertains. For example, one would want to lecture about the concept of inelasticity and refer to necessary medication as an example of an inelastic good and then use the Emend or chemotherapy example as a way to drive home the lesson. Similarly, a teacher would want to explain the process of cost-benefit decision making and he or she might want to present a more commonly known instance of using cost-benefit analysis (such as a government regulation) before launching into the hospital example to show students how individuals frequently use this process in their everyday life. While being just another way to explain these concepts, many students find real-life examples to be more entertaining and memorable than hypothetical ones. When using these examples in class myself, I notice that students seem more enthusiastic and entertained than during other parts of the lecture. While

[8]In actuality, the probability of being hit by a car on your way to the voting booth is often higher than the probability of being the decisive voter, so people choosing to play this strategy really should have stayed home.

these examples are specific to my own treatment, they serve to illustrate how an instructor can use real-life occurrences from their own medical experiences or other significant life events to show how economic principles are present in all things. Using these examples in this way will allow an instructor to reach a wide range of students with a vivid lesson about how economics relates to everyday decisions.

Acknowledgements The author would like to thank Russell S. Sobel and Tami Gurley-Calvez for comments and suggestions. I would also like to thank all of the doctors, nurses, hospital staff, family, friends, teachers, and students who helped me throughout my cancer treatment and recovery.

References

Armstrong L, Jenkins S (2001) Its not about the bike: my journey back to life. Berkley Brooks, New York

Downs A (1957) An economic theory of democracy. Harper & Row, New York

Hall J (2014) Homer economicus: the Simpsons and economics. Stanford University Press, Palo Alto

Hall J (2005) Homer economicus: using the Simpsons to teach economics. J Private Enterprise 20(2):165–176

Leet D, Houser S (2003) Economics goes to Hollywood: using classic films and documentaries to create an undergraduate economics course. J Econ Educ 34(Fall):326–332

Mateer D (2005) Economics in the movies. South-Western Publishing, Nashville

Moss RW (2007) Moss reports: alternative, conventional & innovative cancer treatments. Cancer Communications, Inc, Lemont

Radford RA (1945) The economic organisation of a POW camp. Economica 12(48):189–201

Sexton RL (2006) Using short movie and television clips in the economics principles class. J Econ Educ 37(Fall):406–417

Chapter 7
Textbook Confessions: Government Policies and Market Outcomes

Hugo Eyzaguirre, Tawni Hunt Ferrarini, and Brian O'Roark

Abstract This paper focuses on how government action in the market is presented in Economics Principles textbooks. It looks at whether the government's role (and failure) is addressed in two topics, price controls and trade barriers, which are presumed by many outside of the economics community that they are strategic uses of government resources and will be efficiency enhancing. These topics are covered in all textbooks in our sample, and are typically explained, in economic fashion, as voluntary policies that subvert the market outcome. However, the motivations provided by textbook authors for adopting these measures are woefully inadequate. In particular, while authors regularly bring up the role of special interests when discussing the implementation of trade barriers, those pressures brought to bear in favor of price controls are rarely acknowledged.

7.1 Introduction

The importance of the Principles of Economics course cannot be overstated. It serves as the foundation course for majors, and perhaps more importantly, for most students, this will be their only point of contact with the way economies work. Consequently, Principles becomes the window through which most students will observe and understand how the people living in a world of scarcity make decisions and why those decisions have future consequences. It follows then, that the Principles of Economics textbook plays a central role in guiding the content of

H. Eyzaguirre (✉)
Northern Michigan University, Marquette, MI, USA
e-mail: heyzagui@nmu.edu

T. H. Ferrarini
Lindenwood University, St. Charles, MO, USA
e-mail: tferrarini@lindenwood.edu

B. O'Roark
Robert Morris University, Moon Township, PA, USA
e-mail: oroark@rmu.edu

J. Hall, K. Lawson (eds.), *Teaching Economics*,
https://doi.org/10.1007/978-3-030-20696-3_7

these classes and the instruction received by the students. What is or is not presented in the textbook, therefore, will affect the perspective of students in an out-sized way.

This concern over what is generally covered in Principles has been discussed by Elzinga (1992) and Lopus and Leet (2007). More germane to this essay, others have examined the degree to which specific topics are covered by textbook authors. Lee (1992) focuses on the placement of international topics in textbooks, while Phipps et al. (2012) look at the extent to which textbooks include discussions of entrepreneurship. Hill and Myatt (2007) critique Principles texts for focusing too much on perfectly competitive markets. Levy and Peart (2011) explain between 1960 and 1980 textbooks persistently overestimated economic growth in the Soviet Union.

One of the more studied areas of coverage in Principles texts concerns the emphasis on government solutions to market failure. Fike and Gwartney (2015) examine textbooks in relation to their coverage of public choice, market, and government failure. Market failure is by far more commonly addressed in the texts studied. They conclude that students are being short changed when only the strengths of government policy are addressed as opposed to sharing the strengths and the weaknesses.

Eyzaguirre et al. (2014) find that while the coverage of market failure is a traditional topic in textbooks, government failure does not receive nearly as much attention. Eyzaguirre et al. (2016) examine the extent to which legal and institutional infrastructure provided by government appears in the pages of college textbooks. The reason for this analysis is that most textbooks present market failure as a result of unclear property rights. It would seem somewhat difficult for college students to grasp this point if the coverage of property rights and other relevant institutions is lacking in their textbooks.

Further supporting the contention that government failure is under represented in texts, Coyne and Lucas (2016) discuss the presentation of national defense as a public good. However, of the 50 books in their study, there is rarely a mention of the possibility of government failure in the provision of those public goods. They note that this "leaves students with an incomplete and biased exposure to the government provision of public goods" (Coyne and Lucas 2016, p. 65).

The current paper zeroes in on how government action in the market is presented in texts. Specifically, it looks at whether the government's role (and failure) is addressed in relevant topics. Two important points made in this updated analysis differ from those presented before. First, they correspond to issues where government intervention plays a key role. Second, we extend the analysis by looking at the motivations behind the intervention. We believe this provides a more complete picture of how the economic system works, beyond pure market economics.

Again, as in the previous papers, it is important to distinguish the operation of markets in a free society from the constrained decision-making in the real world. In this particular case, we focus on the constraints imposed by transferring decision-making power from the individuals living in households and operating businesses into the realm of the public (better yet, political) arena where elected officials, policymakers, and appointees make decisions.

Government intervention into the market is addressed in a variety of ways in textbooks. They include:

- Price controls
- Trade barriers
- Fiscal policy (budget deficits)
- Subsidies
- Antitrust policies
- Regulation
- Competition
- Externalities
- Consumer protection (information, standards mandated).

While these subjects are commonplace, they typically are presented with the presumption that they are perfectly strategic uses of government resources, and that they will be efficiency enhancing. Narrowing this list down, we will focus on the first two topics. The primary reason for choosing these two topics is that they are addressed in nearly every Principles text, they are clearly areas where the appropriateness of government intervention can be questioned, and they have recently been discussed in the popular press.

7.2 Methodology

The methodology is similar to our previous work and the existing literature on textbook coverage of a variety of topics. There are quantitative and qualitative methods that have been used.[1] For consistency with our previous work, we will use the textbooks selected in those papers. These texts are presented in Table 7.1. The logic at the time was that these books cover newer and older books spanning a few years old to McConnell et al. (2018) which is in its 21st edition. These books also appear at the top of the list when searching for Principles texts on Amazon. However, we have updated to the latest edition available.

In order to evaluate these texts, we feel an objective criterion is in order. Given that there is not a set of standards for the content of Principles of Economics courses, we resort, as in the past to the Council for Economic Education's Voluntary National Content Standards (referred to from now on as Standards) (Siegfried et al. 2010). The Standards is a document in which Ph.D.s in economics and experts in economic education identify learning milestones for high school students to pass as they prepare to enter a global economy and become productive citizens. While we

[1] We have discussed some of the literature in our previous work. Here, we refer the reader to some of those studies: Lee (1992), Kent and Rushing (1999), Lopus et al. (2008), and Phipps et al. (2012).

Table 7.1 List of textbooks included in the analysis

Title	Edition	Author and year	Publisher
Economics Principles and Policy	13th	Baumol and Blinder (2016)	South-Western Cengage
Principles of Economics	12th	Case et al. (2017)	Prentice Hall
Economics	10th	Colander (2017)	McGraw-Hill Irwin
Modern Principles of Economics	4th	Cowen and Tabarrok (2018)	Worth Publishers
Principles of Economics	7th	Frank and Bernanke (2019)	McGraw-Hill Irwin
Economics: Private and Public Choice	16th	Gwartney et al. (2018)	South-Western Cengage
Economics	6th	Hubbard and O'Brien (2017)	Prentice Hall
Economics	5th	Krugman and Wells (2018)	Worth Publishers
Principles of Economics	8th	Mankiw (2018)	South-Western Cengage
Economics: Principles, Problems, and Policies	21st	McConnell et al. (2018)	McGraw-Hill Irwin
Economics: A Contemporary Introduction	11th	McEachern (2017)	South-Western Cengage
Economics Today	19th	Miller (2018)	Prentice Hall

are concerned about college textbooks, the Standards act as a solid proxy for what students should know at the college level about basic economics and the economy.

Because not all states require economics of their graduating high school seniors, Principles courses at the college level may be the only point of contact between economics and the college student. So, what is covered in a Principles course should at the very least bring all students up to the same level and provide them with a solid foundation in economic reasoning. As the authors of the standards are all themselves college educators, we feel that the Standards provide us with the best available point from which to launch our analysis.

Generally, these standards cover non-controversial topics such as the role of scarcity, incentives, and trade. According to the Standards: The standards focus on the more fundamental economic ideas and concepts that are widely shared by professional economists. Some very important aspects of economics are either quite complex or so controversial that there seems to be no existing consensus. In spite of their importance, such complex or controversial aspects of economics receive less attention in the standards for pedagogical reasons. In addition, those aspects of economics that are more easily separated into independent components account for more of the standards.

7.2.1 Standard Specifics

Because we are focused on price controls, trade barriers, and role of government, let's review the relevant standards for these topics.

Content Standard 8: Role of Prices

At the completion of Grade 12, students will know the Grade 4 and Grade 8 benchmarks for this standard, and also that:

> 4. Government-enforced price ceilings set below the market-clearing price and government-enforced price floors set above the market-clearing price distort price signals and incentives to producers and consumers. Price ceilings can cause persistent shortages, while price floors can cause persistent surpluses.

At the completion of Grade 12, students will use this knowledge to:

> 4. Describe what is likely to happen if the government imposes a price ceiling on gasoline and a price floor on milk.

Content Standard 5: Trade

At the completion of Grade 8, students will know...that:

> 5. Imports are foreign goods and services that are purchased from sellers in other nations.

At the completion of Grade 8, students will use this knowledge to:

> 5. Examine labels of products in their homes and compile a list of imported products and the countries from which they are imported.

Benchmarks: Grade 12

At the completion of Grade 12, students will know...that:

> 2. When imports are restricted by public policies, consumers pay higher prices and job opportunities and profits in exporting firms may decrease.

At the completion of Grade 12, students will use this knowledge to:

> 2. Analyze the political and economic implications of a proposed ban on imported products.

Seeking to evaluate Principles textbooks' coverage of these topics relative to the role of government means we must also evaluate what the Standards say about government failure.

Content Standard 17: Government Failure

At the completion of Grade 12, students will know...that:

> 3. Although barriers to international trade usually impose higher costs than benefits, they are often advocated by people and groups who expect to gain substantially from them. Because the costs of these barriers are typically spread over a large number of people who each pay only a little and may not recognize the cost, policies supporting trade barriers are often adopted through the political process. 4. Price controls, occupational licensing, and reductions in antitrust enforcement are often advocated by special interest groups. Price controls can reduce the quantity of goods

Table 7.2 Our scoring matrix

	Government policy	Political interests	Special interests
No mention	0	0	0
Only a mention	1	1	1
An explanation	2	2	2

> and services produced, thus depriving consumers of some goods and services whose value would exceed their cost.

At the completion of Grade 12, students will use this knowledge to:

> 3. Explain why a political leader would support an idea that helps only a few while harming many, such as a tariff on imported luggage. 4. Explain the statement: Removing rent controls in New York City is good economics but bad politics. Also, explain who would gain and who would lose as a result of a 10 percent ceiling on credit card interest rates.

Reading these standards as a whole we identify three elements as suitable to our analysis of price controls and trade barriers. First, the situation being analyzed is entirely created by government policies, be they forays into controlling market prices or limitations on free trade. Second, the motivations behind the policies include particular political interests. Finally, the motivations behind the policies include particular economic benefits advocated for by special interests.

Because our focus here is on qualitative measurements of the textbook coverage of price controls and trade barriers we develop an index to identify which books cover which topics and in what way. The index used is quite simple. A book receives a score of zero if there is no mention, a score of one if there is a mention, and a score of two if there is also an explanation. We view this index as qualitative because we do not try to make distinctions between a strong and a weak explanation, a clear or confusing explanation, a thorough or partial explanation, and so on. The only distinction we look for is between a mention and an explanation.

For each subject we identify if the authors address the policy as government based, if political interests are discussed, or if special interests are mentioned, and if these subjects are mentioned, are they further explained. We can represent this simple methodology with the matrix shown in Table 7.2.

Based on this matrix, the maximum number of points a textbook could earn for each of the selected topics is six.

7.3 Textbook Coverage

7.3.1 Price Controls

When discussing price controls, all texts do an admirable job of explaining this as government policy. This should not be surprising. Price controls imply the absence

Table 7.3 Textbook discussion of price controls

Textbook	Government policy	Political interests	Special interests	Total
Baumol and Blinder (2016)	2	1	1	4
Case et al. (2017)	2	0	0	2
Colander (2017)	2	2	1	5
Cowen and Tabarrok (2018)	2	0	0	2
Frank and Bernanke (2019)	2	0	0	2
Gwartney et al. (2018)	2	0	1	3
Hubbard and O'Brien (2017)	2	0	1	3
Krugman and Wells (2018)	2	1	2	5
Mankiw (2018)	2	0	1	3
McConnell et al. (2018)	2	0	0	2
McEachern (2017)	2	0	0	2
Miller (2018)	2	0	0	2
Average	2	0.33	0.58	2.92
Percentage	100.00	16.67	29.17	48.61

of the price mechanism to clear the market, in fact it is made illegal. That can only come as a result of government policy. However, when we look into the second and third elements the findings are not so favorable. Except for Colander (2017), which is the only text that offers an explanation, there are only two books that even mention of political interests. In the case of special interests, the results are a little better. Six books mention special interests, but only Krugman and Wells (2018) go on and explain the role they play in the adoption of this policy.

While all books refer to minimum wages as a government policy (the score is 2 out of 2 points for each) identifying the role of political and special interests is lacking. The average score for a book in these two areas is only 0.33 and 0.58 points, respectively. You can see the results in Table 7.3. The comparison among textbooks is illustrated in Fig. 7.1. We found that Colander (2017) and Krugman and Wells (2018) do better than the rest which as we will discuss later is at odds with our findings in our two previous papers.

To get a better sense of the different treatment of price controls we show a sample of quotes from some of the textbooks.

- Cowen and Tabarrok (2018, p. 152)

> One of the primary reasons for price controls may be that the public, unlike economists, does not see the consequences of price controls. People who have not been trained in economics rarely connect lineups with price controls.

- McConnell et al. (2018, pp. 160, 162)

> ...government sometimes concludes that supply and demand will produce prices that are unfairly high for buyers or unfairly low for sellers. So government may place legal limits on how high or low a price or prices may go... In all these cases, good intentions lead to bad economic outcomes.

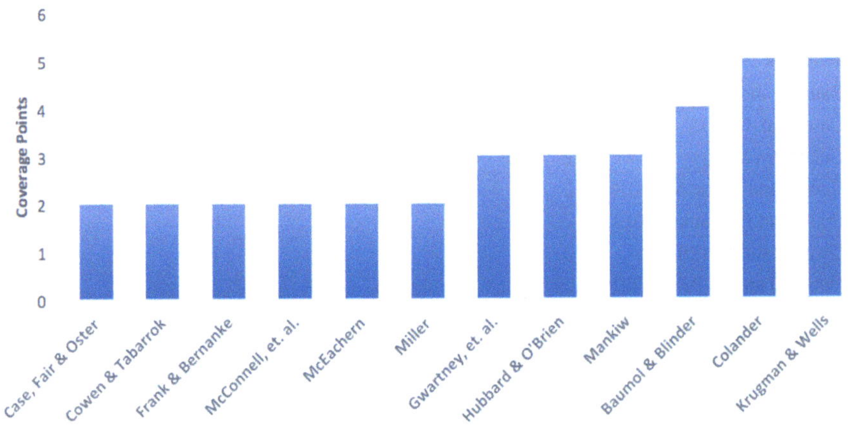

Fig. 7.1 Textbooks by coverage points for price controls

- Krugman and Wells (2018, p. 130)

> ...there is often a strong political demand for governments to intervene in markets. And powerful interests can make a compelling case that a market intervention favoring them is "fair." When a government intervenes to regulate prices, we say that it imposes price controls... Unfortunately, it's not that easy to tell a market what to do. As we will now see, when a government tries to legislate prices—whether it legislates them down by imposing a price ceiling or up by imposing a price floor—there are certain predictable and unpleasant side effects.

- Colander (2017, p. 105)

> Since politicians tend to focus on the short run, we can expect rent control to continue to be used when demand for housing suddenly increases.

From these quotes, we can observe a variety of approaches to covering the explanation of why price controls exist in the first place. A close look at them reveals there is tremendous variation in using fundamental economics to explain how special interests and policymakers respond to incentives in order to capture rents by using the political system to draw benefits to themselves and serve their narrow interests at the expanse of many, many others.

7.3.2 *Trade Barriers*

In the case of trade barriers, we observe better results than in the case of price controls when it comes to connecting this policy with motivation and incentives. Again, all of the textbooks explain the role of the government creating the situation under analysis. Only in four cases, Baumol and Blinder (2016), Case et al. (2017), Mankiw (2018), and Miller (2018), there is no mention or discussion of any of the

Table 7.4 Textbook discussion of price controls

Textbook	Government policy	Political interests	Special interests	Total
Baumol and Blinder (2016)	2	0	0	2
Case et al. (2017)	2	0	0	2
Colander (2017)	2	1	2	5
Cowen and Tabarrok (2018)	2	1	2	5
Frank and Bernanke (2019)	2	1	1	4
Gwartney et al. (2018)	2	2	2	6
Hubbard and O'Brien (2017)	2	1	2	5
Krugman and Wells (2018)	2	1	2	5
Mankiw (2018)	2	0	0	2
McConnell et al. (2018)	2	2	2	6
McEachern (2017)	2	1	2	5
Miller (2018)	2	0	0	2
Average	2	0.83	1.25	4.08
Percentage	100.00	41.67	62.50	68.06

motivations behind the policy. The rest of the textbooks contain at least a mention of political interests driving the policy, while only Gwartney et al. (2018) and McConnell et al. (2018) provide a discussion of these driving interests. Still the overall results are somewhat disappointing with an average score of 0.83.

The texts, as a whole, are more comprehensive in their coverage of the role of special interests. We see that seven of the books not only mention, but also discuss the role special interests play in adopting trade barriers. The proclivity of discussing the involvement of special interests results in a score of 1.25 when analyzing trade barriers, far higher than the score earned in their analysis of price controls.

The results for each textbook can be seen in Table 7.4 and a comparison among them provided in Fig. 7.2.

To get a better sense of the different coverage of trade barriers we include a sample of quotes from some of the textbooks.

- Mankiw (2018, p. 182)

> Economists and the public often disagree about free trade... Only 29 percent of those polled said free international trade helped, whereas 34 percent thought it hurt. (The rest thought it made no difference or were unsure.) By contrast, economists overwhelmingly support free international trade. They view free trade as a way of allocating production efficiently and raising living standards both at home and abroad.

- Hubbard and O'Brien (2017, p. 309)

> This concentration of benefits and widely spread burdens makes it easy to understand why members of Congress receive strong pressure from some industries to enact tariffs and quotas and relatively little pressure from the general public to reduce them.

- Gwartney et al. (2018, p. 376)

> Regardless of the arguments made by the proponents of trade restrictions, their political attractiveness is primarily the result of their special interest nature. Murray

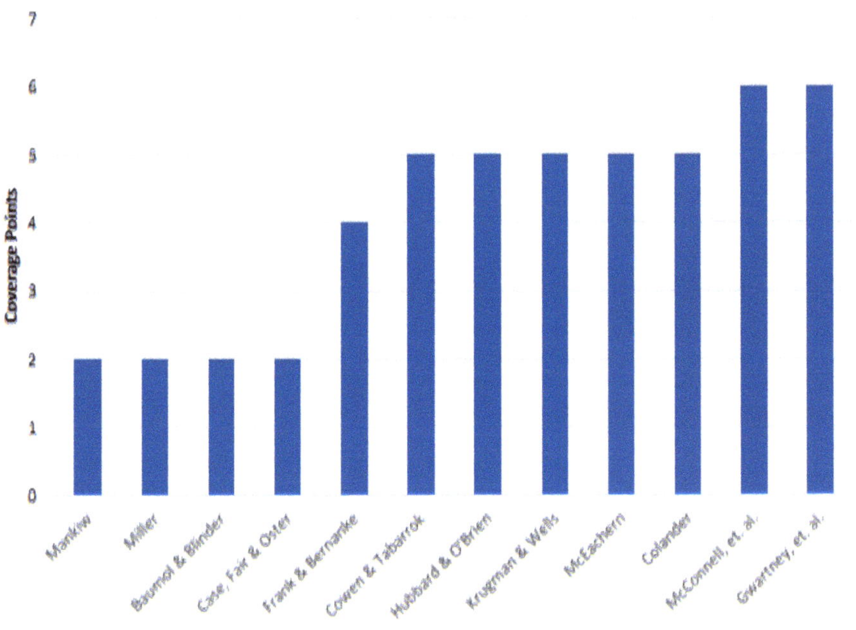

Fig. 7.2 Textbooks by coverage points for trade barriers

> Weidenbaum, former chairman of the President's Council of Economic Advisors, put it this way: "Protectionism is a politician's delight because it delivers visible benefits to the protected parties while imposing the costs as a hidden tax on the public."

- McConnell et al. (2018, p. 819)

> Study after study finds that the costs to consumers substantially exceed the gains to producers and government. A sizable net cost or efficiency loss to society arises from trade protection. Furthermore, industries employ large amounts of economic resources to influence Congress to pass and retain protectionist laws. Because these rent-seeking efforts divert resources away from more socially desirable purposes, trade restrictions impose these additional costs on society as well.

These quotes indicate that the authors of the textbooks reviewed are more skeptical of the role political and special interests play in the setting of trade policy than they are of these influences in price controls.

7.4 Comparing with General Government Failure Coverage

To wrap up our analysis, we want to see how the results in this paper coincide with the findings in our previous papers about a textbook's coverage of government failure (see Eyzaguirre et al. 2014, 2016). In our previous papers, we show different ways to measure the coverage of government failure. In general, a book's rank is relatively consistent regardless of the measure used, so for simplicity of comparison we picked the number of topics covered in a chapter or section on government failure. We expect that the authors who have a better coverage of government failure will also expend effort detailing the political and special interests' influence on price control and trade barrier policy.

The most salient finding is that some of the texts that performed better regarding the general coverage of government failure did not do well with the price controls and trade barriers coverage, and vice versa. The most notable one is the case of Krugman and Wells (2018). This book earned the lowest rating on how much of their material was devoted to discussing government failure, but they are at or near the top in ratings for the topics covered in this paper.

The opposite occurs with Cowen and Tabarrok (2018). They ranked very well in our previous papers but relatively poorly, compare to the coverage of topics in this paper.

This comparison between our prior papers and the current one raises an interesting question. If all the results were similar, then we could simply state that some textbooks are lacking in their coverage of these important issues. Having found some notable differences though, we are forced to ask: "does this mean the coverage of government failure is not as bad as we thought or is it even worse?"

One final issue arises concerning consistency within each textbook. An illustration of what we mean can be seen in the Krugman and Wells (2018) textbook. When discussing market failure, they say "When markets don't achieve efficiency, government intervention can improve society's welfare. That is, when markets go wrong, an appropriately designed government policy can sometimes move society closer to an efficient outcome by changing how society's resources are used" (Krugman and Wells 2018, p. 15).

However, when they discuss price controls the authors suggest that "powerful interests can make a compelling case that a market intervention favoring them is 'fair.' "...those who benefit from the controls are typically better organized and more vocal than those who are harmed by them... government officials often do not understand supply and demand analysis! It is a great mistake to suppose that economic policies in the real world are always sensible or well informed" (Krugman and Wells 2018, p. 130).

If we analyze these quotes together, we could conclude that when there are market failures, government intervention could be very helpful in improving society's welfare, but when we are talking about price controls there are interests influencing policies and as a result the government does not understand supply and demand analysis. This raises an important concern. At what point does the government become smart enough to deal with market failures? The government is the same no matter when it is intervening. It would be illogical to think that the corrective power of government in the case of some market failures is pure and unbiased, while in other instances, the pull of special interests leads to irresponsible applications of policy.

7.5 Conclusion

We began this paper suggesting that the textbook used in a Principles class is of utmost importance. This instrument of instruction provides students an insight into economics that they are unlikely to get anywhere else in their college education or throughout life. As such, we hope the materials covered are comprehensive, and provide a realistic look at the world into which our students will soon be embarking.

Such an analysis of textbooks gives us pause. In these books we see a wide and varied amount of coverage when it comes to price controls and trade barriers. Each of these topics is explained as a voluntary policy that seeks to subvert the market outcome. However, the motivations given for adopting these policies are woefully inadequate. In neither case is there much attention paid to the political intrigue that leads to the adoption of these policies. Similarly, there is very little effort made at explaining the role of special interests in adopting price controls. However, when trade barriers are discussed, the tone changes and a significant majority of the texts we evaluated bring up the role of special interests.

More curious to us though is that when comparing the result of this paper to our previous work there appears to be some significant inconsistencies in some of the books reviewed when it comes to the overall presentation of government failure. A text that provides a thorough discussion on government failure generally should extend this discussion to specific policies. Furthermore, students should not be led to believe that, when moving into the political arena where price and trade policy are debated, government has a clear eye for fixing some perceived problems such as determining a minimum wage but is otherwise incapacitated by special interest lobbying when trying to set trade policy. We would expect textbook authors to be more consistent in their presentation than this.

References

Baumol WJ, Blinder AS (2016) Economics: principles & policy, 13th edn. South-Western Cengage Learning, Mason

Case KE, Fair RC, Oster SE (2017) Principles of economics, 12th edn. Prentice Hall, Upper Saddle River

Colander D (2017) Economics, 10th edn. McGraw-Hill Irwin, New York

Cowen T, Tabarrok A (2018) Modern principles of economics, 4th edn. Worth Publishers, New York

Coyne C, Lucas D (2016) Economists have no defense: a critical review of national defense in economics textbooks. J Private Enterprise 31(4):65–83

Elzinga KG (1992) Eleven principles of economics. South Econ J 58(4):861–879

Eyzaguirre H, Ferrarini TH, O'Roark JB (2014) Textbook confessions: government failure. J Private Enterprise 29(3):159–175

Eyzaguirre H, Ferrarini TH, O'Roark JB (2016) Textbook confessions: of failures, markets, and government. J Econ Finance Educ 15(2):60–71

Fike R, Gwartney J (2015) Public choice, market failure, and government failure in principles textbooks. J Econ Educ 46(2):207–218

Frank R, Bernanke B (2019) Principles of economics, 7th edn. McGraw-Hill Irwin, New York
Gwartney JD, Stroup RL, Sobel RS, MacPherson DA (2018) Economics: private and public choice, 16th edn. South-Western Cengage Learning, Mason
Hill R, Myatt A (2007) Overemphasis on perfectly competitive markets in microeconomics principles textbooks. J Econ Educ 38(1):58–77
Hubbard RG, O'Brien A (2017) Economics, 6th edn. Prentice Hall, Upper Saddle River
Kent C, Rushing FW (1999) Coverage of entrepreneurship in principles of economics textbooks: an update. J Econ Educ 30(2):184–188
Krugman P, Wells R (2018) Economics, 5th edn. Worth publishers, New York
Lee DY (1992) Internationalizing the principles of economics course: a survey of textbooks. J Econ Educ 23(1):79–88
Levy D, Peart S (2011) Soviet growth and American textbooks. J Econ Behav Organ 78(1–2):110–125
Lopus JS, Leet DR (2007) Ten observations on high school economics textbooks. Citizenship Soc Econ Educ 7(3):201–214
Lopus JS, Paringer L, Leet DR (2008) The treatment of the role of government in high school economics textbooks. J Private Enterprise 24(1):155–163
Mankiw NG (2018) Principles of economics, 8th edn. South-Western Cengage Learning, Mason
McConnell CR, Brue SL, Flynn SM (2018) Economics: principles, problems & policies, 21st edn. McGraw-Hill Irwin, New York
McEachern WA (2017) Economics: a contemporary introduction, 11th edn. South-Western Cengage Learning, Mason
Miller L (2018) Economics today, 19th edn. Prentice Hall, Upper Saddle River
Phipps BJ, Strom RJ, Baumol WJ (2012) Principles of economics without the Prince of Denmark. J Econ Educ 43(1):58–71
Siegfried J, Krueger A, Collins S, Frank R, MacDonald R, McGoldrick K, Taylor J, Vredeveld G (2010) Voluntary national content standards in economics, 2nd edn. Council for Economic Education, New York

Chapter 8
University and High School Economics Educators Partnership: A Model from La Crosse, Wisconsin

Adam Hoffer and Andrew Beckstrom

Abstract This paper presents a case study detailing the formation of a partnership between university and high school economics educators. We found that local high school economics teachers craved the specialized knowledge possessed by university economics faculty. Through a simple partnership consisting of face-to-face meetings, emails, and a one-day conference, the economics faculty provided valuable insight to help improve the high school economics curriculum. The university faculty hope to see better-educated and more interested economics students as those high school students enter college.

8.1 Introduction

Collegiate instructors have a vested interest in high school pedagogy. Students who are poorly taught or bored by a subject in high school will be less encouraged to take that course in college. Students receiving AP credit, thus skipping the principles-level college courses, are expected to bring that principles-level knowledge forward when taking higher-level courses within the discipline. Collegiate faculty are, thus, affected by the pedagogical choices made by instructors earlier in the student educational pipeline.

This fact is not new to college faculty. However, high school (and earlier) pedagogy receives little academic discussion, and even less academic research, in most fields. Much of the academic publications focused on university—high school partnerships are more than two decades old (Epstein 1995; Goodland 1993;

A. Hoffer (✉)
University of Wisconsin-La Crosse, La Crosse, WI, USA
e-mail: ahoffer@uwlax.edu

A. Beckstrom
Onalaska High School, Onalaska, WI, USA
e-mail: becan@onalaskaschools.com

J. Hall, K. Lawson (eds.), *Teaching Economics*,
https://doi.org/10.1007/978-3-030-20696-3_8

Richmond 1996). The few that exist within the field of economics do not specifically address economics pedagogy (Castleman and Page 2015; Castleman et al. 2015; Arnold et al. 2015).[1]

This paper presents a case study and replicable model for a partnership between university and high school economics educators. The goals of the partnership were straightforward. The college faculty wanted to provide insight into the high school curriculum, hoping to encourage greater interest and student learning; ideally, those students would then feed students into the university courses. The high school faculty wanted classes that were more engaging and more in-touch with real-world events and policies; the high school faculty could tap into the wealth of knowledge and experience possessed by the university faculty to improve their classes.

The case study presented below provides examples specifically pertaining to the economics curriculum, but model can be easily adapted to another field. The primary takeaway from the first year of the partnership between university and high school faculty was that there were significant gains from exchange for both parties at very low monetary and time costs.

8.2 Motivation

Twenty states currently mandate that high school students complete an economics course prior to graduating (Council for Economic Education 2016). In part due to the efforts of the Council for Economic Education (CEE) and their now 200 national affiliates—state councils and university centers for economic education—the importance of economic education is becoming more widely recognized.

Pedagogically, most high school economics curriculum caters to the AP economics exam. While the AP economics exam achieves its goals of (1) being easy to score, using multiple choice questions, and (2) covers most of the topics covered in a typical collegiate principles course, the AP test promotes the exact ritualistic and memorization-based pedagogy from which collegiate economics is moving away (Rousu et al. 2015; Holder et al. 2015; Hoffer 2015). The result is often a dismal high school course that self-fulfills economics' nickname, "the dismal science."

Further, high school economics teachers usually have little training in economics and even less training in economics pedagogy. College economics majors rarely become high school teachers. Teaching majors rarely specialize in economics; many never take an economics course their entire college career.

High school economics courses typically fall under the umbrella of social studies, and are therefore taught by a social studies teacher—an individual who may specialize in fields ranging from history to cultural studies. These are not the individuals we would expect to have a specialty or well-developed background in

[1] A growing body of literature describes community, school, and university partnerships for financial education and literacy (Hagedon et al. 2016).

economics. We provide an anecdotal example by describing the background of the high school economics teacher with whom we partnered.

8.3 High School Teacher Background

I (Andrew Beckstrom) teach Economics and AP Microeconomics in La Crosse, WI. I have been teaching Economics for 4 years now and my first year teaching I identified an issue that I had with being an Economics teacher; I wanted (and needed) to learn more!

My background in economics and teaching is as follows. I graduated from the University of Wisconsin–Eau Claire in 2004 with a teaching certification and dual major in Spanish and history. I took both principles of microeconomics and macroeconomics in my undergraduate education. I taught full time as a Spanish teacher at River Falls High School from 2004 to 2005. I then moved to Sparta High School to teach Spanish until 2011 and then to Onalaska High School—my current employer—where I still teach Spanish.

Prior to the 2013 school year, I took and passed the Economics Praxis, certifying me to teach any economics course in grades 6–12 (I already had a certification in teaching social studies due to my history major and undergraduate education). I now have an even split of my teaching responsibilities between economics classes and Spanish classes.

There are many topics that I needed to learn more about in the field of Economics to make the class "real" and "meaningful" for my students. Whether it is health care, education, taxes, fiscal policy, the environment, minimum wage, government intervention, etc., I carried into class a basic economic understanding but I wanted more. To fill this gap I read, watched documentaries, and had local professionals come into my class and present where I would learn along with my students.

In 2015, I had a UW-La Crosse education major that was interested in teaching economics. I agreed to allow him to student teach in my class. He introduced me to many things his economics professor and research advisor (same person—the author of this manuscript) was teaching him. I became much more interested and contacted the economics department in the Fall of 2016 to set up a meeting and hold a question and answer session. As I met and worked with the UW-La Crosse faculty, I discovered that they had an extremely deep understanding of the issues I wanted to educate myself on and that they were also willing to share their knowledge and help.

We then organized the Coulee Region Economics Conference to share these ideas with a larger audience. We brought ten high school teachers from the region to interact with the UW-La Crosse faculty and develop better pedagogy for our high school classes.

8.4 University—High School Partnership

In 2016 we (Hoffer and Beckstrom) launched a partnership between the economics department at the University of Wisconsin–La Crosse and local economics high school teachers. The first year of the partnership consisted of (1) an on-campus meeting, (2) a series of email/forum exchanges, (3) a one-day conference, and (4) a series of individual follow-up meeting.

The initial on-campus meeting was geared toward broad-ranging pedagogy and economic philosophy. The initial meeting was also an opportunity for real-time questions and answers and two-way feedback on goals and learning outcomes. The meeting was held on-campus to facilitate attendance from many university faculty.

Following the on-campus meeting, the high school teacher had several questions and areas in which he wanted more examples or greater depth. Email exchange was the best means of facilitating conversation and sharing of examples, notes, and ideas. At the end of this section, we provide a slightly edited and formatted version of an email exchange between the two of us that arose from this conference/partnership. There were other such exchanges between high school teachers and faculty as well.

Expanding to high school teachers in the region, we held a one-day conference at the local high school. The agenda for the conference is listed below. The goals of the conference were to (1) introduce more high school teachers to the university faculty and (2) provide pedagogy examples from the university faculty to the high school teachers. The conference schedule was:

Coulee Region Economics Conference Schedule

Where: Onalaska High School

7:45 – Registration (Coffee and Muffins provided)

8:00 – Dr. Donna Anderson (UW-L) – Economics of Sex, Race and Ethnicity

9:00 – Dr. Adam Hoffer (UW-L) – Sports Economics

10:00 – Dr. Al Gedicks (UW-L) – Metallic Sulfide Mining in Wisconsin

11:00 – Lunch and Best Practice Share (Sandwiches, Chips, Fruit and Cookies provided)

12:30 – Dr. John Nunley (UW-L) – Labor Economics

1:30 – Dr. Nabamita Dutta (UW-L) – International Economics/Economic Development

8.5 Q&A Email Exchange on Political Economy

Note: H denotes High School Teacher (Beckstrom) and U denotes University Professor (Hoffer)

H: What do you think of my overarching goal for the course: Upon completion of this course will you be able to pick up a newspaper, read an article and think like an economist? My goal is that the students will be able to do so.

U: I think most of us would agree that getting our students to 'think like an economist' is our primary goal. Teaching this is difficult and broad assessment may be even more challenging. We focus on 'critical thinking' within specific learning objectives. I like to think, can my student explain why economists agree that trade is good. They can still disagree as long as they can explain why economists think trade is good.

H: The essential question that I have for the "types of economies" unit is: "To what extent does 'the invisible hand' rule the US economy? To what extent does it rule other world economies? How do I attempt to teach this?"

U: Again, this is complex, but I like what you are doing here. Anecdotally, this is how I phrase it when I teach:

The goal of economics is to make the best use of our scarce resources. How do we do that? Hayek, Friedman, and Adam Smith provide some of the clearest answers. The field of economics was launched by Adam Smith attempting to answer a single question: Why are some countries wealthy(ier) and other countries poor(er). It turns out the answer Smith found in 1776 is the same answer that holds true today. Some countries use economics, enforce property rights, and use markets more than other countries. Yes, it is that simple. The Economic Freedom of the World Index (EFW) is a perfect insert here.[2]

The EFW measures the extent to which basic economic principles are used across the globe. 50 years ago the "types of economies" question would have been talked about differently: which works best: communism, socialism, or capitalism. By 1989, the answer was definitive. Capitalism – letting individual people make economic decisions rather than a central government – won. Using Heritage's Economic Freedom Index: the least capitalistic countries in 2015 were North Korea, Iran, and Venezuela (Miller and Kim 2015). The US is still top 20 (but falling). [Note: you can prod some interesting thoughts and discussions here. Anyone want to move to Venezuela? The Venezuelan government controls prices. Venezuelan shortages now have their own wikipedia page (food, clothing, toilet paper, you name it.) "Packs of Condoms in Venezuela Now Cost $755. Venezuela's faltering economy is so out of control that a pack of 36 condoms now costs close to the monthly minimum wage, and even then they're difficult to find" (Regan 2015).

H: When I talk about government and economics, this is what I do and where I am looking for some advice. Step 1 – First I use the Heritage Index of Economic Freedom (IEF) website. I look at how and why the countries got their ranking. Why did North Korea get a 1? Why did Cuba get a 29? Why did France get a 65? US a 79? In my estimation this is one of the most important concepts for a high school student to understand because it shows them how the government influences our lives. Step 2 – This is where I teach about the public good and why it's created. My thinking is that it makes sense here because to a certain extent an economy that is less free on the heritage.org website might offer more public goods. Of course that can vary. Step 3 – Why does the US get the ranking it has? What are specific examples of how the US is pulled closer to 0 on this scale? How is the US pulled toward 100?

U: I like the focus on the US. I would grab the latest report and see what the authors say about the US's change in rank. I think the biggest recent decline was due to a decline in the Sound Value of Money category. Quantitative Easing I-III really hurt.

H: Things that decrease the US's Economic Freedom score:

- The Corn Market – The government has interfered with the corn market. It has provided subsidies to farmers to promote the corn industry that wouldn't be as strong without its help. In doing so it has helped corn farmers in Iowa but hurt shrimp fishermen in Louisiana (because of the pesticide run off). It has reduced the % of money that we (US consumers) spend on food so we can buy more of other things but it has made a less healthy food supply because this makes our meat more high in fat and we have

[2]The Economic Freedom of the World report referred to here is Gwartney et al. (2018). There are two indexes of Economic Freedom, the other is Miller and Kim (2015).

more high sugar foods and drinks because high fructose corn syrup is cheaper. This also contributes to higher obesity and diabetes and consequently health care costs.

- Epipen – The US government has made a decision to allow Epipen to be a monopoly. By interfering in this market it has promoted innovation, research and everything that went into the creation of the Epipen therefore providing more incentive for future innovation but has hurt consumers of the Epipen to a certain extent as they will pay a higher price.
- GM Bailout – The government interfered with the invisible hand here by keeping GM afloat. Without government intervention GM may have sank. It kept more jobs in the US possibly but it interfered with the forces of the free market.
- Not participating in the TPP – Should the US not expand free trade to the countries in the TPP it would reduce the power of the economy to provide its consumers with the maximum amount of goods and services possible and reduce markets available for domestic companies. Adam Smith wouldn't like that.
- Minimum Wage – By not making wages fully 'Darwinian' the US government is doing something that has a social and political benefit (not saying it's the 'best' idea but there are arguments for it) but interferes with the invisible hand.

Things that increase the US's Economic Freedom Score

- NAFTA – The opposite of what I wrote with the TPP
- Garbage Removal in Onalaska – Most countries in Europe, for example, have government contracted garbage removal. In essence this price and service is controlled by the government. In Onalaska (and the US) the garbage removal service is decided on by multiple companies bidding and local officials deciding on what's best. So there is still government control here but it has to pass through what I call an 'invisible hand filter'.
- Lower Taxes – I don't know if this is the best way to approach this but the idea that some businesses want "the government to get out of the way" "less taxes" "less regulation."
- Less Regulation – On Twitter I've seen the hashtag #BetterWay put out by conservatives that refers to how large our regulatory agencies are in the US. Trump boasting about how he's avoided paying taxes. The example I have brought up is the FDA to counter this idea. Would you want to eat steak if the same meat regulations were in place today as were in 1900?

U: Ok, so there is A LOT there. I would focus on the simple, marginal changes. The corn subsidies are clear. The taxes and trade agreements are clear. I would probably leave it at that (plus whatever new things are in the most recent report).

H: Step 4 – Get examples from other countries and their scope of government. For example, when I lived in Costa Rica about every third day this road would flood because of the terrible drainage system they had. These 2 stores would have to shut down because no one could get to them. Or bigger examples like how is health care different in the US vs Canada. Step 5 – Debate. This is where I indicated I'm kind of stuck. How do I turn this into something we can debate in class? How do I scale it down so it's manageable for high school students? Or, maybe the most important question ... is this an activity I should do? Maybe it's too big?

U: This is way too big and too broad. I wouldn't expect PhD economists to be able to debate on such a broad array of government policies and practices. I would really narrow it down. It is hard for students to 'see the unseen' and describe counterfactuals. Using your meat regulation example above, I would still consume meat if the production regulations hadn't changed since 1920. Why? If a meat producer made a bunch of people sick, people would stop buying their goods, maybe they would be sued, and their competitors would take over. Constantly we see innovation outpace regulation. I might limit the debate to trade deals or issues that students can more fully grasp.

H: Is there anything else I can add into my class to make it more exciting?

U: Here is a link to a fun economics project: www.rockonomix.com. I will be assigning the project for my college students, but the first high school competition occurred this past spring. The website should have all the basic information, but I would be happy to talk about more details later if you like.

8.6 Conclusion

Fundamental economics tells us that producers will only find success if they supply what is demanded; local information is often possessed only by local individuals; and specialization and exchange facilitate gains from trade to all voluntary participants. We applied these basic tenants to create a partnership between local university and high school economics educators.

Our local high school teachers craved information on public policy and economic applicability. That information was bountifully supplied in a university hallway located only a few miles from the teachers who demanded access to that knowledge. Despite more than a century of close geographical coexistence, no formal partnership evolved until last year.

As university economics faculty, we were happy to supply low-cost information on our fields of specialization to local high school teachers who could then use that information to better-educate the early pipeline economics students. In exchange, we hope to observe better-educated students and potentially attract more students to our college program.

Attracting more and better-educated students would not only grant us higher preference for scarce university budget funding, but it would also allow us to pass along even better students to employers or graduate programs further along in the pipeline.

References

Arnold KD, Soto EB, Wartman KL, Methven L, Brown PG (2015) Post-secondary outcomes of innovative high schools: the big picture longitudinal study. Boston College Department of Education, Mimeo

Castleman BL, Page LC (2015) Summer nudging: can personalized text messages and peer mentor outreach increase college going among low-income high school graduates? J Econ Behav Organ 115(1):144–160

Castleman BL, Owen L, Page LC (2015) Stay late or start early? Experimental evidence on the benefits of college matriculation support from high schools versus colleges. Econ Educ Rev 47(1):168–179

Council for Economic Education (2016) Survey of the states: economic and personal finance education in our nation's schools. Council for Economic Education, New York

Epstein JL (1995) School/family/community partnerships. Phi Delta Kappan 76(9):701

Goodland JI (1993) School-university partnerships and partner schools. Educ Policy 7(1):24–39

Gwartney J, Lawson R, Hall J (2018) Economic freedom of the world: 2018 annual report. Fraser Institute, Vancouver
Hagedon EA, Schug MC, Suiter M (2016) A collaborative approach to financial literacy in the Chicago public schools. J Private Enterprise 31(1):79–90
Hoffer A (2015) A classroom game to teach the principles of money and banking. Cogent Econ Finance 3(1):1–13
Holder K, Hoffer A, Al-Bahrani A, Lindahl S (2015) Rockonomix. J Econ Educ 46(3):443
Miller T, Kim AB (2015) 2015 Index of economic freedom. The Heritage Foundation, Washington
Regan H (2015) A 36-pack of condoms in Venezuela now costs $755 at official rates. Time. 5 February
Richmond G (1996) University/school partnerships: bridging the culture gap. Theory Into Pract 35(3):214–218
Rousu MC, Corrigan JR, Harris D, Hayter JK, Houser S, Lafrancois BA, Onafowora O, Colson G, Hoffer A (2015) Do monetary incentives matter in classroom experiments? Effects on course performance. J Econ Educ 46(4):341–349

Chapter 9
A Classroom Experiment: The Redistribution of Quiz Scores

Gordon Smith

Abstract Taking the lead from a news story that circulated through the Internet regarding a classroom experiment on socialism, a similar set of experiments were run using quiz scores. In this set of experiments, quiz scores were redistributed in two ways. The first method was to redistribute the scores across the entire classroom. The second method was to redistribute the scores across two different quizzes. Before the experiment, students were asked for their opinion regarding financial redistribution within society in general. After the experiment, students were asked for their opinion regarding grade redistribution within the classroom. The experiments were broadly designed to gauge opinions regarding redistribution and the effect of the saliency of the good on those opinions. With 2 years of data, preliminary results are mixed. The results from the first year of the experiment indicated that students were significantly less willing to redistribute grades than they were financial resources. However, that was not the case for the second year. In fact, for this group of students, they were more willing to redistribute grades than financial resources. This reversal in results has created an opportunity to extend the experiment to additional quizzes through the end of the semester.

9.1 Introduction

On several occasions, a story has popped up regarding a classroom experiment in which the professor gave the students an opportunity to experience, in a tangible way, the rewards and consequences of a socialist-type system (Dupree 2014; O'Dea 2016). In the experiment, the professor agreed to give each student the same grade based on the average for the class. After the first test, the higher performing students were upset because their individual efforts were not fully rewarded. The grade they received as part of the class was lower than the grade they achieved on the

G. Smith (✉)
Anderson University, Anderson, SC, USA
e-mail: gsmith@andersonuniversity.edu

J. Hall, K. Lawson (eds.), *Teaching Economics*,
https://doi.org/10.1007/978-3-030-20696-3_9

test. However, the lower performing students were happier with the outcome, as their overall class grade was higher than what they had achieved on the test. After the second test, the overall class average was much lower. The higher performing students invested little effort in trying to improve their scores since they did not receive the full value of their work. The lower performing students, seeing the value they had initially gained from the higher performing students on the previous test, also invested less effort than they had on the first test. By the time the third test was complete, the average for the class had sunk to the lowest grade possible, and remained there until the end of the course.

Regardless of whether the story is true or not, it does provide a basis for determining students' opinions regarding the redistribution of things of value (Snopes 2016). The story focuses on grades as a substitute for money. The implied assumption is that students identify both money and grades as having value, but in general, only one of them is truly "owned" by the student; grades. In this context, the redistribution of quiz scores was designed as an experiment to test, in general terms, whether or not the assumed saliency or ownership of an item had an impact on students overall feelings regarding the redistribution of that item.

9.2 Literature Review

Though the research on classroom experiments is extensive, the research on classroom experiments to measure student's opinions regarding income redistribution is more limited. Durante et al. (2014) ran a laboratory experiment to determine individuals' preferences for redistribution based on the sources of income (earned or unearned) and the level of participation in the experiment (active participant or observer). They found some level of redistribution is desired, but the desire was impacted by whether or not the individual earned the income or was given the income through some distributional mechanism. In addition, they found that individuals' preferences for redistribution were impacted by the rules determining the initial distribution based on effort. The more random the distribution (the less control the individual had over the rules that determined the initial distribution by effort), the more in favor of redistribution. Assandri et al. (2017) followed up with a similar experiment which looked at the effects of risk preferences on the desire for income redistribution. They found the more risk averse an individual, the more in favor they were for income redistribution.

Unfortunately, research on classroom experiments used to determine student's opinions on grade redistribution is virtually nonexistent. Many reasons have been debated as to why this is the case (Hanson 2011; McArdle 2011); however, if the experiment could be designed to elicit negligible overall impact on a student's grade, while at the same time produce an immediate sense of the consequences of the actions being taken, then the experiment could have value in determining the reactions of the students to the experiment. Such was the case in the design of this experiment.

9.3 Details of the Experiment

The general design of the experiment was to measure students' responses to the redistribution of wealth, or value (quiz scores), within an economy (the classroom). The experiment was divided up into two separate redistribution designs. The first experiment redistributed scores across all students in the classroom. In this context, the experiment looked at the redistribution of wealth within an economy. The second experiment redistributed scores across two separate quizzes. In this context, the experiment looked at the redistribution of wealth across time.

9.3.1 The First Experiment: The Fairness/Equity Quiz

For the Fairness/Equity quiz, before the quiz was distributed, students were told the quiz was unique in that the average score of the class would be applied to every student's grade. The quiz itself was an objective, content-related quiz. The quiz was worth a total of five points and contained five multiple-choice questions. There were no questions on the quiz regarding income or grade redistribution.

The quiz before the first experimental quiz, students were given a 1-point extra credit opportunity (to be applied to their current quiz). The extra credit was a question regarding the redistribution of income within the U.S. economy. The question was an opinion question, but was phrased in four slightly different ways. The two answer choices were "in favor of" or "opposed to."

I am ______ the government redistributing income to those at or below the poverty level ($24,600 for a family of four).

I am ______ the government redistributing my income to those at or below the poverty level ($24,600 for a family of four).

I am ______ the government redistributing income to those at or below the poverty level ($24,600 for a family of four) in order to create greater financial equity in our society.

I am ______ the government redistributing my income to those at or below the poverty level ($24,600 for a family of four) in order to create greater financial equity in our society.

The unique form of the question was randomly distributed within the class. The aim of the question was to determine if students' opinions would vary based on the way the question of the redistribution of income was phrased. The 2016 results are presented in Table 9.1 and the 2017 results in Table 9.2.

Table 9.1 First experiment 2016

Question		In favor of	Opposed to
A	I am ______ the government redistributing income to those at or below the poverty level ($24,600 for a family of four)	9	8
B	I am ______ the government redistributing my income to those at or below the poverty level ($24,600 for a family of four)	4	13
C	I am ______ the government redistributing income to those at or below the poverty level ($24,600 for a family of four) in order to create greater financial equity in our society	4	14
D	I am ______ the government redistributing my income to those at or below the poverty level ($24,600 for a family of four) in order to create greater financial equity in our society	8	8

Table 9.2 First experiment 2017

Question		In favor of	Opposed to
A	I am ______ the government redistributing income to those at or below the poverty level ($24,600 for a family of four)	3	15
B	I am ______ the government redistributing my income to those at or below the poverty level ($24,600 for a family of four)	3	13
C	I am ______ the government redistributing income to those at or below the poverty level ($24,600 for a family of four) in order to create greater financial equity in our society	4	13
D	I am ______ the government redistributing my income to those at or below the poverty level ($24,600 for a family of four) in order to create greater financial equity in our society	0	16

9.3.2 *The Second Experiment: Receive Now/Pay Later Quiz*

For the Receive Now/Pay Later quiz, students were once again told before the quiz was distributed that the quiz was unique. In this case, everyone taking the quiz would receive a score of 90% (4.5 out of 5) regardless of the true score they received on the quiz. However, the degree to which they individually fell short of 90% on their quiz was the amount (number of points) they would have to make up on the next quiz. This quiz and the proceeding were also objective, content-related, multiple-choice quizzes with no questions regarding income or grade redistribution.

For the last quiz in which the students' had to make up the point differential between their true score and the 90% score they were automatically given, a 1-point extra credit opportunity was also provided. The extra credit was similar to the previous extra credit opportunity, except for the fact that two questions were posed instead of one. The first of the two questions was phrased in four slightly different ways. The two answer choices were "in favor of" or "opposed to."

I am _____ Professor Smith redistributing points in the class to those students at or below a passing grade (70).

I am _____ Professor Smith redistributing my points in the class to those students at or below a passing grade (70).

I am _____ Professor Smith redistributing points in the class to those students at or below a passing grade (70) in order to create greater equity in the class.

I am _____ Professor Smith redistributing my points in the class to those students at or below a passing grade (70) in order to create greater equity in the class.

Once again, the uniqueness of the question was randomly distributed within the class with the aim of determining if students' opinions would vary based on the way the question regarding the redistribution of grades was phrased. The results from this second experiment in 2016 can be found in Table 9.3 and 2017 can be found in Table 9.4.

Finally, an additional question was asked in connection to the second experiment. The students were asked for their preference in terms of the two quizzes: "Of the two

Table 9.3 Second experiment 2016

Question		In favor of	Opposed to
A	I am _____ Professor Smith redistributing points in the class to those students at or below a passing grade (70)	3	15
B	I am _____ Professor Smith redistributing my points in the class to those students at or below a passing grade (70)	1	16
C	I am _____ Professor Smith redistributing points in the class to those students at or below a passing grade (70) in order to create greater equity in the class	2	14
D	I am _____ Professor Smith redistributing my points in the class to those students at or below a passing grade (70) in order to create greater equity in the class	2	15

Table 9.4 Second experiment 2017

Question		In favor of	Opposed to
A	I am _____ Professor Smith redistributing points in the class to those students at or below a passing grade (70)	4	13
B	I am _____ Professor Smith redistributing my points in the class to those students at or below a passing grade (70)	2	12
C	I am _____ Professor Smith redistributing points in the class to those students at or below a passing grade (70) in order to create greater equity in the class	5	12
D	I am _____ Professor Smith redistributing my points in the class to those students at or below a passing grade (70) in order to create greater equity in the class	2	12

Table 9.5 Quiz preference 2016

F/E	RN/PL	Both	Neither
9	3	5	51

Table 9.6 Quiz preference 2017

F/E	RN/PL	Both	Neither
15	3	1	43

special quizzes (Fairness/Equity quiz and the Receive Now/Pay Later quiz), I most prefer the following." The answer choices were "The Fairness/Equity quiz," "The Receive Now/Pay Later quiz," "Both quizzes," "Neither quiz." The 2016 results are in Table 9.5 and the 2017 results in Table 9.6.

9.4 Statistical Tests

Three tests were run on the data. The first test was a paired dependent sample test to determine if there was a statistical difference in the response rates on similar questions (A, B, C, and D) between the first and second experiment. The response rates were calculated as the percentage of "in favor of" responses from the total number of responses provided. For 2016, the computed t-statistic was 3.6358 with a p-value of 0.0359. For 2017, the computed t-statistic was -1.4632 with a p-value of 0.2396. Based on these results, 2016 indicated a statistical difference between the average response rates, while 2017 indicated no statistical difference. A one-tailed test on the 2016 data indicated a statistically lower "in favor of" response rate between the first and second experiment at the 0.05 level of significance. In this case, students were more in favor of redistributing income than redistributing points.

The second test was a paired dependent sample test to determine if there was a statistical difference in the response rates on similar questions for each of the two experiments between 2016 and 2017. For the first experiment, the computed t-statistic was 1.8185 with a p-value of 0.2468. For the second experiment, the computed t-statistic was -2.8773 with a p-value of 0.0603. Based on these results, the first experiment indicated no statistical difference in the average response rate, while the second experiment did indicate a statistical difference. A first glance, this seems a little unusual given the large decline in favorable response rates for questions A and D, but these differences were offset by similar response rates for questions B and C. For the second experiment, the rate of favorable responses increased for all four questions between the 2 years, confirmed by a statistically significant one-tailed test on greater favorable responses at the 0.05 significance level.

The third experiment was a paired dependent sample test to determine if there was a statistical difference in quiz preferences between 2016 and 2017. The four preferences were Fairness/Equity (F/E), Receive Now/Pay Later (RN/PL), Both types (Both), and Neither type (Neither). The computed t-statistic was zero, indicating no statistical difference on the average preference for type between the 2 years. By a large majority, students preferred neither one of the two quizzes, but the slight drop-off in this preference between 2016 and 2017 was made up for by the slight increase in preference for the Fairness/Equity quiz.

9.5 Conclusion

In general, the group of students surveyed for this experiment was fairly conservative, so the results are not too surprising. The overall desire for redistribution was predominantly in the minority. However, the trends between the 2 years of the experiment were interesting. For the 2016 group, there is a significantly less favorable attitude towards redistribution after the experiment than before the experiment. This was not the case for the 2017 group. This was true both across years and across questions. The experiment itself seemed to have a greater impact in terms of a general dislike for redistribution on the 2016 group, but a greater impact for acceptance or approval on the 2017 group. It will be interesting to see in what direction the trends move in the future. As the idea of socialism and shared outcomes gains a wider audience both in our undergraduate institutions and in society in general, one would expect a greater impact on students' opinions as it regards redistribution and a greater willingness to engage and promote redistribution even as it regards those items which are more salient in nature, such as grades.

References

Assandri M, Maffioletti A, Piacenza M, Turati G (2017) Risk attitudes and preferences for redistribution: New evidence from the lab. CESifo Econ Stud 64(3):489–515

Dupree W (2014) This teacher rocks! entire class fails when Obama's socialism experiment fail. www.teapartytribune.com. 11 January

Durante R, Putterman L, van deer Weele J (2014) Preferences for redistribution and perception of fairness: an experimental study. J Eur Econ Assoc 12(4):1059–1086

Hanson R (2011) Natural hypocrisy. http://www.overcomingbias.com/. 26 April

McArdle M (2011) Should we redistribute grades like we do income? www.theatlantic.com. 4 May

O'Dea D (2016) Letter: socialism gets failing grade. www.nwfdailynews.com. 3 February

Snopes (2016) Fact check: socialism grade averaging. https://www.snopes.com/. 15 August

Chapter 10
Making Economics Stick with Econ Beats

Abdullah Al-Bahrani and Leith Thompson

Abstract Economic educators interested in incorporating project-based learning can incorporate Econ Beats in their classrooms. Using student reported measures of learning we evaluate students' perception of the efficacy of Econ Beats, a project that requires students to remake popular music into economic terms. The project is also a team-based learning exercise. Our data includes 275 students at the college level and 90 students at the high school level. Students report that they are excited to work on Econ Beats at rates higher than other group projects. Students report that they enjoyed the project and learned economic concepts and definitions. Educators considering active learning or incorporating a transdisciplinary approach to teaching economics can implement Econ Beats.

10.1 Introduction

The goal for introductory courses is to help students develop and retain knowledge in economics. However, retention of economic concepts is limited (Walstad and Allgood 1999). The goal of these courses is for students to be able to apply basic economic concepts years later (Salemi 2005). On average, business students that took a Principles of Economics course score 62% on the economics portion of the exit senior exams (Allgood et al. 2015). Increasing student knowledge and retention of economic concepts has been a focus for economic educators since Becker and Watts (1996) highlighted the limitation in teaching economics. To date, economic educators have used varied teaching methods in hopes of attracting more students, engaging them in and out of class, and finally to increase economic literacy and concept retention. They have used active learning (Hoyt 2003), technology (Elliot

A. Al-Bahrani (✉)
Northern Kentucky University, Highland Heights, KY, USA
e-mail: albahrania1@nku.edu

L. Thompson
Burwood Girls High School, Croydon, NSW, Australia
e-mail: leith.thompson4@det.nsw.edu.au

J. Hall, K. Lawson (eds.), *Teaching Economics*,
https://doi.org/10.1007/978-3-030-20696-3_10

2003), cooperative learning (Deerfield 2018; Emerson and Taylor 2004; Odell 2018; Imazeki 2015; McGoldrick 2012), and other forms of interdisciplinary teaching (Al-Bahrani et al. 2017a; Holder et al. 2015).

In this paper, we evaluate the student reported measure of learning during a semester-long student project called Econ Beats.[1] The student project proposed in Al-Bahrani et al. (2017a) uses project-based learning, music, interdisciplinary collaboration, and team-based learning to help students learn economic language and concepts. The project is designed to help develop students' soft skills, leverages music to help teach economic concepts and language, and to increase engagement in economic courses. We use a pre-survey to measure students' excitement to participate in the non-traditional assignment and a post-survey is distributed to measure the change in student views. The surveys are approved by the Institutional Review Board (IRB). We report the results in aggregate to comply with IRB reporting requirements. The success of Econ Beats at the college level has increased interest in applying the project at the high school level. We also provide information on how involved high school students perceived the project. We find that college level students are more excited to work on Econ Beats when compared to other group projects, and that the benefits of the project are apparent to them even before they begin the work. At the end of the project, students report that the project did improve their ability to learn economic concepts and definitions. They report enjoyment from working on the project and willingness to working with their groups.

10.2 Literature

To improve student retention of economics and to increase literacy, Salemi (2005) and Hansen et al. (2002) propose a "less is more" approach to principle level courses. The authors suggest that principle level courses have become more complex and include more topics than optimal. To increase "stickiness" they suggest reducing the content and focusing educational efforts towards a smaller subset of concepts. The difficulty in this approach is that educators rarely agree on which topics to use (Frank 1998). Consequently, we have not seen a reduction in the concepts covered, but an increase. Educators at the principle level course remain puzzled on best practices to boost student learning. Teaching methods have begun to move away from the traditional "Chalk and Talk" approach that economics education was historically fond of (Becker and Watts 1996), thus creating an evolution of active learning (Buckles and Hoyt 2006) such as cooperative learning (McGoldrick 2012). Think-Pair-Share or Flipped Classrooms (Roach 2014) have helped increase retention of concepts. Other new teaching methods have simply developed due to increased use of and advances in technology.

[1]For examples of the assignment visit www.econbeats.com.

Team-based learning (TBL) has also received some attention due to its impact on student outcomes. Imazeki (2015) delivers tips on how to introduce team-based learning into classes and provides evidence that TBL increases student engagement. Odell (2018) finds that TBL incorporation in economics courses increases grades, engagement, and over all interest in economics. Emerson and Taylor (2004) find that cooperative learning has a positive effect on student learning. The design of Econ Beats as an assignment leverages cooperative learning and team-based learning to enhance the educational experience.

Our current students are "digital natives" and welcome projects that use digital equipment and technology (Welch and Bonnan-White 2012). Educators looking to increase the connection to material need to leverage the tools and environments that the current generation embraces (Al-Bahrani et al. 2016). We should therefore expect that the use of digital media, social media, and music will create a better connection between students and the content that they are learning (Al-Bahrani et al. 2017b), thus increasing student retention of information and learning outcomes. There has been an increase in the use of these innovative tools since Becker and Watts (1996) criticized economists for the deficiency in variety of teaching methods. However, efforts to measure efficacy of the newly introduced teaching methods are limited, mainly due to the difficulty of educational experimental design (Al-Bahrani et al. 2017a). Even in our research we must resort to student evaluation of the project using pre- and post-surveys to measure student engagement with the project. We recognize that the limitations to using student evaluations as a measure of student learning have been well documented and must be considered (Uttl et al. 2017). However, we believe that student evaluations of teaching and instruction can provide valuable information on classroom environment and culture. By asking students directly we can measure how the project empowered students' learning (Levy-Feldman and Libman 2017).

10.3 The Project

The Econ Beats assignment requires students to remake a popular song into economic terms. Al-Bahrani et al. (2017a) provide a detailed description of the assignment design and include a rubric to help educators incorporate the assignment into their classes. To summarize, the assignment is a semester-long, team-based project where students work to produce a music video highlighting their understanding of economic concepts. Students are evaluated on the economic content, the creativity of the storyline, the video production, and audio quality. The project concludes with a public screening and voting by the audience for the best video. The screening of all videos is the highpoint of the semester and is the first time that all students see each other's projects. To incentivize effort and generate excitement, the winning team receives a cash prize. The website www.econbeats.com provides examples of previous submissions and the winners from each semester.

10.4 Student Self-reported Experience

We collected data from five semesters of Principles of Macroeconomics and Microeconomics courses which culminated to a total of 275 enrolled students. The Econ Beats assignment was administered in all classes. Students were informed of the project during the first day of class and the grading requirements were included in the syllabus. The pre-survey was administered during the class period after the drop-add week. Thus, it is possible that students who did not want to participate in the assignment dropped the course before they took the survey. Consequently, the results might be biased in favor of the assignment; however, we also cannot surmise probability of withdraw reasoning.

The pre-survey amassed data on student's majors, enrolled semester hours, and asked a set of questions to determine their perception of the assignment. Since Econ Beats is a non-traditional assignment, and is innovative in its union of music, audio, video, and economics, we were interested in capturing students' view on this assignment. Table 10.1 reports student answers to the pre-survey questions about their perception. The response and opt-in rate to the pre-survey study was 67%.[2] Out of the students that participated in the study, roughly 91% of the students reported that they read and understood the Econ Beats guidelines. This is reassuring since the documentation was included with the syllabus, which educators assume goes unread. More important is the variation between Q2, Q3, and Q5. It was made clear to students that Econ Beats project requires students to work in groups made out of Economics students and students from Electronic Media and Broadcasting (EMB).

Table 10.2 reports the fraction of students that responded agree or strongly agree to questions 2, 3, and 5. Only 49% of the students said they either agree or strongly agree that they enjoy working in groups. However, 67% of the respondents said

Table 10.1 Pre-survey questions

Question	Strongly agree	Agree	Neither agree nor disagree	Disagree	Strongly disagree	*n*
I read and understand the Econ Beats guidelines	56	108	12	3	0	179
I am excited to work on the Econ Beats project	48	76	36	19	4	183
I am excited to work with students from other classes	40	69	57	14	3	183
I believe that the Econ Beats project will show how much I have learned this semester	38	86	42	13	4	183
I enjoy working in groups	21	69	57	24	12	183

[2]To fulfill IRB requirements, the survey was administered outside of class and through an anonymous online link.

Table 10.2 The fraction of respondents that answered agree or strongly agree

Question	Mean
I am excited to work on the Econ Beats project	0.678 (0.469)
I am excited to work with students from other classes	0.596 (0.492)
I enjoy working in groups	0.492 (0.501)

Standard deviation reported in parentheses

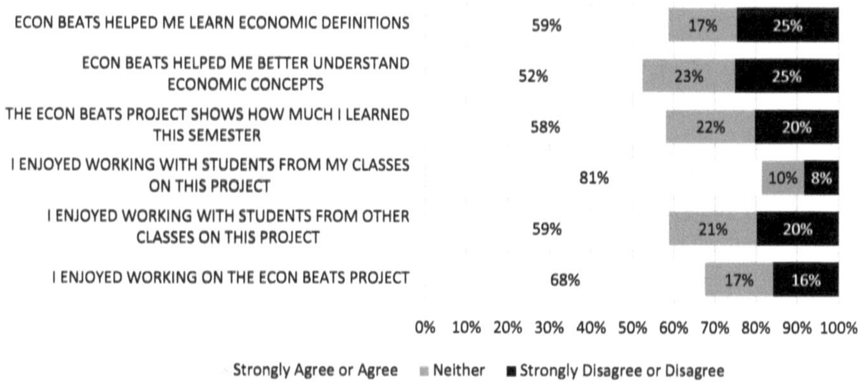

Fig. 10.1 Student response to the Econ Beats post-survey

they are excited to work on the Econ Beats project—implicit indication of positive anticipation to work with their economics group members—and 59% agreed or strongly agreed that they are excited to work with EMB students. The response to questions 2 and 5 highlights the difference in students' perception of Econ Beats relative to other group projects; they view Econ Beats more favorably, and the difference is statistically different. Thus, the design and directions provided to students appear to enhance motivation to work in groups within and across classes compared to group projects in general.

Assigning group projects can be difficult and does raise concerns among students of the free-rider problem. According to Brooks and Ammons (2003), projects that have the following features increase students' willingness to work in groups: (a) early implementation, (b) multiple evaluation points, and (c) specific evaluative criteria, all of which are part of the Econ Beats project. Finally, 68% of students went into the Econ Beats project believing that the project will be indicative of what they learned during the semester.

At the end of the semester, students were asked similar questions in the post-survey. Figure 10.1 reports the questions asked and the distribution of answers; 253 out of 275 students responded. The higher participation rate in the post-survey (92%) compared to the pre-survey (68%) is another measure of student engagement and interest in the class.

Experientially, 68% of students reported that they strongly agreed or agreed with the statement that they enjoyed the Econ Beats project. Students also enjoyed working with other members in their class, 83% of students reported that they strongly agreed or agreed with that statement. Considering absorption, students reported that their project represented what they learned during the semester, 58% and 52% reported that they strongly agree or agree with the statements that Econ Beats helped them better understand economic concepts and economic definitions, respectively.

10.5 The High School Extension

As part of a focus to encourage student engagement in senior high school Economic education in Australia, an Econ Beats trial was introduced in a 10 week "Our Economy-Commerce" introductory course at the junior high school level (14–15 years old). The trial was applied to 90 students. Thompson and Al-Bahrani (2018) provide detailed information on how Econ Beats was incorporated into the Australian High School curriculum.

Data on student engagement was not collected in previous years and therefore comparing student interest pre and post Econ Beats is difficult. Our personal experience is that student engagement and interest in this course was noticeably higher than in previous years. When issued the project, students were markedly more receptive to this assignment style relative to a traditional format of assessment for this type of content. One student was overheard relaying the assignment to another student who had been absent when the project was assigned, explaining "We have an assessment notification, but don't worry, it's a really fun task!"

Group sizes at the high school level were made smaller and, unlike with the college level assignment, time was given in class to work in their groups. In class instruction provided support to students who needed content support and other students who were "English as a Second Language" learners. Initially, ESL students were fairly reluctant upon receipt of the Econ Beats assignment; however, with teacher support during the lyric development phase, students in the end reported thorough enjoyment of the project. Music selected by these students also reflected their cultural background, creating a greater feeling of inclusion in the classroom for the students.

Econ Beats did experience some challenges in the high school classroom, including performance anxiety; concern over "free riders"; and some wariness about the true efficacy of the project. We believe this latter concern is rooted in the fact that learning is often invisible to students, especially if it is an enjoyable project. Again, as digital natives, the high school students showed no reluctance in using any of the required technology to complete the project. Although several students reported having to master new software to complete the task, they did not perceive this as detracting from their enjoyment of the activity. Econ Beats in this way provided valuable cross-curricular learning.

Initial reports from students were that the project was fun, unusual, and creative. After beginning work on the lyrics, students realized, however, that the project involved deeper learning. Students generally reflect that "This is fun, but we've had to really learn more about what we're singing!" or "This is fun, but hard." Several groups intentionally chose topics that were only superficially covered in class, so they could learn more about the topic, allowing for differentiation of learning within the high school classroom. Those students had to engage in their own research and deeper learning in order to formulate vocabulary and context into lyrics for the video.

Any concerns students had over free riders and group dynamics were minimal, although when present, it created a learning opportunity for an important life skills lesson. This criticism is present with any group project, with Econ Beats however, there is enough variety in differing roles required to complete the project that all learners were able to find a contribution they were happy to make. Our experience is that the existence of free riders was possibly reduced than with a more traditional type of group project. In this way, Econ Beats was able to facilitate the benefits of group work with fewer of the typical conundrums. This especially benefits the nature of collaborative work, which has been shown to encourage greater inclusion within the classroom (Thousand et al. 2002).

When surveyed, students reported the most enjoyable aspect of the project was being able to work with music, collaboratively and creatively. Students were very enthusiastic about the unusual nature of the project and overwhelmingly positive when comparing Econ Beats to a more traditional form of assessment. In this way, Econ Beats has enabled a greater motivation and engagement in learning the economic concepts. Further research is required to ascertain the improvements in retention.

Previous research focused on active learning (Hoyt 2003; Emerson and Taylor 2004; Odell 2018; Imazeki 2015; McGoldrick 2012) shows that increased engagement in the learning process contributes to positive learning outcomes. As follows, Econ Beats has been a success in the high school economics classroom, enabling greater motivation and engagement in learning introductory Economics concepts.

10.6 Not All Students Love Econ Beats

Introducing new teaching methods into the classroom is difficult for both instructors and students. Introducing innovative, non-traditional assignments that require working in groups is even more challenging. When introducing Econ Beats, the difficulty lies in students' ability to see the immediate connection of how creating a music video will increase their learning of economic concepts. Moreover, the reluctance of working in groups, which always exists, is amplified for those students that do not see the connection between the assignment and the learning outcomes.

Qualitative questions administered in the pre-survey capture some of the student apprehension. Table 10.3 presents some student comments that indicated their reluc-

Table 10.3 Student reported concerns in the pre-survey

Concern	Issue
A group size of eight is too large to effectively incorporate everyone's opinions	Group size
Finding times that work for everyone	Time availability
Getting the vocals and video shots	Production
Group projects tend to have one or two people who have busy outside of class lives and are unable to meet regularly. While we always will have to work with groups after college, we won't have the expectancy to work 40 h AND have 15 h of class AND find time for group work. The idea of group work to prepare us for later on is a great concept, but I find it's hard to balance it at this level of our lives	Time availability
I am not very comfortable in front of a camera and will probably experience anxiety because of it	Production
I am a non-traditional student by age. Most traditional students have a preconceived stereotype of older students in a younger majority class. This is not an excuse to do less, but only an observation when participating in group assignments or projects	Group dynamic
I am concerned about exactly how much outside classroom work it is going to entail. I work full time, have a 2 year old, and go to school full time. I also hope the groups are not too big, having to keep in contact with a larger amount of people would be difficult	Group dynamic and time availability
I'm concerned about the filming of the video. I'm fine with the assignment, but I am camera shy and can't sing	Production
My concern is that I think that the making of the video and lyrics is going to take a lot a time and might make us lose focus on other important things, like exams or homework	Non-traditional assignment
I'm scared that I'm not creative and extroverted enough for this assignment. This assignment is a chance for those who are bad test-takers to shine. I'm the opposite. I am a great test-taker and not confident in a group setting. I also worry that the size of the group will hinder the quality since we have to collaborate and compromise more than in past years. The schedules lining up are worrisome as well	Non-traditional assignment

tance to participate in the project. We present these comments so that instructors considering incorporation of Econ Beats are better prepared to mitigate student concerns.

The selected concerns reflect the broad range of concerns submitted. Most students were concerned with time availability, exactly how much out of class time they needed to devote to this project is dependent on a combination of their skills and quality expectations. Additionally, students made it clear that working with groups becomes difficult as group size increases. Students did mention the "free-rider" problem in their concerns. The other concerns have to do with production of the music video and audio quality, not all students have the skill set required to create the project. Instructors interested in this assignment can group students by their technology skill set using a pre-survey. Finally, due to the non-traditional aspect of this assignment, some students did not see how this can complement their learning and suggested that this assignment would distract from their ability to learn the content. It has been our experience that educators at times have the same concern, viewing Econ Beats as a substitute away from content. While the Econ Beats assignment is not a test taking assignment, there is no reason to believe that the overall effect is that students perform worse in exams. However, to better determine the efficacy of this assignment an experimental design study is required.

10.7 Conclusion

In this article we provide student self-reported data on their learning and engagement in classes that use Econ Beats as a class project. The data is collected over five semesters and includes 275 college level students. We also provide feedback from 90 high school students enrolled in an Australian Economics course. Economic educators looking to introduce active learning, and project-based learning can incorporate Econ Beats.

Students reported excitement to work on the project at levels higher than working on traditional group projects. The rubrics and guidelines provided by Al-Bahrani et al. (2017a) helped students to feel more enthusiastic about the project. After the completion of the project students reported that the project helped them learn economic concepts and definitions. At the high school level students indicated similar preference for Econ Beats as an assignment.

Incorporating new teaching methods can be arduous for instructors. Having tools that are well revered by students and that encourage real-life learning can reduce the cost of implementation. Our experience at the high school and college level suggests that teachers should consider Econ Beats as a teaching tool.

References

Al-Bahrani A, Holder K, Patel D, Sheridan BJ (2016) The great digital divide: using popular media to teach economics. J Econ Econ Educ Res 17(2):105–111

Al-Bahrani A, Libis B, Drabik S, Gibson J (2017a) Econ Beats: a semester long, interdisciplinary, project-based learning assignment. J Econ Finance Educ 16(3):1–11

Al-Bahrani A, Patel D, Sheridan BJ (2017b) Evaluating Twitter and its impact on student learning in principles of economics courses. J Econ Educ 48(4):243–253

Allgood S, Walstad WB, Siegfried JJ (2015) Research on teaching economics to undergraduates. J Econ Lit 53(2):285–325

Becker WE, Watts M (1996) Chalk and talk: a national survey on teaching undergraduate economics. Am Econ Rev 86(2):448–453

Brooks CM, Ammons JL (2003) Free riding in group projects and the effects of timing, frequency, and specificity of criteria in peer assessments. J Educ Bus 78(5):268–272

Buckles S, Hoyt G (2006) Using active learning techniques in large lecture classes. In: Teaching economics: more alternatives to chalk and talk. Edward Elgar, Cheltenham, pp 75–88
Deerfield A (2018) A quantile regression analysis of the effects of cooperative learning on learning outcomes. Working paper
Elliot C (2003) Using a personal response system in economics teaching. Int Rev Econ Educ 1(1):80–86
Emerson TL, Taylor BA (2004) Comparing student achievement across experimental and lecture-oriented sections of a principles of microeconomics course. South Econ J 70(3):672–693
Frank RH (1998) Some thoughts on the micro principles course. In: Walstad WB, Saunders P (eds) Teaching undergraduate economics: a handbook for instructors. Irwin McGraw–Hill, New York, pp 13–20
Hansen WL, Salemi MK, Siegfried JJ (2002) Use it or lose it: teaching literacy in the economics principles course. Am Econ Rev 92(2):463–472
Holder K, Hoffer A, Al-Bahrani A, Lindahl S (2015) Rockonomix. J Econ Educ 46(4):443
Hoyt GM (2003) How to make economics the fulfilling social science. South Econ J 70(1):201–206
Imazeki J (2015) Getting students to do economics: an introduction to team-based learning. Int Adv Econ Res 21(4):399–412
Levy-Feldman I, Libman Z (2017) Student assessment and good teaching. In: Aloni N, Weintrob L (eds) Beyond Bystanders. Sense Publishers, Rotterdam, pp 205–217
McGoldrick K (2012) Using cooperative learning exercises in economics. In: Hoyt GM, McGoldrick K (eds) International handbook on teaching and learning economics. Edward Elgar, Northampton
Odell K (2018) Team-based learning and student performance: preliminary evidence from a principles of macroeconomics classroom. Int Rev Econ Educ 29(1):44–58
Roach T (2014) Student perceptions toward flipped learning: new methods to increase interaction and active learning in economics. Int Rev Econ Educ 17(1):74–84
Salemi MK (2005) Teaching economic literacy: why, what and how. Int Rev Econ Educ 4(2):46–57
Thompson L, Al-Bahrani A (2018) Incorporating Econ Beats in the Australian high school economics curriculum. Working paper
Thousand JS, Villa RA, Nevin AI (2002) Creativity and collaborative learning: the practical guide to empowering students, teachers, and families. Paul H Brookes Publishing Company, Baltimore
Uttl B, White CA, Gonzalez DW (2017) Meta-analysis of faculty's teaching effectiveness: student evaluation of teaching ratings and student learning are not related. Stud Educ Eval 54(1):22–42
Walstad W, Allgood S (1999) What do college seniors know about economics? Am Econ Rev 89(2):350–354
Welch BK, Bonnan-White J (2012) Twittering to increase student engagement in the university classroom. Knowl Manag E-Learn 4(3):325–345

Chapter 11
Navigating the Economics Major: The Effect of Gender on Students' Degree Pathways

Laura J. Ahlstrom and Carlos J. Asarta

Abstract Although nationwide a small percentage of students complete an economics degree, many students who initially select another major switch into economics or add it as a second major. Prior research has found that women are less likely to earn an economics degree and that students may consider degrees in business and economics to be substitutes. The purpose of this study is to assess gender disparities in students' economics degree attainment based on differences in students' initial major selections and grades received in their introductory microeconomics course. Findings indicate that both male and female students who initially choose to major in economics have a high probability of graduating with an economics major. Students who complete an economics major or minor come from a large selection of initial majors. Male and female students also are found to respond differently to introductory microeconomics grades.

11.1 Introduction

For many students, the college degree selection process is a dynamic one. Although some students choose an initial major and remain in it through graduation, many students change majors at some point in their academic careers (Astorne-Figiari and Speer 2017; Dickson 2010; Kugler et al. 2017). Nationwide, less than 2% of undergraduate students earn a bachelor's degree in economics (Siegfried 2016; Stock 2017). An even smaller proportion of students enter university as economics majors, suggesting that many of the students who earn an economics degree switch into it from another major. Students may also graduate with more than one major, and economics may be a popular choice for a second major (Stock 2017).

L. J. Ahlstrom (✉)
Oklahoma State University, Stillwater, OK, USA
e-mail: laura.ahlstrom@okstate.edu

C. J. Asarta
University of Delaware, Newark, DE, USA
e-mail: asarta@udel.edu

J. Hall, K. Lawson (eds.), *Teaching Economics*,
https://doi.org/10.1007/978-3-030-20696-3_11

Prior research has been conducted on students' persistence in a major and decision to change majors (Astorne-Fiagari and Speer 2017; Dickson 2010; Kugler et al. 2017; Luppino and Sander 2015; Ohland et al. 2004; Ost 2010; Riegle-Crumb et al. 2016; Solnick 1995; Turner and Bowen 1999). Many of these studies, however, analyzed the choices made by students in general or by students who initially selected a STEM (Science, Technology, Engineering, and Mathematics) field. A few studies have assessed students' choices of moving into or out of economics. For instance, a collection of articles has explored students who select between business and economics majors (Asarta and Butters 2012; Marangos 2012; Mumford and Ohland 2011; Salemi and Eubanks 1996). Ashworth and Evans (2001) assessed the likelihood that students would select an economics degree rather than a degree in another field, while Fournier and Sass (2000) analyzed the probability that students would choose an economics degree based on their initial major choice. Kasper (2008) analyzed which academic majors were complements and substitutes to economics. However, with the exception of Chizmar (2000) who explored gender disparities in students' attrition from economics, most of the prior studies have not analyzed the paths students take into or out of economics through the lens of gender.

Female students are underrepresented among economics degree recipients, earning only about one-third of all undergraduate economics degrees (Ball 2012; Bayer and Rouse 2016; Ceci et al. 2014; Goldin 2013; Kim et al. 2002; McElroy 2014; National Center for Education Statistics 2015; Rask and Tiefenthaler 2008; Siegfried 2016). In contrast, nearly half of all graduates in business are female (Ball 2012; Bayer and Rouse 2016). Furthermore, women receive the majority of degrees in other social science fields, including psychology and sociology, and also earn more degrees in STEM fields than in economics (Bayer and Rouse 2016; Ceci et al. 2014). Additionally, while the gender gap in degree attainment in many STEM fields has decreased over the last 20 years, the percentage of economics degrees conferred to women has remained relatively stagnant even though the overall number of economics degrees conferred has increased during that same time (Ball 2012; Ceci et al. 2014; National Center for Education Statistics 2015; Siegfried 2016).

With an emphasis on gender, the purpose of this study is to examine the pathways followed by students graduating with an economics degree based on their initial major choices and grades in their first economics course. We use a series of multinomial logistic regressions to explore the following research questions:

1. Do gender differences in students' initial major selections affect the likelihood of graduating with an economics degree?
2. Do gender differences in students' absolute and relative grades in an introductory microeconomics course affect the likelihood of graduating with an economics degree?

Findings indicate that both male and female students who initially choose to major in economics have a strong probability of completing an economics major and are less likely to earn an economics minor. Students who complete an economics degree also come from a large selection of initial majors, including students who are "undeclared" at matriculation. In addition, the results suggest that male and female students who complete economics degrees are drawn from different initial majors. For example, relative to their same-gender business major peers, male students who earn an economics major are significantly more likely to matriculate as engineering majors, while female economics majors are significantly more likely to join the degree having originally majored in math, computer science, or applied economics. Also, men who enter the university as undeclared business students are significantly more likely than their male declared business major peers to complete an economics major. There is no similar finding for female undeclared business majors. In addition, when it comes to selecting the economics degree, male and female students respond differently to their introductory microeconomics course grades.

11.2 Prior Literature

When undergraduate students are asked to rank their reasons for selecting their college major, interest in the subject and coursework tends to receive the highest rankings (Beggs et al. 2008; Easterling and Smith 2008; Malgwi et al. 2005; Zafar 2013). Evidence suggests that students may have negative attitudes toward economics, considering it to be boring, uninteresting, and impractical (Bansak and Starr 2010; Bollinger et al. 2009; Calkins and Welki 2006; Worthington and Higgs 2004). Calkins and Welki (2006) found that approximately two-thirds of non-economics majors never even considered majoring in economics, believing the subject to be too difficult, confusing, and requiring too much math. Women may have particularly negative opinions of economics. Survey results comparing male and female perspectives toward economics indicate that women are significantly more likely to view economics courses as less practical, less relevant to their lives and careers, and less interesting than courses in other subjects (Bansak and Starr 2010; Bollinger et al. 2009; Jensen and Owen 2000, 2001). Women may also be significantly less likely than men to consider earning an economics degree (Calkins and Welki 2006).

Prior research also suggests that a student's precollege preparation and performance affects his or her major selection (Correll 2001; Davison et al. 2014; Rask and Bailey 2002; Riegle-Crumb et al. 2012; Turner and Bowen 1999; Wang and Degol 2013). In particular, students' performance on standardized exams significantly affects their choice of major (Correll 2001; Davison et al. 2014; Rask and Bailey 2002; Riegle-Crumb et al. 2012; Turner and Bowen 1999; Wang and Degol 2013). Students who earn higher scores on standardized math exams are more likely to select a quantitative major, while those with higher verbal scores are more likely to choose a major in a non-quantitative field (Correll 2001; Davison et al. 2014; Luppino and Sander 2015; Rask and Bailey 2002; Turner and Bowen 1999). In economics, students who earn higher math SAT scores may be more likely to take economics courses and to choose economics as a major (Ashworth and Evans 2001;

Dynan and Rouse 1997; Rask and Tiefenthaler 2008). Women tend to perform better on the verbal SAT relative to the math SAT; for men, the opposite is true (Davison et al. 2014; Turner and Bowen 1999). As a result, women may be less likely to choose an economics major. On the other hand, findings indicate that gender differences in performance on standardized exams may explain only a small part of the gender gap in economics degree selection (Dynan and Rouse 1997; Emerson et al. 2012; Horvat et al. 1992; Jensen and Owen 2001; Rask and Tiefenthaler 2008).

While students' interests and abilities affect their initial choice of major, students' experiences in their college courses influence their final degree selection (Malgwi et al. 2005). Since many students first exposure to economics is in college, the experiences students have in their introductory economics courses may affect their propensity to earn an economics degree. In fact, one study found that two-thirds of students who earned an economics degree selected their major after completing a principles of microeconomics course (Mumford and Ohland 2011). Approximately 25% of these students switched into economics from a math-intensive major, specifically math, engineering, or physics.

Students' grades in their college classes are a significant predictor of their major selection. Evidence suggests that the grades a student earns in courses within their selected major are positively correlated with persistence in that major (Chizmar 2000; Griffith 2010; Ohland et al. 2004; Ost 2010; Riegle-Crumb et al. 2016). Alternatively, when students perform poorly in their initial major, they may be more likely to switch majors (Griffith 2010; Kugler et al. 2017; Mumford and Ohland 2011; Ohland et al. 2004; Ost 2010; Riegle-Crumb et al. 2016). In economics, some evidence suggests that women perform worse than men in their introductory economics courses (Ballard and Johnson 2005; Dynan and Rouse 1997; Elizinga and Melaugh 2009; Emerson et al. 2012). Other studies indicate that there is no significant gender difference in introductory economics course performance and that women may even outperform men (Johnson et al. 2014; Rask and Tiefenthaler 2008; Swope and Schmitt 2006; Terry 2002). Even if no gender disparities in economics course performance exist, women may need higher grades than their male peers to select economics as a major (Emerson et al. 2012; Goldin 2013, 2015; Owen 2010; Rask and Tiefenthaler 2008).

Comparing grades across subjects allows students to evaluate their relative academic strengths, and questions of how relative grades affect major choice selection have been explored in the literature. Several research studies show that students with higher grades in their economics courses relative to their grades in other courses are significantly more likely to major in economics (Ahlstrom and Asarta 2019; Emerson et al. 2012; Jensen and Owen 2001; Rask and Tiefenthaler 2008). In one survey of undergraduate economic majors, over half of the students said they chose an economics major because they performed well in their introductory economics courses and thought the subject was interesting (Jones et al. 2008). Research also suggests that women may be particularly sensitive to their relative course grades and may choose majors in departments that, on average, offer higher grades (Butcher et al. 2014; Goldin 2015; Rask and Tiefenthaler 2008). On many college campuses, economics departments offer courses where students tend to receive lower grades than in courses offered by many other departments (Bar et al. 2009; Butcher et al. 2014; Kostal et al. 2016). Consequently, fewer women may select economics as their major.

Students may view economics and business as substitute degrees, so several studies have explored a student's major selection process between the two (Asarta and Butters 2012; Astorne-Fiagari and Speer 2017; Brasfield et al. 1996; Marangos 2012; Salemi and Eubanks 1996). For instance, Salemi and Eubanks (1996) explored the rise and fall of economics majors at the University of North Carolina at Chapel Hill, coining the term "Discouraged-Business-Majors" to describe students who could not fulfill the requirements to become business majors and selected the less-demanding economics major. Additional studies have found some support for the Discouraged-Business-Major hypothesis (Asarta and Butters 2012; Marangos 2012; Mumford and Ohland 2011). However, Asarta and Butters (2012) also find evidence suggesting that some students who initially select a business degree may be encouraged by their performance in economics courses, ultimately switching into an economics major.

Many variables affect a student's college major selection, including interest in the subject, ability, and performance in college classes. Research indicates that women are significantly less likely to select economics as their major and that gender differences in students' absolute and relative grades in their introductory economics courses significantly affect their propensity to select an economics major. Few studies, however, have analyzed economics degree selection based on students' initial college major choices, and most of them have not assessed gender differences. More research is needed to explain the gender differences in pathways to economics degree completion, hence the reason for this study.

11.3 Background and Data

11.3.1 Background

The data used in this study comes from the University of Delaware (UD), a land-grant and comprehensive institution with an enrollment of approximately 18,000 undergraduate students (Institutional Research and Effectiveness 2018). The University offers programs at its main campus in Newark for both undergraduate and graduate students, as well as opportunities for continuing studies students. Additionally, UD operates an undergraduate Associate in Arts Program at several satellite campuses in Delaware. UD offers more than 150 undergraduate majors, which are divided among six colleges. Students may be admitted into an intended major directly, or they may matriculate as undeclared majors. Students may also be admitted as undeclared majors within a college (e.g., business undeclared or engineering undeclared). In Fall 2016, the University offered admission to 69.5% of the undergraduate applicants. Admitted students generally have a high school GPA in the range of 3.55–3.95 and an average combined SAT score ranging from 1200 to 1350 (Institutional Research and Effectiveness 2018). At the Newark campus, women represent 58% of undergraduate enrollment. Approximately 37% of students are Delaware residents. Over 70% of the students at the Newark campus are white, and about 5% are international students (Institutional Research and Effectiveness 2018).

The Department of Economics is housed within the Alfred Lerner College of Business and Economics. Students may complete three different economics degrees: a Bachelor of Science (B.S.) in economics, a Bachelor of Arts (B.A.) in economics, and a minor in economics. Both of the economics majors require students to complete 30 credit hours in economics as well as letter grades of C- (the equivalent of 1.67 on a 4.0 scale) or better in all economics courses. The B.S. degree requires the completion of a calculus course as well as a quantitative proficiency requirement of nine additional credits in mathematics or business courses that require calculus. The B.A. degree does not require a calculus course, but students must demonstrate proficiency in an ancient or modern foreign language at the intermediate level or better. The minor in economics requires completion of 18 credit hours in economics. There is no math or language requirement for the minor.

All students who complete a degree in business or economics must pass Introduction to Microeconomics, the first economics course offered at UD, with a C- letter grade or better. Other students may choose to take Introduction to Microeconomics to fulfill a University requirement or as an elective. For many students, Introduction to Microeconomics is their first formal exposure to economics. Some students take an economics course in high school, but many matriculating freshmen may have had very little exposure to the field of economics prior to college. Although all states in the USA include economics in their curricular standards, not all of them require school districts to implement the economics standards. Moreover, half of these states require school districts to offer an economics course in high school, while only 22 states require students to complete a high school economics course to graduate (Council for Economic Education 2018). As result, the level of exposure to economics content prior to enrolling in Introduction to Microeconomics is diverse.

11.3.2 Data

The data come from the administrative records of 1470 male and 667 female undergraduate students who completed Introduction to Microeconomics between Fall 2006 and Spring 2014, and who graduated by Winter 2016.[1] Each student record contains demographic characteristics, measurements of precollege ability, and college coursework. Student records also contain information about the

[1]The University of Delaware awards degrees four times a year: February, May, August, and December.

Table 11.1 Summary of student variables

Variable	Description
Female	1 if student is female
Minority	1 if student is non-white
Age at micro	Student's age in years at microeconomics
SAT math	Student's SAT Math score divided by 10
SAT verbal	Student's SAT Verbal score divided by 10
Economics entry	1 if student's initial major was in economics
Business entry	1 if student's initial major was in business
Math/CSci/Ap Econ entry	1 if student's initial major was in math, computer science, or applied economics
Bus undeclared entry	1 if student's initial major was in business undeclared
Engineering entry	1 if student's initial major was in engineering
Natural sciences entry	1 if student's initial major was in the natural sciences
Social sciences entry	1 if student's initial major was in the social sciences
Hum/Health/Edu entry	1 if student's initial major was in the humanities, health sciences, or education
Undeclared entry	1 if student's initial major was undeclared
Non-fresh at micro	1 if student had greater than 27 cumulative credits at microeconomics
Multiple majors	1 if student graduated with more than one major degree
Micro grade	Student's microeconomics course grade
Relative micro grade	Student's micro grade/cum GPA from micro term but without micro grade
Econ major	1 if student graduated with a B.S. or B.A. in economics
Econ minor	1 if student graduated with a minor in economics

students' initial major(s) and degrees earned, including both majors and minors.[2] Table 11.1 describes the variables used in this study.

Table 11.2 provides the descriptive statistics, by gender, for the full sample of students who completed Introduction to Microeconomics. Male students ($n = 1470$) comprise about 69% of the students in the sample and are, on average, significantly older than their female counterparts. The mean math SAT score is significantly higher for men than for women, but female students have a significantly higher mean verbal SAT score. A significantly larger proportion of women took Introduction to Microeconomics after their freshman year. All students in the sample selected only one major at matriculation. There is no significant gender difference in the proportion of students in the sample who matriculated as economics majors. Over half of the men in the sample initially declared business as their major, which is a significantly larger proportion than the 43.5% of female business majors. On the other hand, no significant gender difference exists in the share of male and female

[2]Students may complete multiple majors and/or minors at the University of Delaware.

Table 11.2 Summary statistics for students, full sample

	Male students		Female students		Mean
Variable	Mean	SD	Mean	SD	Diff
Minority	0.189	0.389	0.177	0.382	
Age at micro	18.218	0.689	18.100	0.687	***
SAT math	644.395	67.564	630.900	65.763	***
SAT verbal	593.469	70.782	602.489	74.284	**
Non-fresh at micro	0.386	0.487	0.459	0.499	***
Economics entry	0.027	0.161	0.019	0.138	
Business entry	0.507	0.500	0.435	0.096	**
Math/CSci/Ap Econ entry	0.041	0.200	0.075	0.264	**
Bus undeclared entry	0.197	0.398	0.168	0.374	
Engineering entry	0.127	0.333	0.067	0.251	***
Natural sciences entry	0.045	0.207	0.060	0.238	
Social sciences entry	0.061	0.239	0.076	0.266	
Hum/Health/Edu entry	0.039	0.193	0.076	0.266	***
Undeclared entry	0.154	0.361	0.190	0.393	*
Multiple majors	0.305	0.460	0.364	0.482	**
Micro grade	3.024	0.707	3.023	0.688	
Relative micro grade	1.027	0.307	0.951	0.201	***
Econ major	0.202	0.402	0.121	0.327	***
Econ minor	0.239	0.426	0.240	0.427	
N	1470		667		

Note: $*p < 0.05$; $**p < 0.01$; $***p < 0.001$

students who entered as undeclared business majors. Nearly twice the number of male students matriculated as engineering majors, while women significantly outnumbered men in the humanities, health sciences, and education fields by almost two to one. Additionally, a significantly larger proportion of women matriculated into the fields of math, computer science, and applied economics. In contrast, no significant gender difference exists among students whose initial major was in the natural sciences or in a non-economics social science domain. Finally, women were significantly more likely to enter the university as undeclared majors and to complete multiple majors.

The mean Introduction to Microeconomics grade for both men and women is 3.02, which is equivalent to a B letter grade on a 4.0 scale. Although there is no significant gender difference in students' absolute grades in Introductory to Microeconomics, the mean relative microeconomics grade is significantly higher for male students than for female students. Students' relative microeconomics grades are calculated by dividing their absolute grades in Introduction to Microeconomics by the grades they received in all other courses that were taken during the same term. For men, the average relative microeconomics grade is slightly above one, suggesting that male students performed as well as, if not somewhat better, in Introduction to Microeconomics than in their other courses. Women's mean relative microeconomics grade is less than one, indicating that the women in the sample performed slightly worse in Introduction to Microeconomics than in the other courses they completed that semester.

Consistent with prior research, female students are less likely to earn an economics degree. Specifically, the percentage of female students who graduated with an economics major is significantly lower. Twenty percent of the male students completed an economics major, compared to only 12% of the female students. In contrast, no significant gender difference exists among students who earn minors in economics.

11.4 Methodology

Using a series of multinomial logistic regressions, we analyze students' economics degree selection. We first estimate the probability that a student will graduate with an economics degree for the full sample of students, using as the reference group students who select business as their initial major. Recognizing that male and female students may have different propensities to earn economics degrees, we run separate regressions for men and women using Eq. 11.1:

$$\begin{aligned} Pr^{\mathrm{M,F}}(EconMajor/EconMinor/Non = 1) &= \beta_0 + \beta_1 Minority_i \\ &+\beta_2 AgeatMicro_i + \beta_3 AgeatMicro_i^2 + \beta_4 SATMath_i \\ &+\beta_5 SATVerbal_i + \beta_6 Non\text{-}FreshatMicro_i + \beta_7 EconomicsEntry_i \\ &+\beta_8 EngineeringEntry_i + \beta_9 Hum/Health/Educ_i \\ &+\beta_{10} Math/CSci/ApEconEntry_i + \beta_{11} NaturalSciencesEntry_i \\ &+\beta_{12} SocialSciencesEntry_i + \beta_{13} UndeclaredEntry_i \\ &+\beta 14 MultipleMajors_i + \beta_{15} MicroGrade_i + \beta_{16} RelativeMicroGrade_i \\ &+\beta_{17} AcaYr06\text{-}07_i + \beta_{18} AcaYr07\text{-}08_i + \cdots + \beta_{24} AcaYr13\text{-}14_i + \epsilon_i \end{aligned} \tag{11.1}$$

Student demographics characteristics, including their minority status and age at the time of taking Introduction to Microeconomics, are incorporated into the model. In addition, we control for student ability by including students' math and verbal SAT scores. Since SAT scores are reported in units of 10 (e.g., 550 and 560), students' math and verbal SAT scores were divided by 10. Transforming the SAT scores in this manner allows for easy interpretation of the marginal effect of a one-unit increase in a student's math or verbal SAT score. The model also includes students' initial majors at the time of matriculation as well as a dummy variable to control for students who graduated with more than one major. In addition, we include students' absolute and relative Introduction to Microeconomics grades. We also incorporate fixed year effects by including dummy variables for the academic year in which a student completed Introduction to Microeconomics.

Next, we run a second regression, presented in Eq. 11.2, for students who matriculated into Lerner College of Business and Economics. The reference group for this regression is students who declared a specific business major, such as accounting or marketing, upon admission. This model also includes a dummy variable for students who initially entered as business undeclared students to assess if students who have a general interest in business may be more likely to select an economics major than their declared business major peers.

$$\begin{aligned} &Pr^{\mathrm{M,F}}(EconMajor/EconMinor/Non = 1) = \beta_0 + \beta_1 Minority_i \\ &+\beta_2 AgeatMicro_i + \beta_3 AgeatMicro_i^2 + \beta_4 SATMath_i \\ &+\beta_5 SATVerbal_i + \beta_6 Non\text{-}FreshatMicro_i + \beta_7 EconomicsEntry_i \\ &+\beta_8 BusUndeclaredEntry_i + \beta_9 MultipleMajors_i \qquad (11.2) \\ &+\beta_{10} MicroGrade_i + \beta_{11} RelativeMicroGrade_i \\ &+\beta_{12} AcaYr06\text{-}07_i + \beta_{13} AcaYr07\text{-}08_i + \cdots + \beta_{19} AcaYr13\text{-}14_i + \epsilon_i \end{aligned}$$

11.5 Results

11.5.1 Economics Degree Selection for Full Sample of Students

Table 11.3 presents the average marginal effect estimates, by gender, for the full sample of students using the multinomial logistic regression of economics degree selection. For both men and women, neither a student's minority status nor age at the time of completing Introduction to Microeconomics is significantly correlated with economics degree selection. Students' math and verbal SAT scores are not significant predictors of choosing an economics major for either gender although female students' math SAT scores are significant, positive predictors of earning an economics minor. Both male and female students who select economics as their initial major are significantly more likely to graduate with an economics major and are significantly less likely to complete a minor in economics.

The magnitude of the coefficients is larger for female students who select economics majors at entry for both economics major and minor degree selection. Women whose initial major is economics are 73.7% more likely than females whose initial major is in business (the reference group) to earn an economics major relative to a non-economics degree, whereas male students who enter college as economics majors are only 50.1% more likely to earn an economics major than their other business peers.

Table 11.3 Average marginal effects for economics degree selection, full sample

	Male		Female	
Variable	Econ major	Econ minor	Econ major	Econ minor
Minority	0.005	0.004	0.018	0.015
	(0.025)	(0.027)	(0.030)	(0.044)
Age at micro	−0.233	−0.827	−0.471	0.668
	(0.392)	(0.447)	(0.356)	(0.760)
Age at micro^2	0.007	0.022	0.012	−0.018
	(0.010)	(0.012)	(0.009)	(0.021)
SAT math	−0.001	−0.001	−0.003	0.006*
	(0.002)	(0.002)	(0.002)	(0.003)
SAT verbal	0.002	0.00003	0.003	0.002
	(0.002)	(0.002)	(0.002)	(0.003)
Non-fresh at micro	0.006	0.006	−0.015	0.0003
	(0.024)	(0.026)	(0.028)	(0.038)
Economics entry	0.501***	−0.175***	0.737***	−0.193***
	(0.071)	(0.036)	(0.081)	(0.049)
Engineering entry	0.103*	0.135**	0.164	0.174*
	(0.045)	(0.042)	(0.090)	(0.079)
Hum/Health/Educ entry	0.186**	0.038	0.317**	−0.007
	(0.069)	(0.055)	(0.087)	(0.063)
Math/CSci/Ap Econ entry	0.104	−0.126**	0.299***	−0.128**
	(0.066)	(0.043)	(0.085)	(0.047)
Natural sciences entry	0.217***	0.028	0.330**	0.050
	(0.060)	(0.052)	(0.102)	(0.086)
Social sciences entry	0.139**	0.129*	0.276**	0.146*
	(0.051)	(0.054)	(0.084)	(0.072)
Undeclared entry	0.279***	−0.102***	0.225***	−0.039
	(0.038)	(0.029)	(0.055)	(0.042)
Multiple majors	0.249***	−0.216***	0.091**	−0.200***
	(0.025)	(0.020)	(0.028)	(0.031)
Micro grade	−0.055**	0.126***	−0.009	0.047
	(0.021)	(0.027)	(0.025)	(0.034)
Relative micro grade	0.199**	−0.200	0.190**	−0.123
	(0.068)	(0.115)	(0.068)	(0.119)
Micro grade (overall)	0.121***	−0.193***	0.068***	−0.086***
	(0.020)	(0.024)	(0.020)	(0.028)
Academic year dummies	Yes	Yes	Yes	Yes
Observations	1470	1470	667	667
Log likelihood	1258.063	1258.063	486.916	486.916

Notes: Robust standard errors are in parentheses. The reference group is students whose initial major was in a business field. The academic year dummy coefficients are available upon request
$^*p < 0.05$; $^{**}p < 0.01$; $^{***}p < 0.001$

Gender differences in economics major selection also exist among students who matriculate into a major outside of Lerner College of Business and Economics, relative to those who select business majors at entry. Men whose initial major is engineering are 10.3% more likely than male business majors to complete an economics major, but the result is not significant for females who originally matriculate into engineering. Students of both genders whose initial majors are in the natural sciences, social sciences, and the humanities, health sciences, or education are significantly more likely to complete economics majors than students who initially matriculate into business majors. Additionally, women who enter as math, computer science, or applied economics majors are 29.9% more likely to complete economics majors than female students in the reference group (business majors). Male math, computer science, and applied economics majors, however, are not significantly more likely to earn economics majors than students who select business majors at entry. Both male and female students who are admitted as undeclared majors have significantly higher probabilities of earning economics majors compared to business students, but the coefficient is larger for the men. Finally, men who earn more than one major degree are 24.9% more likely to earn an economics major, compared to females who have a 9.1% higher probability of earning an economics major if they graduate with more than one degree.

Some significant gender differences in economics minor selection are also apparent. Both male and female students who originally matriculated as engineering majors are significantly more likely to earn economics minors when compared to their business major peers, though the size of the coefficient is stronger for women. Females who are engineering majors at entry are 17.4% more likely than students in the reference group to complete minors in economics, whereas their male counterparts are only 13.5% more likely than students in the reference group to earn an economics minor. For both male and female students, matriculating as a social science major is a significant positive predictor of graduating with an economics minor. Male students who enter as undeclared majors are significantly less likely to earn a minor in economics; however, there is no significant effect on earning an economics minor for women who matriculate as undeclared majors. In addition, initial math, computer science, and applied economics majors of both genders are about 13% less likely to earn an economics minor than their initial business major counterparts. Furthermore, students of both genders who graduate with multiple major degrees are significantly less likely to complete an economics minor.

Consistent with prior research, male and female students exhibit different responsiveness to their grades (Emerson et al. 2012; Goldin 2015; Horvat et al. 1992; Rask and Tiefenthaler 2008). Female students' absolute microeconomics grades alone are not a significant predictor of completing an economics major, while male students' absolute grades are significantly and positively correlated with completing an economics major. However, the average marginal effect coefficients for the absolute *Micro grade* variable indicate the effect that a student's introductory microeconomics grade has on the probability of selecting an economics degree, holding the relative grade measure constant. The overall marginal effect of the introductory microeconomics grade actually comprises both the absolute and relative grade measures. Therefore, the *Micro grade (overall)* composite measure accounts for the influences of both variables on the probabilities. Additionally, the average marginal effect coefficients for a student's relative introductory microeconomics grade measure offer information about the effect that a change in a student's average introductory microeconomics course grade has on the probability of selecting an economics degree, holding constant the absolute microeconomics grade.

The overall introductory microeconomics grade measure correlates in a positive and significant way with earning an economics major for students of both genders and significantly decreases students' likelihoods of completing an economics minor. Furthermore, both male and female students' relative introductory microeconomics course grade measures are positively associated with completing an economics major. In contrast with previous research on students' relative microeconomics grade measures, however, the size of the effect is roughly equivalent for both men and women. Conversely, for students of both genders, the relative introductory microeconomics course grade measure does not significantly affect completion of an economics minor.

11.5.2 Economics Degree Selection for Business Majors at Matriculation

We now turn our attention to the estimation of Eq. 11.2 so that we can explore the pathways followed by students who chose business majors at entry. Table 11.4 presents the average marginal effect estimates for the regression on economics degree selection among students who matriculated into Lerner College of Business and Economics. As with the findings from the full sample, students' minority status is not a significant predictor of economics degree completion for either gender. Male students' math SAT scores do not significantly affect their economics degree selection, but female students' math SAT scores are a significant positive predictor of earning an economics minor. In addition, men's verbal SAT scores significantly affect the probability of earning an economics degree. Though the effect sizes for both coefficients are small, men who earn higher verbal SAT scores are significantly more likely to earn an economics major, but significantly less likely to earn an economics minor. In contrast, women's verbal SAT scores are not significant predictors of their likelihood of completing an economics degree.

The results presented in Table 11.4 also indicate that there are significant gender differences in students' economics degree selections based on their initial major selection. The reference group is students who initially matriculated with a declared business major. Both male and female students who matriculate as economics majors are significantly more likely to earn economics majors than their declared business major peers. The size of the coefficient is larger for women, who are 60.7% more likely to earn an economics degree than female students who originally matriculated as business majors. Male economics majors are 50.6% more likely to complete economics majors than their declared business major counterparts.

Table 11.4 Average marginal effects for economics degree selection, business students only

	Male		Female	
Variable	Econ major	Econ minor	Econ major	Econ minor
Minority	0.033	−0.008	0.038	−0.069
	(0.031)	(0.035)	(0.037)	(0.048)
SAT math	−0.002	0.003	−0.003	0.011*
	(0.002)	(0.002)	(0.002)	(0.004)
SAT verbal	0.004*	−0.005*	0.003	−0.003
	(0.002)	(0.002)	(0.002)	(0.004)
Non-fresh at micro	−0.034	0.013	−0.007	−0.013
	(0.028)	(0.036)	(0.026)	(0.051)
Economics entry	0.506***	−0.138***	0.607***	−0.067
	(0.080)	(0.039)	(0.127)	(0.090)
Bus undeclared entry	0.066*	−0.059*	0.014	−0.022
	(0.026)	(0.028)	(0.022)	(0.047)
Multiple majors	0.188***	−0.217***	0.016	−0.075
	(0.027)	(0.025)	(0.018)	(0.045)
Micro grade	0.018	0.097*	0.094*	−0.021
	(0.021)	(0.041)	(0.041)	(0.054)
Relative micro grade	0.077	−0.095	−0.313*	0.122
	(0.050)	(0.186)	(0.148)	(0.193)
Micro grade (overall)	0.044***	0.066	−0.003	0.017
	(0.015)	(0.034)	(0.016)	(0.032)
Academic year dummies	Yes	Yes	Yes	Yes
Observations	785	785	303	303
Log likelihood	596.526	596.526	161.260	161.260

Notes: Robust standard errors are in parentheses. The reference group is students whose initial major was in a declared business field. The academic year dummy coefficients are available upon request

$^{*}p < 0.05$; $^{**}p < 0.01$; $^{***}p < 0.001$

Additionally, men who enter as economics majors are significantly less likely to complete minors in economics rather than non-economics degrees, but this variable is not a significant predictor of women's economics minor selection. There is also a significant gender difference in economics degree selection among male and female students who were initially business undeclared majors. Relative to their declared business major peers, male undeclared business students are 6.6% more likely to complete economics majors and 5.9% less likely to complete minors in economics. On the other hand, women who enter as business undeclared students are no more or less likely to earn economics degrees relative to female students who declared business majors at entry. Additionally, men who complete more than one major have an 18.8% higher probability of earning an economics major and a 21.7% lower likelihood of earning an economics minor. In contrast, this variable is not a significant predictor of economics degree selection for women.

The estimation results also indicate that male and female business students respond differently to their grades in introductory microeconomics. Although the average marginal effect coefficient on women's absolute introductory microeconomics grades seems to indicate that they are significant predictors of earning an economics major, the overall introductory microeconomics grade measure is not significantly correlated with female students' economics major selection. Contrary to expectations, women who have a higher relative introductory microeconomics grade measure are significantly less likely to complete an economics major. Thus, the results suggest that female students who matriculate into Lerner College of Business and Economics are less likely to graduate with an economics major when they perform better in Introduction to Microeconomics relative to the grades they receive in other courses. For male students, the relative introductory microeconomics grade measure is not significantly correlated with earning a major in economics. However, the overall introductory microeconomics grade measure for men is a significant, positive predictor of completing an economics major. Finally, for students of both genders, the overall introductory microeconomics measure shows no significant effect on selecting an economics minor.

11.6 Discussion

The results from this study suggest that gender differences in economics degree attainment may exist based on a student's initial major selection. Additionally, the results are consistent with prior studies showing that male and female students respond differently to their grades when selecting economics degrees (Emerson et al. 2012; Horvat et al. 1992; Rask and Tiefenthaler 2008). Moreover, the findings suggest that male and female students display differential responses to their introductory microeconomics grades when both the absolute and relative course grade measures are taken into consideration.

Our work supports prior research findings showing that both male and female students who matriculate as economics majors are likely to earn economics degrees (Chizmar 2000; Fournier and Sass 2000; Mumford and Ohland 2011). Not surprisingly, students whose initial major is economics are less likely to earn an economics minor rather than a non-economics degree. Additionally, women who initially select economics as their major may be even more likely than their male peers to graduate with a bachelor's degree in economics. These findings suggest that students who choose economics as their major prior to entering college may have developed an interest in the subject during their adolescent years, possibly as a result of completing an economics course.

Although students whose initial major is in business comprise a large percentage of the students who graduate with an economics major, particularly among men, our results indicate that students with a declared business major have a lower probability of completing an economics major than students who initially select majors outside of Lerner College of Business and Economics. Many students may consider business and economics to be substitutes, but the results presented here indicate that female students who select business majors at matriculation are much less likely than their male counterparts to complete a major in economics, suggesting that women may be less inclined to view the two degrees as substitutes. This finding is consistent with prior research suggesting that students who choose an economics major do not necessarily do so because they view it as a close substitute to business (Jones et al. 2008).

Gender differences are apparent, however, in male and female students' propensities to switch into economics based on their major at matriculation. Men who enter as engineers are significantly more likely to earn an economics major, while female engineering majors are no more or less likely to earn an economics major than a non-economics degree when compared with female business students. On the other hand, female math, computer science, and applied economics majors have a significantly higher probability of earning an economics major relative to female business students. These findings are somewhat consistent with prior research that indicates a large proportion of students who graduate with an economics major originally select a math-intensive field for their major (Mumford and Ohland 2011).

In addition, both male and female students whose initial majors are in the natural or social sciences as well as the humanities, health sciences, or education are also more likely to earn economics majors when compared to their business major counterparts although the magnitudes of the coefficients are stronger among women. Since the University of Delaware offers a humanities-oriented B.A. degree in economics, many of these students may switch into the B.A. in economics major or add it as a second degree. Studies have found that men who enter into traditionally female majors, such as education or psychology, may be more likely to change majors than women who enter traditionally male majors, such as economics (Kugler et al. 2017; Riegle-Crumb et al. 2016). The results from this study may offer some support for these conclusions.

The findings from this study also provide support for research showing that male and female students respond differently to their introductory microeconomics course grades (Emerson et al. 2012; Goldin 2015; Rask and Tiefenthaler 2008; Sabot and Wakeman-Linn 1991). For men who matriculate into Lerner College of Business and Economics, their relative Introduction to Microeconomics course grades do not significantly affect their propensity to earn an economics major. However, men's overall introductory microeconomics grades are a significant, positive indicator of completing a major in economics. This finding may not be that surprising, given that students who complete a degree in business must pass Introduction to Microeconomics with a C- letter grade or better. In addition, business majors may be more likely to pass their introductory economics courses than students of other majors; however, they are significantly less likely to pass intermediate microeconomics than economics majors (Bosshardt and Watts 2005). Students who major or minor in economics at the University of Delaware must complete an intermediate microeconomics course. Thus, it is possible that the grades male students receive in intermediate microeconomics courses may be more important predictors of their propensity to earn an economics degree than the grades they earn in Introduction to Microeconomics, a question that deserves future attention in the literature.

Among female students, the overall effect of the Introduction to Microeconomics grade is a significant predictor on the selection of an economics major only for women who matriculate into a major outside of Lerner College of Business and Economics. For these women, the absolute Introduction to Microeconomics grade has a significant positive correlation with economics major selection. In contrast, women's relative Introduction to Microeconomics grades are a significant predictor of graduating with an economics major in both the overall and business student samples. For women in the full sample, the relative Introduction to Microeconomics grade is positive and significant. However, for the subsample of women who matriculate into Lerner College of Business and Economics, earning a higher relative introductory microeconomics grade significantly decreases their probability of completing a major in economics. Moreover, the size of the parameter for the relative introductory microeconomics grade is more than three times the magnitude of the absolute introductory microeconomics grade. These results suggest that female students may be more responsive to their relative economics grades than their absolute economics grades, which is consistent with prior research comparing the effect of female students' absolute and relative economics grades (Emerson et al. 2012; Rask and Tiefenthaler 2008).

The results presented in this study also suggest that female business majors may respond differently to their introductory microeconomics course grades than women who initially select other majors. One possible explanation for this difference is based on research into the reasons behind college major selection for business students. For example, Easterling and Smith (2008) found that business students were less concerned about whether or not their major was a good fit with their aptitude than students who selected other majors. Another possible explanation is that female business majors may have more negative views of economics compared to women who initially select other majors. Students who matriculate into Lerner College of Business and Economics must complete Introduction to Microeconomics as part of their required business core courses. Thus, women who matriculate as business majors may take Introduction to Microeconomics solely because it is a requirement for a business degree. Conversely, students who select an initial major outside of a business discipline may choose to take economics as an elective. Because female students are less likely to take economics courses in general, women who take Introduction to Microeconomics as an elective course may have more interest in and positive attitudes toward economics.

11.7 Conclusion

The results from this study indicate that students who matriculate as economics majors have a high probability of graduating with an economics major. Given this significant finding, providing students with access to quality economic education at the K-12 level is important. Research indicates that taking a high school economics course is a significant predictor of economics major selection (Ashworth and Evans 2001). Students who complete an Advanced Placement (AP) Microeconomics or Macroeconomics course may also be more likely to select an economics major, particularly if they earn a score of 4 or 5 on the AP Microeconomics or Macroeconomics exam (Avery et al. 2016; Morgan and Klaric 2007). Female students may be particularly influenced by access to economic education at the K-12 level. Evidence suggests that completing a high school course in a subject is a more significant factor in a female student's college major selection than it is for male students (Malgwi et al. 2005). In addition, students who complete a high school economics course may perform better in college-level economics courses, though the findings are mixed (Ashworth and Evans 2001; Ballard and Johnson 2005; Brasfield et al. 1996; Lopus 1997; Melican et al. 1997). The majority of states, however, do not require students to complete a high school economics course for graduation (Council for Economic Education 2018), though an increase in state economics mandates since the late-1990s has increased the percentage of students who do complete a high school economics course (Walstad and Rebeck 2012).

In addition, prior research indicates that students' academic interests and ability expectations are often formed during their adolescent years, prior to entering college (Eccles 2009; Konrad et al. 2000; Lapan et al. 1996). Providing high quality economic education to students before they enter college may improve students' beliefs about economics and their economics ability, resulting in an increase in economics majors at matriculation. Unfortunately, the content and quality of K-12 economics courses varies significantly (Lopus 1997; Walstad 2001). Teacher training in economics is a particular issue. Research indicates that there is a positive correlation between teachers' economic knowledge and their students' achievement in economics (Butters et al. 2011, 2013; Swinton et al. 2012). Economics is often taught by social studies teachers, many of whom take fewer than two college-level economics courses prior to graduating from college (Walstad 2001; Bosshardt and Watts 1994, 2005; Walstad and Watts 2015). Moreover, nearly one-third of high school social studies teachers, and more than half of the elementary teachers who are certified in social studies, never complete an economics course in college (Bosshardt and Watts 2005; Walstad and Watts 2015).

For teachers who have already received their degrees, attendance at workshops, in-service programs, and post-graduate coursework aimed at improving teachers' economics content knowledge and instructional pedagogy may improve student achievement in economics (Swinton et al. 2012; Cargill et al. 2008; Butters et al. 2011). Students may also view their high school grades and achievement as evidence of their relative academic strengths and weaknesses, choosing a major in which they believe they have a comparative advantage (Riegle-Crumb et al. 2012; Correll 2001). Thus, improving teacher training in economics and the quality of K-12 economics instruction may yield more students who enter college as economics majors.

In summary, this study uses a series of multinomial logistic regressions to assess how male and female students' majors at the time of matriculation and grades in their introductory microeconomics course affect their propensities to graduate with economics degrees. Future research endeavors may want to examine student perceptions, comparing how male and female students who initially major in business perceive their introductory microeconomics grades relative to male and female students who initially select other non-business majors. Additional research may also want to explore how non-business majors perceive the economics major. In the end, these additional research inquiries, along with the findings presented in this chapter, will help us better understand the process by which male and female students select, persist, and graduate with economics majors.

References

Ahlstrom LJ, Asarta CJ (2019) The gender gap in undergraduate economics course persistence and degree selection. AEA papers & proceedings 109:255–260

Asarta CJ, Butters RB (2012) The discouraged-business-major hypothesis revisited: could economics be the encouraged-business-major? J Econ Educ 43(1):19–32

Ashworth J, Evans JL (2001) Modeling student subject choice at secondary and tertiary level: a cross-section study. J Econ Educ 32(4):311–320

Astorne-Fiagari C, Speer JD (2017) Are changes of major major changes? The role of grades, gender, and preferences in college major switching. University of Memphis, Working Paper

Avery C, Gurantz O, Hurwitz M, Smith J (2016) Shifting college majors in response to advanced placement exam scores. National Bureau of Economic Research, Working Paper No. 22821

Ball JA (2012) The gender gap in undergraduate business programs in the United States. J Educ Bus 87(5):260–265

Ballard C, Johnson M (2005) Gender, expectations, and grades in introductory microeconomics at a US university. Fem Econ 11(1):95–122

Bansak C, Starr M (2010) Gender differences in predispositions towards economics. East Econ J 36(1):33–57

Bar T, Kadiyali V, Zussman A (2009) Grade information and grade inflation: the Cornell experiment. J Econ Perspect 23(3):93–108

Bayer A, Rouse CE (2016) Diversity in the economics profession: a new attack on an old problem. J Econ Perspect 30(4):221–242

Beggs JM, Bantham JH, Taylor S (2008) Distinguishing the factors influencing college students' choice of major. Coll Stud J 42(2):381–394

Bollinger CR, Hoyt GM, McGoldrick KM (2009) Expanding teaching and learning horizons in economic education, Nova Science, New York, chap Chicks don't dig it: gender, attitude, and performance in principles of economics classes, pp 43–65

Bosshardt W, Watts M (1994) Instructor effects in economics in elementary and junior high schools. J Econ Educ 25(3):195–211

Bosshardt W, Watts M (2005) Teachers' undergraduate coursework in economics in the baccalaureate and beyond longitudinal study. J Econ Educ 36(4):400–405

Brasfield DW, Harrison D, McCoy J, Milkman M (1996) Why have some schools not experienced a decrease in the percentage of students majoring in economics? J Econ Educ 27(4):362–370

Butcher KF, McEwan PJ, Weerpana A (2014) The effects of an anti-grade-inflation policy at Wellesley College. J Econ Perspect 28(3):189–204

Butters RB, Asarta CJ, Fischer TJ (2011) Human capital in the classroom: the role of teacher knowledge in economic literacy. Am Econ 56(2):47–57

Butters R, Asarta C, Thompson E (2013) The production of economic knowledge in urban and rural areas: the role of student, teacher, and school characteristics. J Agric Appl Econ 45(1):1–15

Calkins LN, Welki A (2006) Factors that influence choice of major: why some students never consider economics. Int J Soc Econ 33(8):547–564
Cargill TF, Jurosky J, Wendel J (2008) Implementing economics standards: a pilot transition program. J Econ Educ 39(2):126–134
Ceci SJ, Ginther DK, Kahn S, Williams WM (2014) Women in academic science: a changing landscape. Psychol Sci Public Interest 15(3):75–141
Chizmar JF (2000) A discrete-time hazard analysis of the role of gender in persistence in the economics major. J Econ Educ 31(2):107–188
Correll SJ (2001) Gender and the career choice process: the role of biased self-assessments. Am J Sociol 106(6):1691–1730
Council for Economic Education (2018) Survey of the states: economic and personal finance education in our nation's schools 2018. Council for Economic Education, New York, NY
Davison ML, Jew GB, Davenport ECJ (2014) Patterns of SAT scores, choice of STEM major, and gender. Meas Eval Couns Dev 47(2):118–126
Dickson L (2010) Race and gender differences in college major choice. Ann Am Acad Polit Soc Sci 627(1):108–124
Dynan KE, Rouse CE (1997) The underrepresentation of women in economics: a study of undergraduate economics students. J Econ Educ 28(4):350–368
Easterling DS, Smith K (2008) A factor-analytic investigation of students' perceptions regarding purpose, choice of major, and future work. J Coll Character 10(2):1–19
Eccles J (2009) Who am I and what am I going to do with my life? Personal and collective identities as motivators of action. Educ Psychol 44(2):78–89
Elizinga KG, Melaugh DO (2009) 35,000 principles of economics students: some lessons learned. South Econ J 76(1):32–46
Emerson TLN, McGoldrick K, Mumford KJ (2012) Women and the choice to study economics. J Econ Educ 43(4):349–362
Fournier GM, Sass TR (2000) Take my course, "please": the effects of the principles experience on student curriculum choice. J Econ Educ 31(4):323–339
Goldin C (2013) Notes on women and the economics undergraduate major. Newsletter of the Committee on the Status of Women in the Economics Profession Summer, 4–6
Goldin C (2015) Gender and the undergraduate economics major: notes on the undergraduate economics major at a highly selective liberal arts college. Harvard University, Working Paper
Griffith AL (2010) Persistence of women and minorities in STEM field majors: is it the school that matters? Econ Educ Rev 29(6):911–922
Horvat J, Beaudin BQ, Wright SP (1992) Persisting in the introductory economics course: an exploration of gender differences. J Econ Educ 23(2):101–108
Institutional Research and Effectiveness (2018) UD facts and figures. University of Delaware, Newark, DE
Jensen EJ, Owen AL (2000) Why are women such reluctant economists? Evidence from liberal arts colleges. Am Econ Rev 90(2):466–470
Jensen EJ, Owen AL (2001) Pedagogy, gender, and interest in economics. J Econ Educ 32(4):323–343
Johnson M, Robson D, Taengnoi S (2014) A meta-analysis of the gender gap in performance in collegiate economics courses. Rev Soc Econ 72(4):436–459
Jones S, Hoest E, Fuld R, Dahal M, Colander D (2008) What economics students think of the economics major. Middlebury College Department of Economics, Discussion Paper
Kasper H (2008) Sources of economics majors: more biology, less business. South Econ J 75(2):457–472
Kim D, Markham FS, Cangelosi JD (2002) Why students pursue the business degree: a comparison of business majors across universities. J Educ Bus 78(1):28–32
Konrad AM, Ritchie Jr JE, Lieb P, Corrigall E (2000) Sex differences and similarities in job attribute preferences: a meta-analysis. Psychol Bull 126(4):593
Kostal JW, Kuncel NR, Sackett PR (2016) Grade inflation marches on: grade increases from the 1990s to 2000s. Educ Meas Issues Pract 35(1):11–20

Kugler AD, Tinsley CH, Ukhaneva O (2017) Choice of majors: are women really different from men? National Bureau of Economic Research, Working Paper
Lapan RT, Shaughnessy P, Boggs K (1996) Efficacy expectations and vocational interests as mediators between sex and choice of math/science college majors: a longitudinal study. J Vocat Behav 49(3):277–291
Lopus JS (1997) Effects of the high school economics curriculum on learning in the college principles class. J Econ Educ 28(2):143–153
Luppino M, Sander R (2015) College major peer effects and attrition from the sciences. IZA J Labor Econ 4(1):4
Malgwi CA, Howe MA, Burnaby PA (2005) Influences on students' choice of college major. J Educ Bus 80(5):275–282
Marangos J (2012) The "discouraged-business-major" hypothesis: policy implications. Educ Econ 20(4):430–446
McElroy MB (2014) The 2014 report of the committee on the status of women in the economics profession. American Economic Association (Online)
Melican C, Debebe F, Morgan R (1997) Comparing AP and college student learning of economics. J Econ Educ 28(2):135–142
Morgan R, Klaric J (2007) AP®students in college: an analysis of five-year academic careers. College Board, New York
Mumford KJ, Ohland MW (2011) Student performance in undergraduate economics courses. J Econ Educ 42(3):275–282
National Center for Education Statistics (2015) Digest of education statistics. US Department of Education, Washington DC
Ohland MW, Zhang G, Thorndyke B, Anderson TJ (2004) Grade-point average, changes of major, and majors selected by students leaving engineering. Paper presented at the ASEE/IEEE Frontiers in Education Conference Savannah, GA
Ost B (2010) The role of peers and grades in determining major persistence in the sciences. Econ Educ Rev 29(6):923–934
Owen AL (2010) Grades, gender, and encouragement: a regression discontinuity analysis. J Econ Educ 41(3):217–234
Rask KN, Bailey EM (2002) Are faculty role models? Evidence from major choice in an undergraduate institution. J Econ Educ 33(2):99–124
Rask KN, Tiefenthaler J (2008) The role of grade sensitivity in explaining the gender imbalance in undergraduate economics. Econ Educ Rev 27(6):676–687
Riegle-Crumb C, King B, Grodsky E, Muller C (2012) The more things change, the more they stay the same? Prior achievement fails to explain gender inequality in entry into STEM college majors over time. Am Educ Res J 49(6):1048–1073
Riegle-Crumb C, King B, Moore C (2016) Do they stay or do they go? The switching decisions of individuals who enter gender atypical college majors. Sex Roles J Res 74(9–10):436–449
Sabot R, Wakeman-Linn J (1991) Grade inflation and course choice. J Econ Perspect 5(1):159–170
Salemi MK, Eubanks C (1996) Accounting for the rise and fall in the number of economics majors with the discouraged-business-major hypothesis. J Econ Educ 27(4):350–361
Siegfried JJ (2016) Trends in undergraduate economics degrees, 1991–2014. J Econ Educ 47(1):89–93
Solnick SJ (1995) Changes in women's majors from entrance to graduation at women's and coeducational colleges. Ind Labor Relat Rev 48(3):505
Stock WA (2017) Trends in economics and other undergraduate majors. Am Econ Rev 107(5):644–649
Swinton JR, Scafidi B, Woodard HC (2012) The impact of the Teaching High School Economics workshop for teachers on student achievement. East Econ J 38(3):401–416
Swope KJ, Schmitt PM (2006) The performance of economics graduates over the entire curriculum: the determinants of success. J Econ Educ 37(4):387–394
Terry A (2002) Student performance in the introductory corporate finance course. J Financ Educ 28(Fall/Winter):28–41

Turner SE, Bowen WG (1999) Choice of major: the changing (unchanging) gender gap. Ind Labor Relat Rev 52(2):289–313
Walstad WB (2001) Economic education in US high schools. J Econ Perspect 15(3):195–210
Walstad WB, Rebeck K (2012) Economics course enrollments in US high schools. J Econ Educ 43(3):339–347
Walstad WB, Watts M (2015) Perspectives on economics in the school curriculum: coursework, content, and research. J Econ Educ 46(3):324–339
Wang M, Degol J (2013) Motivational pathways to STEM career choices: using expectancy-value perspective to understand individual and gender differences in STEM fields. Dev Rev 33(4):304–340
Worthington AC, Higgs H (2004) Factors explaining the choice of an economics major: the role of student characteristics, personality and perceptions of the profession. Int J Soc Econ 31(5/6):593–613
Zafar B (2013) College major choice and the gender gap. J Hum Resour 48(3):545–595

Chapter 12
Taking a Path Less Traveled: Mastering 'Metrics Without a Textbook

Alice Louise Kassens

Abstract Causality plays a central role in economics instruction, save econometrics. There, attention switches to the restrictive classical linear regression assumptions, violations of them, and the search for the "true" model. Current textbooks encourage this pedagogy. In contrast, empirical economic research increasingly focuses on research design and determining causality. To prepare students for the labor market, undergraduate econometric instruction should focus on the "doing" of econometrics rather than econometric theory, a task that may necessitate forgoing the traditional textbook. This manuscript offers an example of a design-based course taught in the fall of 2017, which follows Angrist and Pischke's *Mastering 'Metrics*.

12.1 Introduction

In the standard undergraduate economic education, causality is a central theme from the beginning. The effect of price on quantity demanded and supplied, as defined by the rules of demand and supply, respectively, takes center stage in the principles courses. Causality is reinforced in the field courses and driven home in theoretical detail in the intermediate courses. A strange deviation occurs in econometrics, a course now required in most programs. The focus shifts toward the problems with the linear model and relatively little attention is paid to causality. For some students, this shift may render the subject a confusing add-on to the curriculum rather than a natural path from the intermediate courses and an obvious method of testing theories learned. Additionally, unless destined for a doctoral program in economics, the standard econometrics course falls short of preparing students for the "doing" of econometrics in the labor market.

A. L. Kassens (✉)
Roanoke College, Salem, VA, USA
e-mail: kassens@roanoke.edu

J. Hall, K. Lawson (eds.), *Teaching Economics*,
https://doi.org/10.1007/978-3-030-20696-3_12

Existing econometric textbooks encourage the focus on econometric theory rather than causality and do little to address current methods used in practice. We leave students to learn those methods on their own. There is a rich debate among scholars concerning econometrics as a science, but relatively little regarding its pedagogy. That area is growing and is turning toward the standard course structure and its disconnect with the "doing" of econometrics. This manuscript contributes to that discussion and offers an example from a one semester, undergraduate, designed-based course, which forgoes a standard textbook and is inspired by various works by Angrist and Pischke (2015), particularly *Mastering 'Metrics.*

12.2 Background

The practice of econometrics has a dark history, marred by devilish criticisms by economic celebrities, including John Maynard Keynes, who referred to it as "black magic" in his 1939 work in which he outlined his problems with the linear model (Keynes 1939). Others dismissively spoke of "pretend tools" (Worswick 1972) and "measurement without theory" (Koopmans 1947). Perhaps due to lingering sensitivity to these remarks, empirical economic work remains seemingly obsessed with seeking the "true" model. Hendry reminds us that econometrics, not econo-"mystics" (Hendry 1980), is defined as "the advancement of economic theory in its relation to statistics and mathematics" (Frisch 1933).

Discussion of the problems plaguing econometrics moved from voodoo and hocus-pocus to more worldly issues such as: (1) correlation versus causation (Black 1982), (2) lack of sensitivity tests (Leamer 1983), (3) absurd assumptions (Pratt and Schlaifer 1984), (4) fragile inference (Leamer and Leonard 1983; McAleer et al. 1985), and (5) model selection (Cooley and LeRoy 1981; McAleer et al. 1985). Seeking to take the "con" out of econometrics during the 1980s, more attention was paid to sensitivity analysis. The changes increased the credibility of the field, but most of the highbrow bickering ignored the central theme of causality in economic theory, best dealt with through research design. The causality-focused practice of econometrics grew substantially in recent decades with the use of natural experiments, instrumental variables, and differences-in-differences.

While David Card, Alan Kruger, Joshua Angrist, Jörn-Steffen Pischke, and others involved in the causality revolution made a tremendous impact on the practice of empirical econometrics, for the most part, the introductory econometrics courses remain in the Dark Ages. Additionally, little literature exists concerning econometric pedagogy. Sowey reviewed the teaching of econometrics in 1983, but the pedagogy discussion was left largely alone for 15 years despite the radical changes in empirical possibilities due to technological innovation (Sowey 1983). Kennedy (1998) took the issue up next, and lamenting student understanding of sampling distributions, followed by Becker and Greene (2001) who commented upon the insistence of "chalk and talk" teaching methods despite the increased availability of computing power and the ability to "do" econometrics in the classroom. Now, 17 years after Becker and Greene's (2001) comments, econometric instruction is largely unchanged. Most classes use statistical software, as shown in the next section of this manuscript, but the instruction continues to focus on the linear model and econometric theory rather than causality. Hoping students will independently see the importance of the causality preached in the principles and intermediate courses with the relentless mathematical abstraction and distraction is akin to George expecting Elaine to succeed on the IQ test taken in the raucous Dream Café (Leopold 1991).

The doing of econometrics is not only increasingly empirical (Angrist et al. 2017), but greater attention is paid to research design and causality than in its dark days. If we expect our students to be prepared for the labor force and capable doers of empirical research, we need to teach the subject the way it is practiced. The traditional or standard econometric pedagogy needs to shift toward a design-based approach, else risk sending students out into the world capable of regurgitating the proof of the unbiasedness of beta under strict conditions which rarely hold, but not proficient in devising a research design yielding what people really want to know: What is the causal effect of X on Y, ceteris paribus? This is the case made by Angrist and Pischke (2017, 2015). The remainder of this manuscript outlines the current structure of econometric courses, henceforth called the "standard" approach, and offers an example of an alternative, design-based approach discussed at length by Angrist and Pischke.

12.3 Issue

To provide an overview of the current undergraduate introductory econometrics landscape, the top 50 economics programs, as ranked by College Choice (2018) are briefly analyzed.[1] Due to the vast amount of information available online, most information is found using a Google search. In a few cases, the current listed professor was contacted to verify or provide information. The posted degree requirements are used to determine if econometrics is a required course. If so, the most recent syllabus (none later than 2016) is used to assess textbook adopted, software used, and type of curriculum taught.

[1]The selection of the ranking system is irrelevant. College Choice is used simply to have a representation of strong economics programs in the USA. This ranking system is largely driven by tuition and starting salaries.

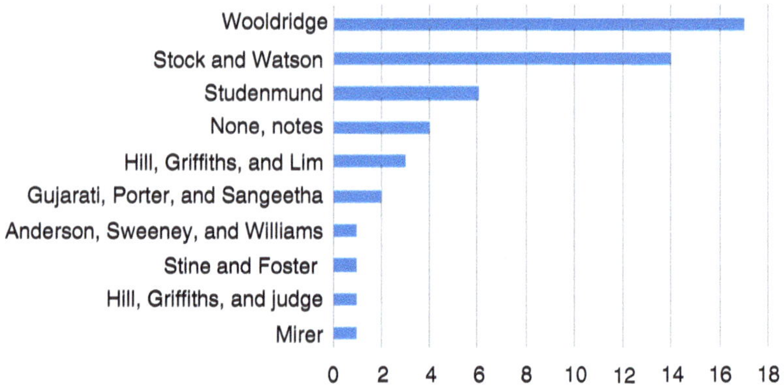

Fig. 12.1 Distribution of textbooks used in introductory econometrics courses, top fifty economics programs (count)

All fifty programs have an introductory econometrics course, and all but four programs require it for at least one economics major.[2] Figure 12.1 shows the distribution of textbooks used in the fifty courses. Wooldridge (2015) and Stock and Watson (2015) dominate the environment, accounting for 62% (31 of 50) of the courses studied. Seven other books (six if the two Hill et al. (2000, 2017) versions are aggregated) account for the remaining course adoptions: Studenmund (2017), Hill et al. (2017), Gujarati et al. (2011), Anderson et al. (2015), Stine and Foster (2017), Hill et al. (2000), and Mirer (1994). All textbooks employ the standard approach. Four faculty opt for no textbook and use individualized notes instead. Figure 12.2 shows the statistical software used by the fifty programs. Stata is the selected software for close to three quarters of the programs. R, Eviews, and Excel are the remaining software selections. One course permits students to use the software of their choice.

The use of statistical software indicates the desire to "do" econometrics in the classroom, but the syllabi and textbooks suggest it is done in the standard way and largely ignores research design. Three programs offer a design-based econometrics course and four either require or suggest reading *Mastering 'Metrics*, a book covering the current design methods used in practice. It is likely that many professors teach econometrics the way that they were taught and have been doing so since they began teaching their own courses. In addition to path dependence and inertia, a third potential reason for employing the standard approach is that available textbooks and supplemental materials follow this structure, making going it alone quite costly.

[2]Some programs have several economics majors, and not all require econometrics. For example, a program may have a theory based major that does not require econometrics and a mathematical based major that does require it.

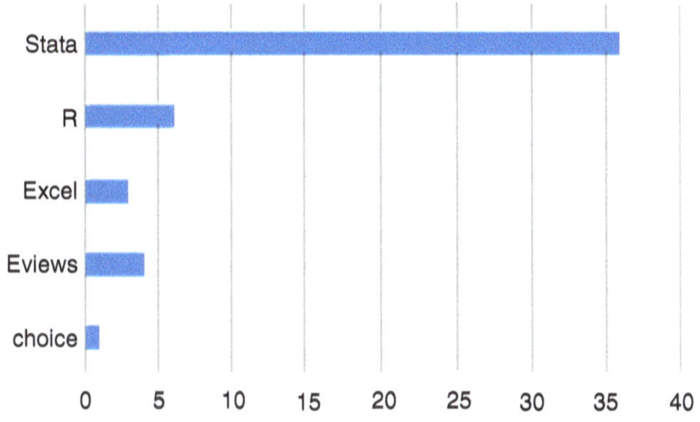

Fig. 12.2 Distribution of statistical software, top fifty economics programs (count)

The applied econometrics that we "do" as researchers varies significantly from the standard approach used in the classroom. The Classical Model is powerful, but at least one assumption is often violated and the results frequently do not estimate a true causal effect. The remainder of this manuscript provides an example of a one semester undergraduate econometrics course that employs the design-based approach and covers regression, instrumental variables, regression discontinuity design, and differences-in-differences. Materials for the course and further discussion are available at: https://kassensmetrics.weebly.com, all aimed at reducing the cost of adopting the design-based approach and hopefully incentive to shift to current econometric pedagogy.[3] It is suggested that faculty read Angrist and Pischke's (2015) *Mastering 'Metrics* and "Through Our Classes, Darkly" (Angrist and Pischke 2017) for support and inspiration. For more advanced students, *Mostly Harmless Econometrics* may be a better fit (Angrist and Pischke 2009).

12.4 Doing Econometrics: An Example

In the 2017 fall semester, this author piloted a design-based undergraduate econometrics curriculum at a small liberal arts college in Southwestern Virginia. At the institution, econometrics is a required course in the economics major with the following prerequisites: MATH 111, a basic math course for the social sciences, INQ 240, a basic statistics course within the general education curriculum, and either ECON 321 or 322, Intermediate Microeconomics or Intermediate Macroeconomics, respectively. Due to the size of the major, only one section is taught each year

[3]Other courses, both graduate and undergraduate, lean toward the designed-based approach. This author does not suppose that she is the first. The website for *Mastering 'Metrics* (http://masteringmetrics.com) shares several sample syllabi from courses around the world.

Table 12.1 Topics by week, standard and design-based courses

Week	Standard	Causal-focused
1	Introductions/what is economics	Introduction/the big picture
2	Review of statistics	Review of statistics
3	OLS	Analysis and interpretation of randomized trials
4	OLS	Analysis and interpretation of randomized trials
5	Using regression analysis	Regression basics
6	The classical model	Regression basics
7	The classical model	Regression basics
8	*Fall break*	
9	Hypothesis testing/specification	Using multivariate regression
10	Specification/multicollinearity	Heteroskedasticity/serial correlation
11	Multicollinearity/serial correlation	Instrumental variables
12	Serial correlation/heteroskedasticity	Instrumental variables
13	*Thanks giving break*	
14	Dummy dependent variables	Regression discontinuity
15	Prediction	Difference-in-difference

and always by the same professor. The 2017 edition of the econometrics course is the thirteenth time the professor taught the course, and the first time the standard approach was not employed. Seven students, six of whom are seniors, enrolled in 2017 course, which is on the lower end of the typical student enrollment range, although ideal for attempting a modified pedagogical approach. Seven students constitute a small sample; thus, this study does not include a statistical analysis. Rather it provides a description of the course structure, outcomes, and modifications.

Table 12.1 details the topics covered for the standard (2005–2016) and design-based (2017) versions of the course. The full syllabus for the design-based course is shown in the Appendix. The standard course required Studenmund's textbook and generally followed its chapter order and topics (Studenmund 2017). Students used Stata until 2015, when SAS was adopted due to the zero explicit cost associated with SAS OnDemand and the University Edition. Assessment was based upon five homework sets, two tests, an empirical paper, and a final exam. The average grade over the 12 years was a C (2.0 on a 4.0 scale). Based upon test answers, students largely memorized terms and proofs each year. Additionally, student papers were often incoherently divided into portions addressing the standard violations of the Classical Linear Regression Assumptions without a clear understanding of the material. Too much focus was placed on the R-squared statistic and violations of the classical assumptions and too little on modeling and results. The improper focus is not surprising given the structure of the course and textbook. Frustrated by the poor outcomes, the professor was nonetheless reluctant to alter the course due to the associated costs and lack of a new course model template or textbook. In short, it was obvious that something needed to change, but it was not obvious what those changes should be.

After reading Angrist and Pischke (2017) in the summer of 2017 and visiting the complementary webpage, an alternative path became clear (Angrist and Pischke 2017). A new, design-based course was developed over the summer of 2017 for introduction in the fall of 2017. Table 12.1 catalogs the changes. The theme of the course is the "doing" of econometrics with a focus on causality and modeling rather than the classical model and violations of its assumptions. The course diverges from the standard model after week two. A thorough discussion of what is meant by causality and why it is a challenge to model is followed by an introduction to the gold standard for establishing causality, randomized trials. An emphasis is placed on the erroneous relationships that are frequently produced when a problem is not modeled correctly. *Mastering 'Metrics* provides several examples and the instructor details an example in class using employer wellness based programs and the health and productivity benefits perhaps incorrectly attributed to them.[4]

The rest of the semester covers the more commonly used models in applied economics: (1) regression, (2) instrumental variables, (3) regression discontinuity design, and (4) differences-in-differences. The first two methods are typically covered in the standard course, but the designed-based approach focuses less on the econometric theory behind the estimates and more on how the methods are used to disentangle causal effects and their interpretation. The latter is the task of empirical economists and likely creates the most value added to undergraduate economic education, particularly for those not planning on attending graduate school. Regression discontinuity design and differences-in-differences models are not typically covered in a standard course, but each are potential methods for untangling the causality web and are frequently used in practice.

Assessment in the revised course remains the same, save dropping one test, but no formal textbook is adopted since they all follow the standard approach. Instead, *Mastering 'Metrics* is assigned and complemented with lecture notes authored by the professor and data sets available on the *Mastering 'Metrics* website.[5] Course homework assignments frequently require students to reproduce at least one table from the chapter of focus using the adopted course software, SAS. The published journal articles the tables come from are thoroughly discussed in *Mastering 'Metrics*, with particular focus on design and causality. Reproducing the tables after covering the topic in class emphasizes teaching by example rather than in abstraction: students "do" the econometrics. Additionally, students can quickly see if their results are "right" by matching them to those in the book. Stata do files reproducing the tables are available online, so similar assignments should be modified if Stata is the software of choice to avoid student "copy-and-pasting" and incentivize learning. The causality theme is repeated throughout the semester in

[4]The wellness program example is detailed at: https://kassensmetrics.weebly.com.

[5]The lecture notes are available on the course website. The website for *Mastering 'Metrics* offers several resources, including the data sets and Stata do files for most tables included in the book. Additionally, upon request, faculty have access to pdfs of all tables, which simplifies creating lecture slides and other course materials.

lecture and assignments. Sample homework and test questions are shown in the Appendix and the course website.

12.5 Outcomes

Grades are not always strongly correlated with student learning, but scores for the fall 2017 course were considerably higher than the norm. This was neither due to above average student ability, which was consistent with past semesters, nor a more relaxed grading practice by the professor. Other qualitative observations of improved student learning were the intentional and specific attention to causality in their semester papers and detailed reflection and critique of the effectiveness of their research design on the final exam. Additionally, students displayed a more accurate use of terminology, paid adequate attention to results and potential policy implications, and relied less on a single goodness of fit measure, namely the R-squared statistic in their papers. Finally, class discussion and pre-class chattering among students was at a higher level than previous semesters. Students spoke knowledgably about the material rather than trying to impress with large words that they didn't fully understand (e.g., "heteroskedasticity" and "multicollinearity"). In short, students were better empiricists, both actively and conversationally, after following the designed-based approach. The above is not evidence of causality, but is informative to others considering altering their course structure.

Students did not complain about the absence of a standard textbook. Many appreciated saving money and enjoyed the humor laced throughout *Mastering 'Metrics*. The complementary lecture notes and PowerPoint slides authored by the professor were frequently accessed (according to the course software log) and students reported that they were helpful, particularly on the more challenging material. At the request of the students, a "synthesis" document bringing the lessons together and showing the big picture was posted. These documents served as another way to emphasize the importance of modeling and the course focus on causality.

12.6 Adjustments

A few changes are anticipated for the fall 2018 edition of the course. The topics covered will remain the same, but the timing and relative intensity of some will be adjusted. Students commented that they were not comfortable with SAS until toward the end of the semester.[6] One student suggested hosting a SAS Boot Camp

[6]As noted on the syllabus, students go through the SAS Programming I course throughout the semester in addition to in class applications. This e-course is available at no explicit cost from SAS. Faculty may request course materials as well to assist in student learning.

at the start of the semester. To this end, the first 2 weeks of the fall 2018 course will include a boot camp after the basic course introductions. To make time for the boot camp, three paper discussions from the 2017 schedule will be eliminated as students reported little benefit from them. This will free up four and a half hours of class time. Additionally, more time will be spent on the regression discontinuity design and differences-in-differences models by spending slightly less time on regression, but without sacrificing content. Finally, the professor will produce videos covering the more challenging topics for students to review when needed.

12.7 Conclusion

Causality plays a central role in undergraduate economic education until the econometrics course, where it is forsaken. Instead, we teach our students the classical linear regression model, including its restrictive assumptions and, if possible, how to detect and correct violations of the assumptions. Economic research is increasingly empirical, placing emphasis on research design and the search for causality. Currently, four methods are most frequently used to disentangle causation in economic research: (1) regression, (2) instrumental variables, (3) regression discontinuity design, and (4) differences-in-differences, but we largely leave our students to learn these methods on their own. The disconnect between econometric pedagogy and practice must be corrected for the sake of our students and the effectiveness of their education. Unfortunately, traditional econometric textbooks continue to push the standard approach, making the adoption of the design-based approach costly.

This manuscript outlines a course and provides the materials used following the design-based approach. The course tracks a non-traditional path and does not adopt a standard textbook. Rather Angrist and Pischke's *Mastering 'Metrics* is the primary reading material, complemented with resources authored by the professor. Anecdotal evidence suggests the production of more competent "doers" of empirical economic research compared to those following the traditional path. Apart from the few, minor adjustments, the described course will be taught again in subsequent semesters. Faculty members are encouraged to read the associated works by Angrist and Pischke, use the materials provided by this author and her course webpage, and the forthcoming resources from Marginal Revolution to change course and travel down the design-based path.

Acknowledgements Thank you to Josh Hall and participants at the 2018 APEE Annual Conference for their comments and suggestions and to my fall 2017 ECON 448 class for piloting the revision. I am appreciative for the encouragement and support from Josh Angrist. I am most grateful to Michael Enz who first brought "Through Our Classes Darkly" to my attention and reviewed drafts of this manuscript.

Appendix

ECON 448: INTRODUCTION TO ECONOMETRICS

Dr. Alice Louise Kassens • West 234 • 375-2428 (O) • kassens@roanoke.edu

Office Hours are Tuesday & Wednesday 1:00 – 3:00 pm or by appointment

SEEKING THE PATH TO CAUSALITY

Required Text

Angrist, Joshua D. & Pischke, Jorn-Steffen. (2015). *Mastering Metrics.* Princeton: Princeton University Press.

Required e-course

SAS Programming I (link on Inquire, no cost)

Software

SAS Studio

Learning Outcomes

Display a firm grasp of economic knowledge

Demonstrate proficiency in a variety of communication skills

Conduct rigorous economic analysis and research

Demonstrate computer proficiencies for economic analysis

Prerequisites

ECON 321 or 322 or permission; INQ 240

Supplemental Materials

Lecture notes/synthesis

Topic videos/podcasts

Unsolicited Advice

This course is hard. It is a 300-level course. You will be challenged perhaps more than in any previous course. That is OK. Accept the challenge. Rise to the challenge. Show some grit. You will be amazed at what you can accomplish when you dedicate yourself for the entirety of the semester.

COURSE OUTLINE

DATES[A]	**TOPIC/*SUBTOPIC***[B]	**READING**[C]	**ASSIGNMENTS**[D]
AUGUST 30	The Big Picture	MM Introduction Lecture Note 1	Create SAS OnDemand account (use email from Kassens) Programming I Lessons 1-3
SEPTEMBER 4-6	SAS BOOTCAMP Statistics Review	Lecture Note 2	Programming I Lessons 4-7
SEPTEMBER 11-20	Analysis and Interpretation of Randomized Trials	MM Chapter 1 Lecture Note 3	**Homework #1** **Prospectus (Sunday September 16, 5:00 pm, Turnit In)**
SEPTEMBER 25-OCTOBER 12	Regression Basics	MM Chapter 2 Lecture Note 4	**Homework #2** **Literature Review (Friday October 12, 5:00 pm, Turnit In)**
OCTOBER 23-NOVEMBER 1	Instrumental Variables (IV)	MM Chapter 3 Lecture Note 5	**Homework #3** **MIDTERM October 30**
NOVEMBER 6-20	Regression Discontinuity Design (RDD)	MM Chapter 4 Lecture Notes 6	**Homework #4** **Data and Methods (Sunday November 11, 5:00 pm, Turnit In)**
NOVEMBER 27-DECEMBER 6	Differences-in-Differences	MM Chapter 5 Lecture Note 7	**Homework #5** **Final Paper (Friday December 7, 5:00 pm, Turnit In)**
DECEMBER 13			**FINAL EXAM, 8:30 am**

[A] Schedule will adjust as needed and should be considered tentative. Changes to the schedule will be announced.

[B] Lecture notes and other helpful materials will be posted on Inquire for each topic/subtopic.

[C] Several online resources exist to help in your learning of the material including this video series by Ben Lambert. SAS tutorials can be found here.

[D] The site with the data sets referenced in MM are found here. You will be asked to access them on several assignments.

Grade Determination and Details

Attendance (5%) - Students are expected to be in class every day. If you cannot make it to class you must alert me prior the start of class for you to be considered excused. Students will be marked present any day that I take attendance and they are either present or excused. More than three unexcused absences will result in a *full course letter grade reduction.*

Homework (25%) - Homework sets are due at the start of class unless you are told otherwise. *If you are late to class, your assignment is late.* Assignments dropped at Dr. Kassens' office during class are considered late. Late assignments will be accepted with a 10% deduction per hour it is late starting at the deadline. If you have a conflict with the due date you must notify Dr. Kassens at least a week in advance. The associated program file must be attached for each SAS assignment, else suffer a 10% grade penalty. The results for SAS problems must be neatly presented. You will be graded on your presentation.

Prospectus (5%) - A 2-3 page prospectus is due **Sunday September 16** by 5:00 pm via Turnit-In. The homework late penalty will be used. Emailed papers will not be accepted. Your prospectus must include a clear motivation, research question, and hypothesis. Additionally, you must include a developing literature review linking the selected papers to your project. APA guidelines should be followed. Additional details will be given at a later date.

Literature Review (10%) - A 3-5 page literature review is due **Friday October 12** by 5:00 pm via Turnit-In. The homework late penalty will be used. Emailed papers will not be accepted. APA guidelines should be followed. Additional details will be given at a later date.

Data and Methods (10%) - A 3-5 page write-up is due **Sunday November 11** by 5:00 pm via Turnit-In. The homework late penalty will be used. Emailed papers will not be accepted. Your write-up must describe your hypothesis and economic and econometric models. Additionally, you must carefully describe the variables needed and data sources. A screen shot of the first page of your data spreadsheet must be attached, but not included in the page count.

Final Paper (15%) - A 20-25 page final paper is due **Friday December 7** by 5:00 pm via Turnit-In. The homework late penalty will be used. Emailed papers will not be accepted. The program file showing all SAS commands for your project must be included as an attachment, but not included in the page count. APA guidelines should be followed. Additional details will be given at a later date.

Midterm and Final Exam (15% each (30%)) - If you have a conflict with the test(s), you must notify me at least a week in advance and make other arrangements. Late tests for unexcused absences are not given and a zero will be recorded in these cases. Tests will be reviewed, but will be collected by the professor afterwards. All tests are property of the professor. You may come to review your test during office hours. The midterm is currently scheduled for **October 30.** The final exam date is set by the College and cannot be changed. The final exam is **December 13, 8:30-11:30 am.**

You must turn in a certificate for the SAS Programming I e-course to demonstrate completion. Failure to do so by SEPTEMBER 28rd at 5:00 pm will result in a *5-point reduction in your course grade.*

Other Policies and Notices

Expected Number of hours worked per week - As is noted in our catalog, for a one-unit course, students are expected to complete 12 hours of work inside and outside of class each week. Since this is a one-unit course, your expectations should be the same.

Special Services - In order to be considered for disability services, students must identify themselves to the Office of Disability Support Services. Students requesting accommodations are required to provide specific current documentation of their disabilities. Please contact JoAnn Stephens-Forrest, M.S.W., Coordinator of Disability Support Services, at 540-375-2247 or e-mail stephens@roanoke.edu.

If you are on record with the College's Office of Disability Support Services as having academic or physical needs requiring accommodations, please schedule an appointment with Ms. Stephens-Forrest as soon as possible. You need to discuss your accommodations with her before they can be implemented. Also, please note that arrangements for extended time on exams, testing, and quizzes in a distraction-reduced environment must be made at least two full business days *before every test.*

Academic Integrity - This course requires both group and individual work. You are expected to follow the instructions for all assignments, including what are considered acceptable and unacceptable resources. Doing your own work and properly acknowledging the work of others are fundamental and crucial values in an academic environment. Violations of academic integrity will immediately be referred to the proper authorities.

Electronic Devices - Calculators are permitted for exams, but all cell/smart phones, iPods, etc. must be placed at the front of the room prior the exam. Bathroom breaks will not be permitted during tests and exams due to prior bad acts of former students. Cell/smart phones and iPods must be turned off prior any class period. You may use a computer to take notes but you may not log onto the Internet unless you are told to do so by the professor.

ECON 448 HOMEWORK #2

Homework is due **Tuesday October 25** in class. If you are late to class, your homework is late. Please review the homework policy on the syllabus. Complete all problems and attach your SAS programs (NOT LOG) to your answer sheet. You may work in groups, but each person must turn in their own copy of the homework.

1. Go back to your table from problem #2 on Homework #1 and test if each of the differences are statistically significant. Add the standard error for the difference and highlight the differences that are significant. Turn in your updated table and program. HINT: Use the ttest procedure in SAS.

2. The data set LIFE5 contains data for the following variables:

Variable	Definition
$lifeexpect_i$	Life expectancy at birth, in years, in state i, 2010
$medinc_i$	Median household income, in $1,000, in state i, 2010
$uninsured_i$	Percentage of population (ages 0-64) in state i, without health insurance, 2008-2010
$smoke_i$	Percentage of adults in state i who smoked, 2006-2012
$obesity_i$	Percentage of adults in state i who were obese (BMI at least 30), 2006-2012
$teenbirth_i$	Number of births to teenage mothers in state i per 1,000 females aged 15-19, 2010
$gunlaw_i$	Dummy variable = 1 if state i had a firearm law protecting children, 0 otherwise, 2010
$metro_i$	Percentage of population in state i that lived in a metropolitan statistical area, 2010

a. We are interested in the causal effect of gun control laws on life expectancy. Explain, in words, why income, insurance, smoking, obesity, teen birth, and metro status are important controls in our model. Use economic theory in your explanation.
b. Find the means for all variables with (column 1) and without (column 2) gun control laws. Find the difference in means (column 3) and test for the statistical significance of the differences.
c. Comment in words on your findings shown in column 3.
d. Run a regression of life expectancy using all the controls and the gun control dummy. Put your results in column 4.
e. What is the causal effect of gun control laws on life expectancy?
f. Explain potential issues with your regression model (ie. Potential sources of bias.) Be specific.

ECON 448 MIDTERM, FALL 2017

Please log-in to Inquire and download the dataset listed below. Log-in to SAS Studio. Upon completion of these tasks, please close Inquire before continuing with the test. Feel free to use Word to type your answers, particularly the essay question. If you type your answer, put your name on it, print it, and turn it in with your test. Print your SAS program generated for the test.

Complete all problems. Place all personal devices that connect to the Internet at the front of the room.

You may use an approved calculator, including the Google calculator.

DATA SET: wage2.csv

NAME: ______________________________

1. [20] A researcher plans to study the causal effect of police on crime using data from a random sample of US counties. He plans to regress the county's crime rate on the (per capita) size of the county's police force.

    a. Explain why this regression is likely to suffer from omitted variable bias. Which variables would you add to the regression to control for the omitted variables and explain why? List at least two.
    b. Pick one of your added variables from a) and use the equation for OVB to determine the sign of the bias. Will the estimated coefficients under- or over-estimate the true impact of the police force on the crime rate? Explain in detail.
2. [20] Essay Question: Explain selection bias, including its definition, how/why it occurs in economics research, and the issues it causes.

    Explain a randomized trial and how it overcomes the issue of selection bias. How was a randomized trial used in Oregon (from the paper we read)? Provide detail.

    Explain how economists use regression to control for selection bias using treatment group(s). Explicitly show a treatment dummy in a regression and discuss how it is interpreted. You may use any regression that you choose.

3. [20] Use the dataset "WAGE2" for this problem. When asked, place your answers in the table that follows. Print your SAS program for this problem.

Variable	**Equation (1)**	**Equation (2)**
Intercept		
Education		
Age		
Marital status		
Race (black = 1)		
Ability	____	
AR2		
N		

Consider the true earnings model:

$$lwage_i = \beta_0 + \beta_1 educ_i + \beta_2 age_i + \beta_3 married_i + \beta_4 black_i + \beta_5 ability_i + \varepsilon_i$$

where lwage = the natural log of monthly wage for person i, educ = years of education for person i, age = age of person i (years), married = marital status dummy variable (= 1 if person i is married), black = race dummy variable (= 1 if person i is black), ability = innate ability of person i. AR2 is the adjusted R^2 statistic and N is the sample size.

a. Initially, you do not have data on ability, and you estimate the following model:
$$lwage_i = \beta_0 + \beta_1 educ_i + \beta_2 age_i + \beta_3 married_i + \beta_4 black_i + \varepsilon_i$$

   Place your estimated coefficients in the column titled "Equation 1" in the table and use notation to indicate the significant coefficients. Define your notation. In words, interpret the estimated coefficients.
b. You decide to use the IQ score of person i as a proxy for innate ability. Estimate the true model using this proxy and write the estimated coefficients in the column "Equation 2." Use the same significance notation that you defined in part a. Interpret the coefficient for ability. Are there changes in the other estimated coefficients? Discuss.
c. Which model do you prefer? Why?
d. Estimate the omitted variable bias (since you have data for ability) assuming 1) education and ability are correlated and the source of the problem and 2) IQ is a good proxy for ability. You should report an actual value. Comment on the size and the sign of the bias and how you arrived at your estimate.

References

Anderson D, Sweeney D, Williams T (2015) Essentials of modern business statistics. Cengage Learning, Boston

Angrist J, Azoulay P, Ellison G, Hill R, Lu SF (2017) Economic research evolves: fields and styles. Am Econ Rev 107(5):293–297

Angrist JD, Pischke JS (2009) Mostly harmless econometrics: an empiricist's companion. Princeton University Press, Princeton

Angrist JD, Pischke JS (2015) Mastering 'Metrics. Princeton University Press, Princeton

Angrist JD, Pischke JS (2017) Undergraduate econometrics instruction: through our classes, darkly. J Econ Perspect 31(2):125–144

Becker WE, Greene WH (2001) Teaching statistics and econometrics to undergraduates. J Econ Perspect 15(4):169–182

Black F (1982) The trouble with econometric models. Financ Anal J 38(2):29–37

College Choice (2018) Best economics degrees. https://www.collegechoice.net/

Cooley TF, LeRoy SF (1981) Identification and estimation of money demand. Am Econ Rev 71(5):825–844

Frisch R (1933) Editorial. Econometrica 1(1):1–4

Gujarati D, Porter D, Gunasekar S (2011) Basic econometrics. McGraw Hill, New York

Hendry DF (1980) Econometrics - alchemy or science. Economica 47(108):387–406

Hill RC, Griffiths W, Judge G (2000) Undergraduate econometrics. Wiley, Hoboken

Hill RC, Griffiths W, Lim G (2017) Principles of econometrics. Wiley, Hoboken

Kennedy PE (1998) Teaching undergraduate econometrics: a suggestion for fundamental change. Am Econ Rev 88(2):487–492

Keynes JM (1939) Professor Tinbergen's method. Econ J 49(195):558–568

Koopmans TC (1947) Measurement without theory. Rev Econ Stat 29(3):161–179

Leamer EE (1983) Let's take the con out of econometrics. Am Econ Rev 73(1):31–43

Leamer EE, Leonard H (1983) Reporting the fragility of regression estimates. Rev Econ Stat 65(2):306–317

T. Leopold, The Café (Director: Tom Cherones, Episode: 307, Originally aired: November 6, 1991)

McAleer M, Pagan AR, Volker PA (1985) What will take the con out of econometrics? Am Econ Rev 75(3):293–307

Mirer T (1994) Economic statistics and econometrics. Pearson, Essex

Pratt JW, Schlaifer R (1984) On the nature and discovery of structure. J Am Stat Assoc 79(385):9–21

Sowey E (1983) University teaching of econometrics: a personal view. Econ Rev 2(2):255–333

Stine R, Foster D (2017) Statistics for business. Pearson, Essex

Stock J, Watson M (2015) Introduction to econometrics. Pearson, Essex

Studenmund A (2017) Using econometrics. Pearson, Essex

Wooldridge J (2015) Introductory econometrics: a modern approach. South-Western, Mason

Worswick GD (1972) Is progress in economic science possible? Econ J 82(325):73–86

Chapter 13
Structured Writing Assignments in an American Economic History Course

Judge Glock, Joshua Hall, and Marcus M. Witcher

Abstract This article describes how our American Economic History capstone writing class is structured to allow students to build upon their own research and writing in order to complete an extensive written piece as the culmination of the class. The course is organized so that students can pursue their own interests across fields in economics, and emerge from it with both a better understanding of a particular field, and a paper that can be used for job and graduate school applications and potential publication. The article relates the lessons learned by the authors during the teaching of the course, and the ways in which the course organization has assisted students with their education and careers.

13.1 Introduction

American Economic History at West Virginia University (WVU) offers students the opportunity to apply intermediate microeconomic and macroeconomic methods to analyze issues from our nation's past. It is the capstone writing course for all economics majors at WVU, and asks seniors to describe and appraise changes in the US economy over the period from the American Revolution to the 2008 financial crisis. Once students have completed the class they are prepared to explain the most important influences on economic growth and development of the USA. In addition to acquiring an appreciation and understanding of economic history, the course is

J. Glock
West Virginia University, Morgantown, WV, USA
e-mail: earl.glock@mail.wvu.edu

J. Hall (✉)
College of Business and Economics, West Virginia University, Morgantown, West Virginia, USA
e-mail: joshua.hall@mail.wvu.edu

M. M. Witcher
University of Central Arkansas, Conway, AR, USA
e-mail: mwitcher1@uca.edu

J. Hall, K. Lawson (eds.), *Teaching Economics*,
https://doi.org/10.1007/978-3-030-20696-3_13

both the capstone and writing course for the economics major. As a result, the class is designed to hone students' research, writing, and presenting skills—preparing them to use the skills they have developed in the classroom to the workplace or graduate school. To this end, we have designed a set of assignments that work in tandem to develop and polish these skills.

The three of us have taught or co-taught this course for the past 5 years at WVU. The design and structure of the course has evolved from when we initially took over the course as we quickly realized that many students did not have the necessary background or interest in doing original research.[1] In addition, we quickly found that students needed regular assignments that could be an input into their final work. Much of successful writing is revision, and so the course evolved to allow for multiple smaller assignments that could be used as inputs into a final paper. In describing our capstone course, we hope to highlight for others what we feel has worked for us so that it might be adapted to other contexts if found useful. In this respect, our work is similar to other economic education research on capstone courses such as McGoldrick (2008), Klein (2013), and Chamlee-Wright et al. (2017).

13.2 Reading Articles and Writing Memos

On the first day of class, following the standard introductions and covering of the syllabus, we ask each student to fill out note cards describing their favorite field of economics, an era of history they find interesting, and a topic they would like to learn more about. Once we have collected the note cards, we review them and assign each student an article in economic history that corresponds with his or her interests. Our goal is to get students started with an article that will interest them. They are expected to read the article, design a presentation, and write a one-page memorandum that details the article's argument and its contribution. If students enjoy their initial article, we encourage them to use the references to explore other articles and books in this literature. If the student wants to go in a different direction, they are at liberty to do so. It is our hope that students find a subject, time period, and subfield of economics that reflects their own interests and we encourage them to explore topics in which they are interested. Ideally, students will discover their topic early in the semester and stick with it throughout. In designing the course, our goal is that each article (three total), memo, and presentation will provide material for the student's final paper. We hate wasted effort and want every assignment in the class to build towards the final product.

This approach has several advantages. First, students often don't know how their interests align with academic research as terminology may change over time but the economics are still very similar. One student, as an Uber driver, was very

[1] To cite but one reason, we do not require that economics majors take econometrics.

interested in economic issues surrounding Uber. So he was assigned Eckert and Hilton's (1972) classic article on jitney regulation in 1910s San Francisco. Another student was a baseball fan and interested in working in a professional front office. He was assigned Baker et al.'s (2004) study of changes in organizational form in nineteenth-century baseball teams.[2] Second, if done well, the memos can be used as inputs into literature review of the final paper. Third, the use of brief memos forces students to hone in on what is interesting in the paper. In addition, since all writing assignments in the class have a revision included, the brevity of the memos makes grading a lot more palatable. Fourth, the real advantage of a capstone course being American Economic History is that no matter the students favorite course during their economics coursework, they should be able to find a way to write in that field. Reading of multiple articles in a field highlights for students how they can approach a topic they care about through the lens of American Economic History. Even a field like international trade—which students used to struggle with in finding research topics—improved considerably after this approach was adopted as seeing articles like Irwin (2000) showed them how they can focus on US history and international trade simultaneously.

13.3 Presentations

Although American Economic History is primarily a writing course, we also require that students present on each article (and the book they review) during the semester. In addition to being a university requirement for writing courses, requiring students to present their findings accomplishes three goals. First, we find that getting in front of their peers leads students to read the article more thoroughly—the threat of public failure seems to be a powerful motivator. Second, in presenting, students are required to analyze how best to present the material to their audience who have not read the article. This leads them to approach the article from another perspective—that of a teacher. We find that this results in a more complete understanding of the material. Finally, presenting gives students the opportunity to receive feedback and ideas about not only the articles they are presenting, but also how those articles might fit together for their larger project. An additional benefit of having the students present is that they get additional experience digesting data and presenting the relevant information in a professional setting. This is undoubtedly a skill they will draw on throughout their careers.

Unlike other courses in the economics curriculum where content is paramount, this approach forced us to explicit recognize that the content of the course would vary from semester to semester. The point of the course is not to do a complete survey of American Economic History. Instead, the goal is to improve the writing,

[2]This student has gone on to work for multiple major league teams.

research, and presentation skills of our students, all while showing them how the study of economic history can inform the present day.

13.4 Mastering the Book Review

In addition to reading, writing, and presenting on three articles during the semester, students are also required to review a book that relates to their topic. Ideally, the book will build on the articles that the student has already read and provide a more detailed understanding of whatever topic in economic history they have selected. We encourage students to get an early start and submit their books for approval as soon as possible during the semester. Students are also encouraged to select books that were released within the last 3 years. Their book review, if it is exceptionally well done, can be submitted to undergraduate journals that publish book reviews or to the few economics journals that still publish book reviews (Hunter 2017). Once students have read their books, they present their findings to the class. The book review presentations usually follow the three article presentations and provide the students with an opportunity to think about how all the secondary sources they have read fit together.

13.5 Final Papers

Every assignment in this course builds on the last and culminates in the student's final paper. Like with everything else, we strive to give students options when it comes to what their final paper will consist of. Initially this was done for pragmatic reasons, since, like many economics departments (Johnson et al. 2012), West Virginia University does not require economics majors to take econometrics. As such, students are presented with three options: the Economic Education Paper, Economic Historian Paper, and the Original Research Paper. Most students select the first or second option as they do not require as much individual research as the research paper. For students who intend to pursue graduate school, however, the third option offers them an opportunity to use the skills they have acquired during their course work to create an original piece of research. These papers can serve as the student's writing sample for graduate school applications and, in the case of exceptional the student, may provide them with a solid first draft that they can convert into a published article.

13.5.1 Economic Education Paper

A large majority of students choose to write on a single topic of economic history, presented in the form of a precis for secondary school teachers who might be interested in teaching the topic to younger students. We have found that articles from the journal *Social Education* that focus on economics are good examples to hand out to the students. One of our favorites is Schug et al. (2015). Again, the goal is to place the student in the position of the teacher and to help them explain the economic concepts and issues in clear language. Students have chosen to work on topics such as the economic influence of the civil rights movement, the effects of the gold standard, the history of gambling, and the relationship between immigration and economic growth. We find that students have usually become significantly more confident in their topic by the end of the semester, and feel comfortable writing and presenting their final paper concerning a subject about which they have acquired some mastery.

Ideally, if a student has stayed on a similar topic throughout the course of the semester, they can use much of their previously written material from their memos and the book review to fill in this final topic. This also gives the student a chance to incorporate revisions and suggestions made by the teacher over the course of the semester, and fully absorb those revisions as part of their final project. This makes the final paper a much-improved piece of work.[3]

13.5.2 Economic Historian Paper

Some students quickly become interested in a single economic historian on whom they have worked, and choose to focus on him or her for the remainder of the course, instead of a singular topic in economic history. Their final paper should therefore be a combination of a brief biography of that economist, along with a summation of his or her work in the field. To model this type of paper, we provide students with published versions of papers in this vein. We have found that this helps students to "see" the correct format and structure of the paper. A good example of a survey paper of one scholar's thought that is just the right length is Myhrman and Weingast (1994).

This paper requires a lot of reading, as students must read a large number of works by one author and then correctly categorize and contextualize the economic historian's contributions. We find that as a result good students who have not had econometrics tend to select into this paper. While no student's paper has yet been of the level to encourage publication, the average quality of these papers tends to be high. In addition, students sometimes find themselves to be extremely moved

[3]This type of scaffolding in economic research is covered in Hall and Harger (2015).

by the contributions made by famous economic historians. For instance, one young woman did an extensive study of Claudia Goldin's work in the field of economic history, with a particular emphasis on her work on the entrance of women into the labor force. The student completed a comprehensive biography and review of Goldin's work, well beyond the level surveyed in her previous memos and those of her classmates. At her final presentation, she pulled back her sleeve to show a tattoo inspired by Goldin's work. Of course, we were appreciative of the enthusiasm this student had shown for economic education.

13.5.3 The Original Research Paper

Few students choose to pursue the original research paper, since it requires the most independent work and econometrics.[4] Yet those who do are best placed to pursue further education in graduate school, with the demonstration of an independent piece of scholarship informed by extensive analysis of the secondary literature in that field gleaned from previous memos and reviews.[5] To help guide students on what the final product might look like, we provide them with copies of economic history articles from letters journals. Some examples are McFerrin et al. (2012), Tarabar and Hall (2015), and Gabriel (2016). We chose letters because we have found that identifying an interesting question, a way to test it, and one good table is a lot of work for students in one semester, especially when revision is required.

Students who have pursued the research paper usually have to consult with the teacher early in the semester, and to find out which secondary literature to consult and which databases might be available for research. Students have worked with data such as Poole and Rosenthal's (2000) DW-Nominate scores, macroeconomic time-series in FRED, Union Army personnel data (Costa and Kahn 2003), IPUMs, and others. Students have worked on topics such as the passage of the Seventeenth amendment, the relationship between the creation of Medicaid and health care spending, and the effects of immigration on political ideology. Students have gone on to use these papers to apply to schools and jobs, and sometimes have had them published in peer-reviewed academic journals (Johnson and Hall 2018).

[4]While a student could technically write an analytical narrative or other form of original economic history research, in our experience even the best students do not have the background to successfully pull off non-empirical original research. The structures of empirical papers in economics provide a clear road map for students that seems to be necessary to producing clear and coherent scholarship.

[5]While the WVU economics major is small relative to the size of the University, on average two of our undergraduates pursue a PhD in Economics. In the last 10 years students have graduated from schools like Michigan State, UC-Irvine, Clemson, and Florida State University.

13.6 Conclusion

West Virginia University's American Economic History capstone course, organized as a structured, cumulative writing and presentation class, has provided students with a unique way to pursue their own interests, develop their writing and presentation skills, and create an original piece of writing or research. Although not every student takes to the exercise, and some have to be pushed to settle on a topic, most in our experience are excited to apply their knowledge of economics to a field in which they have already expressed interest. They are also excited to see their work accumulate into an extensive piece of polished written material. They can see that their labors over the course of their college career and the semester have paid off in a complete work in which they can express some small measure of pride.

References

Baker M, Miceli TJ, Ryczek WJ (2004) The old ball game: organization of 19th-century professional base ball clubs. J Sports Econ 5(3):277–291

Chamlee-Wright E, Hall JC, Grube LE (2017) Cultivating the liberally educated mind through a signature program. J Econ Educ 48(1):34–44

Costa DL, Kahn ME (2003) Cowards and heroes: group loyalty in the American Civil War. Q J Econ 118(2):519–548

Eckert RD, Hilton GW (1972) The jitneys. J Law Econ 15(2):293–325

Gabriel PE (2016) The doughboy premium: an empirical assessment of the relative wages of American veterans of World War I. Appl Econ Lett 23(2):93–96

Hall J, Harger K (2015) Teaching students to 'do' public choice in an undergraduate public sector course. J Econ Finance Educ 14(2):66–75

Hunter D (2017) Review of Charles Calomiris and Stephen Haber, fragile by design: the political origins of banking crises and scarce credit. New Perspect Polit Econ 13(1–2):55–58

Irwin DA (2000) Did late-nineteenth-century US tariffs promote infant industries? Evidence from the tinplate industry. J Econ Hist 60(2):335–360

Johnson C, Hall J (2018) Do National Basketball Association players need higher salaries to play in high tax states? Evidence from free agents. Appl Econ Lett 25(5):359–361

Johnson BK, Perry JJ, Petkus M (2012) The status of econometrics in the economics major: a survey. J Econ Educ 43(3):315–324

Klein CC (2013) Econometrics as a capstone course in economics. J Econ Educ 44(3):268–276

McFerrin R, Norman S, Wills D (2012) Determinants of homestead claims and the expansion of Western settlement. Appl Econ Lett 19(18):1927–1932

McGoldrick K (2008) Doing economics: enhancing skills through a process-oriented senior research course. J Econ Educ 39(4):342–356

Myhrman J, Weingast BR (1994) Douglass C. North's contributions to economics and economic history. Scand J Econ 96(2):185–193

Poole KT, Rosenthal H (2000) Congress: a political-economic history of roll call voting. Oxford University Press, New York

Schug MC, Suiter MC, Wood WC (2015) From the cross of gold to central banking: three key episodes in American financial history. Soc Educ 79(2):82–88

Tarabar D, Hall JC (2015) The Seventeenth Amendment, Senate ideology and the growth of government. Appl Econ Lett 22(8):637–640

Chapter 14
Integrating the Economic Way of Thinking into US History Courses

M. Scott Niederjohn and Colin O'Reilly

Abstract Can the economic way of thinking be integrated into high school and middle school US history courses? We introduce an instrument, the Test of Economic Thinking, to assess student's ability to apply the economic way of thinking. In a pilot study involving 120 high school and middle school students across three states, we implement the Test of Economic Thinking to assess the effectiveness of integrating economic concepts into US history courses using the supplemental *Economic Episodes in American History* textbook. The results indicate that the supplemental textbook improves student's ability to apply economic concepts. The pilot study suggests that integrating the economic way of thinking into high school US history can be fruitful and that the *Economic Episodes in American History* text can be a useful tool to facilitate the integration.

14.1 Introduction

> History matters. It matters not only because we can learn from the past, but because the present and the future are connected to the past by the continuity of a society's institutions (North 1990, p. vii).

Douglass North understood that history matters. In the research that led him to a Nobel Prize in economics, he showed how we learn from our economic past. The institutions that support liberal democracy and economic prosperity are shaped by the historical context (Acemoglu and Robinson 2012). History matters because it enriches the lives of the people who study it.

M. S. Niederjohn
Lakeland University, Plymouth, WI, USA
e-mail: niederjohnms@lakeland.edu

C. O'Reilly (✉)
Creighton University, Omaha, NE, USA

J. Hall, K. Lawson (eds.), *Teaching Economics*,
https://doi.org/10.1007/978-3-030-20696-3_14

Yet, as important as history is, complaints about its teaching abound. Students complain that history is merely an exercise in trivial pursuit. Professors complain that their students are historically inept. High school and middle school teachers say much the same thing: blame all around. The dismal statistics reported by the National Assessment of Educational Progress regarding young people's historical knowledge provides empirical evidence that we have plenty of room for improvement (National Center for Education Statistics 2010).

This chapter focuses on three aspects of economics education. First, we examine how the economic way of thinking can be taught in high school and middle school American history courses. As a universal high school graduation requirement American history courses are an opportunity to infuse the economic way of thinking into the curriculum. Second, an assessment instrument designed to test economic thinking skills is introduced and released to other researchers. Finally, we report on a pilot study using the new instrument to measure the effectiveness of a supplemental text on economics in American history. The pilot study finds that the *Economic Episodes in American History* (EEAH) textbook increases understanding of the economic way of thinking among middle school and high school students.

14.2 Economics: The Missing Link

A complete understanding of history requires a careful integration of key concepts and ideas from several of the social sciences. Several national education organizations emphasize the integration of social sciences into teaching history at the pre-college level. For example, the National Council for History Education (1997) states:

> ... History is indispensable to an ordered view of the natural sciences, the social sciences, and the humanities. In this sense history is the generative subject, through which students gain understanding of, and respect for, human accomplishments in all fields of endeavor.

They go on to explain that geography and history are "constant companions." Studying one without the other is nearly impossible. How can one meaningfully study European settlement of North America without reference to the basic tools of geography? History and civics are similarly linked. Imagine trying to teach a government course without reference to the historical context surrounding the writing of the Declaration of Independence and the Constitution. Similar points can be made for military, diplomatic, and religious history.

Similarly, *Expectations of Excellence: Curriculum Standards for Social Studies*, released by the National Council for the Social Studies (1994), stresses the importance of integrating the key social studies disciplines. Evidence suggest that integrating economics into US history courses can be fruitful (Schug and Niederjohn 2008). The NCSS urges educators to use its standards in both integrated and single discipline configurations—a task requiring teachers to have solid subject matter knowledge and the appropriate instructional tools.

Where is economics in all this? Most often, it is the missing link. The connection between history and economics is rarely made, but it is nonetheless fundamental. The year 1776, for example, produced not one but two documents of historical importance to the new nation. One, of course, was the Declaration of Independence. The other was Adam Smith's (1776) *Wealth of Nations*. The founders had read Smith (Fleischacker 2002). Thomas Jefferson had a copy in his library and considered it the best work of its kind. The ideas of Smith were subsequently imbedded into key parts of the Constitution. As a result, the Constitution established a framework for the efficient conduct of economic affairs. It defined the protection of private property and specified that contracts would be enforced in even-handed fashions; it stipulated rules for bankruptcy, an important element since bankruptcy implies a failure to fulfill contracts. In short, the Constitution created a system of well specified property rights, which aligned incentives, reduced uncertainty, and permitted the development of free markets—essential, in Adam Smith's view, for a productive and prosperous economy. Unfortunately, such economic insights are often completely overlooked in traditional textbooks.

14.3 Integrating Economics Can Strengthen Historical Understanding

Integrating economics into history can help learning in two ways: First, understanding historical events requires the application of basic economic concepts. For example, it is impossible to understand the economic success of the American colonies without a grasp of the institutions inherited from the British such as rule of law, protection of private property rights, and openness to trade. Or, consider the Great Depression, a cataclysmic event in US history. Despite its importance, our textbooks are woefully out of date in the treatment of this topic. They continue to portray the stock market crash of 1929 as major cause of the Great Depression, a view is widely dismissed by economic historians (White 1990). To understand the causes of the Great Depression requires a basic knowledge of monetary policy, fiscal policy, and the importance of international trade.

Second, economics can provide students with a way to prioritize historical content to help them better understand human actions. History often presents students with a confusing array of people, facts, events, locations, and dates. Yet, not all of this information is equally valuable in problem solving. The economic way of thinking provides analytical tools to prioritize the information. It encourages students to focus their attention sharply on the choices individuals made, the costs involved, and the incentives in play. The economic way of thinking takes history beyond the examination of scattered facts and dates and toward a way of thinking critically about people's choices. This is especially important when people's choices seem unexpected or are easily dismissed as being irrational or perhaps involving no choice at all. History viewed through the lens of economic logic is an examination of the choices individuals make and why they make them. The economic perspective also helps students better understand how institutions are shaped by individual choices and, in turn, how these institutions themselves provide incentives that influence people's choices and incentives.

The *Voluntary National Content Standards in Economics of the Council on Economic Education* states: "Institutions evolve and are created to help individuals and groups accomplish their goals (Council for Economic Education 2010, p. iii)." The standard names banks, labor unions, corporations, and legal systems as examples of important economic institutions. The standard also places emphasis on clearly defined and well enforced property rights as essential to a market economy. A focus on the incentives that institutions create is fundamental to getting the economics right in American history (Council for Economic Education 2010).

How might the emphasis on choices, costs, and incentives reveal a deeper understanding of people's behavior in the past? Indentured servitude provides a good example. Indentured servitude is often presented as an institution only slightly better than slavery. In fact, the treatment of indentured servitude in US history textbooks is often placed nearby the early description of slavery—implying that they were similar institutions. A careful application of economic principles such as choice and incentives reveals a different picture. The theoretical tools of economics allow students to sift through the same basic set of facts but to arrive at a different destination.

Indentured servants signed contracts that had the force of law. Their provisions were enforced by the courts. Unlike slavery, this meant that both sides had rights. Both sides—masters and servants—were obliged to fulfill the terms of the contract.

Passage across the Atlantic was expensive. For some individuals who faced tough economic circumstances in England, for example, signing an indenture appeared to be their best choice. A new sort of labor market arose. The market, while far from perfect, by and large allowed the parties involved to accomplish their goals. On the one hand, colonial farmers, artisans, and other business people had high demand for people to work. The colonies always faced labor shortages. On the other hand, many people in England—those willing to take serious risks—were willing to sign indentures in the anticipation of obtaining new economic opportunities in North America.

Much to the dismay of the Spanish and the French, indentured servitude provided the impetus for the widespread settlement of people from Britain in North America. It helps explain how market institutions—and the prosperity they produce—were established in North America and not in South America. And, as quickly as indentured servitude arose, it faded away. Parliament passed no law to eliminate the system. Instead, the incentives changed once again. As the cost of passage across the Atlantic became less expensive, people wishing to come to North America made different choices. Why sign a labor contract when you can save up some money and purchase a ticket?

14.4 A Pilot Study: *Economic Episodes in American History and the Test of Economic Thinking*

Economic Episodes in American History (EEAH) is a textbook supplement designed to provide teachers of US history with a simple tool to sharpen students' historical understanding through the integration of basic economic principles into existing US history courses (Schug and Wood 2011). It includes a broad collection of vignettes from every major period in US history featuring content where economic principles are most relevant. Most importantly, it explicitly teaches the economic way of thinking with a consistent emphasis on importance of individual choices, costs, incentives, institutions, and trade.

A grant was obtained from a national foundation to sponsor workshops for teachers designed to instruct them on how to use the EEAH book within their existing US history courses. The grant provided funding for full day workshops for fifty teachers on EEAH during the summer of 2017. Teachers that attended the workshop received a small stipend and a classroom set of EEAH texts. Further, teachers were introduced to a new assessment instrument called the Test of Economic Thinking (TET) and further stipends were offered to those teachers willing to pre- and post-test their students using this instrument before and after teaching a set of EEAH lessons.

The Test of Economic Thinking is intended to measure how well students are able to apply a problem-solving approach called the "economic way of thinking." This is a system of logical thinking that is based on key assumptions deeply rooted in traditional economic analysis. The economic way of thinking involves the application of one or more well established principles which include, but are not limited to, the following: choices and scarcity, costs, incentives, economic systems, voluntary trade, and primary and secondary effects. The Test of Economic Thinking is designed primarily for high school students and deliberately focuses on only these six principles of economic thinking. Thus, many important principles have been excluded.

The Test of Economic Thinking consists of thirteen situations for students to consider. Students read each situation and then circle the letter of the answer that best reflects the principles of economic thinking. Students are then asked to indicate the top two economic principles that are the most appropriate to apply to the situation under discussion. Using this approach, the Test of Economic Thinking measures two types of thinking skills:

1. the respondent's ability to recognize the best economic explanation underlying a situation and
2. the respondent's ability to predict the outcome of an economic situation.

Each skill is tested in each of the thirteen scenarios making the maximum score on the test twenty-six points. The body of the test and scoring rubric are included as an Appendix.

14.5 Evaluating the *Test of Economic Thinking*

We assess the efficacy of the supplemental Economic Episodes in American History textbook at increasing understanding of basic economic concepts among high school and middle students. Instructors were recruited from three different schools in three different states to participate in the experimental pilot study. Consent from the parents or guardians of the students was obtained for 130 participants and the study received approval from the Creighton University Institutional Review Board.

Data were obtained from two sources. The results from the Test of Economic Thinking were used to measure student understanding of economic concepts and a multiple-choice survey of participants provided a limited set of additional descriptive statistics about the student participants. Full demographic information was not collected to ensure anonymity of participants, all of whom were minors. Ten students that completed consent forms did not complete some other aspect of the study. Participants with incomplete information were not included in the analysis which reduced the sample to 120 participants.

Student performance on the Test of Economic Thinking was measured prior to a semester of instruction supplemented by the EEAH text to establish a baseline level of student understanding. For each of the three instructors at least one section of US history or social studies was designated to receive instruction supplemented by EEAH, the treatment group, and at least one section was designated to serve as a control group. The control sections received traditional instruction. After a year or semester of instruction, students in both the treatment group as well as those in the control group completed the Test of Economic Thinking again.

Many studies assessing the efficacy of a particular teaching method on improving economic reasoning use a study design that involves a group of students that receive treatment and a group that does not (Yamarik 2007; Emerson et al. 2015). However, if assignment to the treatment group is not random, simply comparing the mean score between the treatment and control group will yield biased results. Factors that affect test performance or learning outcomes may be correlated with assignment to the treatment group (Haughton and Kelly 2015). For example, the course section receiving the treatment may happen to contain a disproportionate number of the honors students or be scheduled at a time of day in which students are more focused. To overcome the potential bias, we follow Dickie (2006), among others, by implementing a pre-test-post-test control-group design, also known as a difference-in-difference study design.

The so-called difference-in-difference study design captures variation in student performance along two dimensions. First, we measure performance based on assignment to a treatment or control group. Second, we measure variation over time, with test scores at the start and end of the semester. The difference-in-difference study design allows for the identification of the causal effect of treatment (Angrist and Pischke 2009).

The field experiment yielded pre- and post-test scores for 120 participants that completed the study across ten class sections. The five treatment sections contained 65 students and the five control sections contained 55 students. The largest section included 19 students participating in the study and the smallest had only 4 students participating. See Table 14.1 for the average pre- and post-test scores, the standard deviation of test scores, and the number of students by section. Treatment sections are indicated with an asterisk.

Table 14.1 Descriptive statistics

	Average test score	Standard deviation	Number of students
Section 1			
Pre-test	24%	10%	18
Post-test	23%	10%	
Section 2			
Pre-test	18%	9%	12
Post-test	22%	10%	
Section 3*			
Pre-test	24%	9%	19
Post-test	29%	12%	
Section 4*			
Pre-test	32%	14%	10
Post-test	39%	12%	
Section 5*			
Pre-test	29%	9%	18
Post-test	35%	9%	
Section 6			
Pre-test	22%	6%	9
Post-test	29%	13%	
Section 7*			
Pre-test	28%	8%	10
Post-test	32%	14%	
Section 8			
Pre-test	23%	7%	12
Post-test	27%	9%	
Section 9			
Pre-test	19%	4%	4
Post-test	38%	20%	
Section 10*			
Pre-test	20%	9%	8
Post-test	53%	9%	

Treatment sections are indicated with an asterisk

14.6 Empirical Results

The average post-test score for students in the control sections was 26% and the average score in treatment sections was 36%. However, the treatment group also outperformed the control group by five percentage points on the Test of Economic Thinking prior to treatment, an indication that assignment into the treatment and control sections is most likely not random. Therefore, the large gap between the post-test scores of students that received treatment those that did not cannot be interpreted as causal.

The causal effect of treatment is identified through the difference-in-difference study design as visualized in Fig. 14.1. The difference between the pre-test score and the post-test score constitutes the first difference, which can be calculated for both the group of students that received treatment and for those that did not receive treatment. The second difference is calculated as the difference between the *change* in scores for the control group and the change in scores for the treatment group. Therefore, the effect of using the textbook is the difference in the size of the gap between the first two columns and the gap between the third and fourth columns in Fig. 14.1.

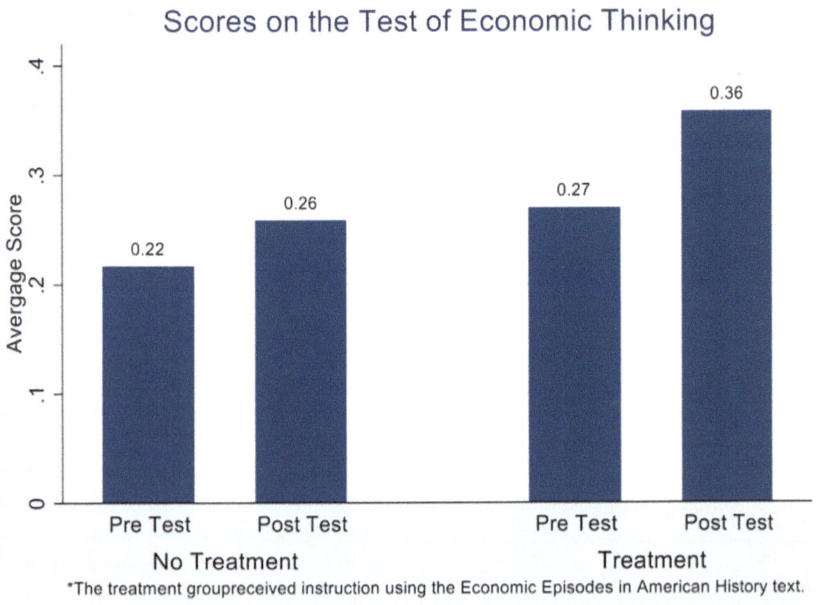

Fig. 14.1 Causal effect of Economic Episodes of American History of economic thinking

The difference between pre- and post-test scores for the control group is four percentage points and the difference between pre- and post-test scores for the treatment group is nine percentage points. As stated before, the causal effect of treatment is the difference between the change in scores of these two groups, in this case five percentage points. Therefore, the effect of treatment by using the EEAH text is to increase scores on the Test of Economic Thinking by five percentage points. But is an improvement of five percentage points large? The standard deviation of test scores is 12 percentage points; therefore, treatment increases performance on the Test of Economic Thinking by almost half of a standard deviation.

To assess the statistical significance and robustness of these findings we conduct difference-in-difference regression analysis as described by Eq. 14.1. The test score, $Score_{it}$, of student i in period t is estimated by $Post_{it}$, a variable indicating if the score corresponds to a pre-test or a post-test and by $Treat_{it}$, a variable that indicates if the student was assigned to receive treatment during the study. The variable of interest is an interaction term between the post-test indicator and the treatment indicator, $Post * Treat_{it}$, which obtains a value of one for observations that correspond to post-test scores for students that received instruction using EEAH text. To control for teacher and school effects that do not change over time we include a teacher fixed effects, μ_i. Some specifications include additional control variables that are included in X_{it}. The estimate of β_3 is therefore the effect size of treatment as shown in Fig. 14.1.

$$Score_{it} = \beta_0 + \beta_1 Post_t + \beta_2 Treat_i + \beta_3 Post * Treat_{it} + \gamma X_{it} + \mu_i + \epsilon_{it} \quad (14.1)$$

The baseline results of the difference-in-difference regression are presented in the first column of Table 14.2. The coefficient on the variable of interest, the post-test-treatment indicator variable, is positive but is not statistically significant. However, once we account for teacher specific effects in Column 2, the effect of treatment is statistically significant at the 10% level. The teacher fixed effects that account for unobserved differences in teacher quality, school quality, and other omitted school level factors have a significant effect on tests scores and improve the fit of the model. The R-squared increases from 0.18 to 0.23 after their inclusion. In Column 2, the estimate of β_3 is 0.046, an indication that treatment using the supplemental text tends to increase scores on the Test of Economic Thinking by 4.6 percentage points.

Additional control variables are added in the subsequent columns of Table 14.2. As a measure of parent's education, we include a variable that indicates if the student's mother has completed high school. The effect is statistically significant, indicating that students with mothers that completed high school have, on average, higher test scores. As a measure of extracurricular involvement, we include a variable equal to one if the student participates in sports during the school year. Participating in sports has a negative and statistically significant effect on test scores. The negative effect may be due to students allocating less time to studying while playing sports or may indicate that students involved in sports are generally less academically inclined. More importantly, the inclusion of these control variables does not alter the estimated treatment effect.

Table 14.2 Effect of the EEAH text on the test economic thinking

Variables	(1) No fixed effect	(2) Fixed effect	(3) FE and controls	(4) FE and controls
Post-test	0.042** (0.019)	0.042** (0.019)	0.042** (0.019)	0.029 (0.018)
Treatment	0.053*** (0.017)	0.040** (0.017)	0.042** (0.018)	0.039** (0.018)
Post*treatment	0.046 (0.028)	0.046* (0.027)	0.046* (0.027)	0.055** (0.027)
Mother's education			0.039** (0.016)	0.038** (0.016)
Sports			−0.049*** (0.017)	−0.050*** (0.017)
Job				−0.00 (0.020)
College				0.011 (0.021)
Constant	0.217*** (0.011)	0.194*** (0.014)	0.195*** (0.020)	0.192*** (0.023)
Teacher FE		X	X	X
Observations	240	240	238	232
R-squared	0.1843	0.233	0.271	0.2741

* indicates 10% level of significance;
** indicates 5% level of significance;
*** indicates 1% level of significance

The final two control variables are included in Column 4. One is an indicator for whether the student self-reports a plan to attend college and the other indicates whether a student is working a job during the school year; neither of these controls are statistically significant. The inclusion of these two controls reduces the sample size to 116 students due to missing data. The loss of these four observations modestly increases the effect size which increases the statistical significance of the treatment effect; however, this is an artifact of the arbitrary loss of four observations.

14.7 Conclusion

Ten sections of US history and social studies consisting of a total 120 students participated in a study of the effectiveness of a supplemental textbook. The supplemental economics textbook, *Economic Episodes in American History* (Schug and Wood 2011), infuses the economic way of thinking into vignettes about US history with the goal of improving student's ability to apply the economic way of thinking.

The pilot study assesses student's ability to apply the economic way of thinking based on their performance on the Test of Economic Thinking, an instrument introduced in the present study. The test was administered at the beginning of the semester and at the end of the semester to assess performance over time. Further, some class sections received treatment in the form of instruction using the supplemental textbook, while others did not. Through this difference-in-difference study design, we identify a positive and marginally statistically significant effect of treatment using the Economic Episodes in American History textbook on test scores. The results indicate that the textbook increases student's ability to apply the economic way of thinking to various scenarios. Specifically, treatment improved scores on the Test of Economic Thinking by about five percentage points. The positive effect is robust to the inclusion of a limited set of control variables.

The results of the pilot study provide modest evidence that the Economic Episodes in American History textbook can help to infuse the economic way of thinking into high school and middle school US history courses. However, some caveats must be noted. The pilot study was conducted on a modest sample of 120 students. Further research on a larger sample is needed to draw more general conclusions and to increase confidence in the results found in this pilot study. In addition, the main effect identified here is only statistically significant at the 10% level. Studies with a larger sample may be able to identify more precise estimates of the effects described in this study.

Appendix: Test of Economic Teaching Teacher Edition

Introduction
The Test of Economic Thinking is intended to measure how students are able to apply a problem-solving approach called the "economic way of thinking." This is a system of logical thinking that is based on key assumptions based on traditional economic problem analysis. The economic way of thinking involves the application of one or more well established principles which include but are not limited to the following: choices and scarcity, costs, incentives, economic systems, voluntary trade, and primary and secondary effects.

Directions
What follows are 13 situations for your consideration. Please read each situation and then circle the letter of the answer that best reflects the principles of economic thinking. Then, please indicate the top two economic principles that you think are the most appropriate to apply to the situation.

Scoring
The best answers are shown in bold font. The directions for scoring follow the Situations.

Scarcity and Choices

Situation 1

Fred and Wilma are a young married couple who are financially well off. Fred runs a finance company and Wilma is a physician. They are discussing how to celebrate their wedding anniversary. Fred wants to spend a week on a Caribbean cruise. Wilma wishes to spend a week in Orlando, Florida, visiting the theme parks and shopping. From an economic perspective, what is the problem Fred and Wilma are facing?

1. Time is an unlimited resource and no choice is necessary.
2. **Time is a limited resource and thus they have to make a choice.**
3. Financial success encourages excessive spending and indulgence.
4. Financial success means people can have all that they want with no sacrifice.

From the following list of economic principles, please choose two which you think are the most important reasons for your answer to Situation 1.

1. People make choices because they face scarcity. (Most important)
2. People's choices involve costs. (Next most important)
3. People respond to incentives in predictable ways.
4. People create economic systems that influence individual decision.
5. People gain when they trade voluntarily.
6. People's choices sometimes create unintended consequences.

Situation 2

Once or twice a week, Robyn arrives at work a few minutes late. Most often she is late because traffic is heavier than expected. Noticing the pattern of tardiness, Robyn's employer explained that a condition of Robyn's continued employment means arriving to work on time. Using economic thinking, what is the source of Robyn's tardiness?

1. Robyn's elected officials are at fault because they fail to fund adequate roads that can handle peak hour traffic.
2. Robyn's employer is at fault because she should offer flexible start times to take account of changing traffic conditions.
3. **Robyn is at fault because to her the benefits of being late to work outweigh the costs.**
4. Robyn's parents and teachers are at fault because they failed to teach Robyn the importance of being punctual.

From the following list of economic principles, please choose two which you think are the most important reasons for your answer to Situation 2.

1. People make choices because they face scarcity. (Most important)
2. People's choices involve costs. (Next most important)
3. People respond to incentives in predictable ways.
4. People create economic systems that influence individual decision.
5. People gain when they trade voluntarily.
6. People's choices sometimes create unintended consequences.

Costs

Situation 3
Luke decides to play his favorite video game instead of studying for tomorrow's math exam. Which of the following best describes the cost of his decision?

1. **Luke's cost for playing his favorite video game were the benefits he would have gained on the math exam if he had used the time to study for the exam.**
2. Luke's decision did not involve money and thus no meaningful cost was involved.
3. Luke's decision reflected his individual preferences so no real cost was incurred.
4. Luke's cost for playing his favorite video game was the time he could have spent being with friends after school.

From the following list of economic principles, please choose two which you think are the most important reasons for your answer to Situation 3.

1. People make choices because they face scarcity. (Next most important)
2. People's choices involve costs. (Most important)
3. People respond to incentives in predictable ways.
4. People create economic systems that influence individual decision.
5. People gain when they trade voluntarily.
6. People's choices sometimes create unintended consequences.

Situation 4
Ricky and Lucy want to enroll their 5-year-old daughter Angela in the local public schools. They are pleased that the local school board and the state provide a free education for children like Angela. From an economic perspective, are they correct in thinking that public school education is free?

1. Yes. Ricky and Lucy do not have to pay tuition for Angela's schooling.
2. No. The benefits of public schools outweigh the costs.
3. Yes. Tax payers support public education at no direct cost to parents.
4. **No. Resources used to pay teachers and buy books are not free.**

From the following list of economic principles, please choose two which you think are the most important reasons for your answer to Situation 4.

1. People make choices because they face scarcity. (Next most important)
2. People's choices involve costs. (Most important)
3. People respond to incentives in predictable ways.
4. People create economic systems that influence individual decision.
5. People gain when they trade voluntarily.
6. People's choices sometimes create unintended consequences.

Situation 5
Elaine lives in an apartment building where all the units are occupied. A new person approaches George, the owner of the building, and offers to pay twice as much rent for an apartment. George is not certain what to do. Finally, he approaches

Elaine with the following deal: George will turn down the new applicant's offer but Elaine must pay a higher rent because George's costs have increased. Elaine disagrees and points out that George's costs have not increased—the taxes, utilities, and maintenance—everything has stayed the same. Using the economic way of thinking, decide whether Elaine or George is correct in his/her analysis?

1. George is correct because the offer from the new applicant changed his implicit costs.
2. **George is correct because charging Elaine a higher rent recognizes what George would give up if he does not accept the new applicant's offer.**
3. Elaine is correct because George's monetary costs have not changed.
4. Elaine is correct because George should only raise rents when incomes of renters like Elaine are keeping pace with inflation.

From the following list of economic principles, please choose two which you think are the most important reasons for your answer to Situation 5.

1. People make choices because they face scarcity. (Next most important)
2. People's choices involve costs. (Most important)
3. People respond to incentives in predictable ways.
4. People create economic systems that influence individual decision.
5. People gain when they trade voluntarily.
6. People's choices sometimes create unintended consequences.

Incentives

Situation 6
Martin and Max started a business that produces popular new apps for smartphones. After all of the business bills were paid, Martin and Max split evenly the income that was left—the profit. From an economic perspective, what is the role of profits for Max and Martin?

1. Martin and Max are earning a profit which should now be passed along to employees and consumers.
2. Martin and Max are learning that earning a profit is almost certain in the app business.
3. Martin and Max are earning a profit that should now be taxed as a normal cost of doing business.
4. **Martin and Max are responding to profit as the reward for providing consumers what they want.**

From the following list of economic principles, please choose two which you think are the most important reasons for your answer to Situation 6.

1. People make choices because they face scarcity.
2. People's choices involve costs.

3. People respond to incentives in predictable ways. (Most important)
4. People create economic systems that influence individual decision. (Next most important)
5. People gain when they trade voluntarily.
6. People's choices sometimes create unintended consequences.

Situation 7
In 1970, proven oil reserves were 531 billion barrels. Today, there are over 1 trillion barrels of proven oil reserves despite that fact that the world oil consumption has increased several times over. From an economic perspective, how is the increase in oil reserves best explained?

1. Government investments in research have resulted in new discoveries for producing oil.
2. **Oil companies can earn increased profits if they are able to discover new sources of oil.**
3. Government regulations require maximum levels of oil production while protecting worker safety.
4. Oil companies with low profits are well positioned to increase levels of production.

From the following list of economic principles, please choose two which you think are the most important reasons for your answer to Situation 7.

1. People make choices because they face scarcity.
2. People's choices involve costs.
3. People respond to incentives in predictable ways. (Most important)
4. People create economic systems that influence individual decision. (Next most important)
5. People gain when they trade voluntarily.
6. People's choices sometimes create unintended consequences.

Economic Systems/Rules of the Game

Situation 8
Lois, a member of the City Council of Big Falls, wants to help low-income families to find less expensive housing. She has proposed that the City of Big Falls approves rent controls on landlords who rent apartments. That is, by law, the price of rent for an apartment will be set at new low rates. What do you predict will be the outcome of this policy if the City Council approves?

1. More low-income families will have access to affordable apartments.
2. **Fewer low-income families will have access to affordable apartments.**
3. Access to apartments for low-income families will remain unchanged.
4. Landlords will take steps to improve their apartments to attract new tenants.

From the following list of economic principles, please choose two which you think are the most important reasons for your answer to Situation 8.

1. People make choices because they face scarcity.
2. People's choices involve costs.
3. People respond to incentives in predictable ways. (Next most important)
4. People create economic systems that influence individual decision. (Most important)
5. People gain when they trade voluntarily.
6. People's choices sometimes create unintended consequences.

Situation 9
Amsterdam is a European city famous for its very narrow, tall, long buildings with narrow, steep stairways built from 1500 to 1600. What is the most likely economic explanation of this unusual architecture?

1. Narrow and tall homes were found to have less risk of flooding from Amsterdam's many canals. This reduced the cost of home insurance.
2. **Amsterdam's property taxes were assessed according to the width of the front of homes. Wider homes were subject to higher taxes.**
3. Narrow and tall homes were the result of limited skills of architects during this time period. This caused home builders to select a simple and low-cost design.
4. Amsterdam's property taxes were assessed according to the height of homes. Taller homes were subject to higher taxes.

From the following list of economic principles, please choose two which you think are the most important reasons for your answer to Situation 9.

1. People make choices because they face scarcity.
2. People's choices involve costs.
3. People respond to incentives in predictable ways. (Next most important)
4. People create economic systems that influence individual decision. (Most important)
5. People gain when they trade voluntarily.
6. People's choices sometimes create unintended consequences.

Voluntary Trade

Situation 10
Goods and services in the USA today can be easily sold across state lines. What would be the likely outcome of granting each of the 50 states the right to tax all incoming goods and services from other states?

1. State tax revenues would increase, reducing state governments' budget problems while increasing each state's prosperity.
2. All states would tax each other's incoming goods and services but there would be no other economic effects.

3. **The USA would become less prosperous because of reduced specialization and trade among the 50 states.**
4. US trade with foreign countries would be reduced because people would have the opportunity to support their own state governments by buying US-made goods from other states.

From the following list of economic principles, please choose two which you think are the most important reasons for your answer to Situation 10.

1. People make choices because they face scarcity.
2. People's choices involve costs.
3. People respond to incentives in predictable ways.
4. People create economic systems that influence individual decision. (Next most important)
5. People gain when they trade voluntarily. (Most important)
6. People's choices sometimes create unintended consequences.

Situation 11
In 2011, the US approved a free trade agreement with South Korea that would eliminate most trade barriers between the two countries. Which country, if either, stands to benefit from this agreement?

1. South Korea will benefit but not the USA.
2. The USA will benefit but not South Korea.
3. **Both South Korea and the USA will benefit.**
4. **Neither South Korea nor the USA will benefit.**

From the following list of economic principles, please choose two which you think are the most important reasons for your answer to Situation 11.

1. People make choices because they face scarcity.
2. People's choices involve costs.
3. People respond to incentives in predictable ways.
4. People create economic systems that influence individual decision. (Next most important)
5. People gain when they trade voluntarily. (Most important)
6. People's choices sometimes create unintended consequences.

Primary and Secondary Effects

Situation 12
In 1990, members of the U.S. Congress approved a 10% excise tax on yachts sold in the USA at a price of higher than $100,000. The goal of the tax was to increase government revenues in a time when the federal government faced high deficits. What result do you think was unexpected by members of Congress?

1. Yacht sales increased as wealthy buyers stepped up spending to help the government reduce the deficit.
2. **Yacht sales decreased and thousands of skilled workers lost their jobs.**
3. Tax revenues from yacht sales increased at a level that was higher than expected and helped to reduce the deficit.
4. Yacht sales remained unchanged because manufacturers passed the increased cost along to yacht buyers.

From the following list of economic principles, please choose two which you think are the most important reasons for your answer to Situation 12.

1. People make choices because they face scarcity.
2. People's choices involve costs.
3. People respond to incentives in predictable ways.
4. People create economic systems that influence individual decision. (Next most important)
5. People gain when they trade voluntarily.
6. People's choices sometimes create unintended consequences. (Most important)

Situation 13
Beginning in the 1990s, government regulators eased the rules for low and moderate income families to obtain home loans. They did not have to make down payments nor did they have to prove they could make the monthly mortgage payments. One goal of the regulators was to increase levels of homeownership. What result do you think was unexpected by the regulators?

1. **Home owners often could not afford the payments and lost their homes.**
2. Home ownership decreased among low and moderate income families.
3. Home sales increased while home buying decreased.
4. Home shortages became widespread as home builders were unable to meet the new demand.

From the following list of economic principles, please choose two which you think are the most important reasons for your answer to Situation 13.

1. People make choices because they face scarcity.
2. People's choices involve costs.
3. People respond to incentives in predictable ways.
4. People create economic systems that influence individual decision. (Next most important)
5. People gain when they trade voluntarily.
6. People's choices sometimes create unintended consequences. (Most important)

Scoring

The Test of Economic Thinking (TET) includes 26 items worth one point each. Thus, the best possible score is 26 points. Students can earn 2 points in each

Situation. Students can earn 1 point for responding correctly to the first multiple-choice question in each Situation. If students respond correctly to the first multiple-choice question in a Situation, they can earn a second point by identifying the correct response to the second question in the same Situation. Identifying the two correct economic principles in any order (most important or next most important) constitutes a correct answer and students can earn 1 more point. We think that if students fail to respond correctly to the first multiple-choice question in a given Situation, they would most likely be guessing when responding to the second question. Thus, the TET is weighted to measure reasoning skills using the specified economic principles.

Intended Audience

- The test is designed primarily for high school students.
- The number of test items is limited due to restrictions in classroom testing time and limited student concentration time.
- Classroom testing will reveal more about the overall difficulty of the test, the time it takes for students to complete it, and much more.

Test Design

- The TET is deliberately focused on only six principles of economic thinking. Thus, many important principles have been excluded. The TET should be regarded in the same way that most other tests are regarded—it is a sampling of student thinking skills rather than a comprehensive examination.
- The TET measures two thinking skills:

  1. the respondent's ability to recognize the best economic explanation underlying a Situation or
  2. the respondent's ability to predict the outcome of an economic Situation.

- The TET measures the respondent's use of economic principles to explain and predict. Two types of Situations are used:

  1. EXPLAIN: Choose or identify the best economic explanation: Situations 1,2,3,4,5, and 6.
  2. PREDICT: Predict the most likely outcome based on economic principles. Situations: 7,8, 9,10,11,12, and 13.

References

Acemoglu D, Robinson JA (2012) Why nations fail: the origins of power, prosperity, and poverty, 1st edn. Crown, New York

Angrist JD, Pischke J (2009) Mostly harmless econometrics: an empiricist's companion. Princeton University Press, Princeton

Council for Economic Education (2010) Voluntary national content standards in economics, 2nd edn. Council for Economic Education, New York

Dickie M (2006) Do classroom experiments increase learning in introductory microeconomics? J Econ Educ 37(3):267–288

Emerson TLN, English LK, McGoldrick K (2015) Evaluating the cooperative component in cooperative learning: a quasi-experimental study. J Econ Educ 46(1):1–13

Fleischacker S (2002) Adam Smith's Reception among the American Founders, 1776–1790. William Mary Q 59(4):897–924

Haughton J, Kelly A (2015) Student performance in an introductory business statistics course: does delivery mode matter? J Educ Bus 90(1):31–43

National Center for Education Statistics (2010) The nation's report card: US history 2010: national assessment of educational progress at grades 4, 8, and 12. US Department of Education, Washington

National Council for History Education (1997) Building a United States history curriculum: a guide to using themes and selecting content. National Council for History Education, Westlake

National Council for the Social Studies (1994) Expectations of excellence: curriculum standards for social studies. National Council for the Social Studies, Washington

North D (1990) Institutions, institutional change and economic performance. Cambridge University Press, Cambridge

Schug MC, Niederjohn MS (2008) Can students learn economics in US history? J Priv Enterp 23(2):167–176

Schug MC, Wood WC (2011) Economic episodes in American history. Wohl Publishing, Morristown

Smith A (1776) An inquiry into the nature and causes of the wealth of nations. Methuen & Company, London

White EN (1990) The stock market boom and crash of 1929 revisited. J Econ Perspect 4(2): 67–83

Yamarik S (2007) Does cooperative learning improve student learning outcomes? J Econ Educ 38(3):259–277